Sport, Rhetoric,
and Political Struggle

POLITICAL COMMUNICATION

FRONTIERS IN

Mitchell S. McKinney and Mary E. Stuckey
General Editors

Vol. 35

The Frontiers in Political Communication series
is part of the Peter Lang Media and Communication list.
Every volume is peer reviewed and meets
the highest quality standards for content and production.

PETER LANG
New York • Bern • Berlin
Brussels • Vienna • Oxford • Warsaw

Sport, Rhetoric, and Political Struggle

Edited by Daniel A. Grano
and Michael L. Butterworth

PETER LANG
New York • Bern • Berlin
Brussels • Vienna • Oxford • Warsaw

Library of Congress Cataloging-in-Publication Data

Names: Grano, Daniel A., editor. | Butterworth, Michael L., editor.
Title: Sport, rhetoric, and political struggle / edited by Daniel A. Grano
and Michael L. Butterworth.
Description: New York: Peter Lang, 2019
Series: Frontiers in political communication; volume 35 | ISSN 1525-9730
Includes bibliographical references and index.
Identifiers: LCCN 2018048532 | ISBN 978-1-4331-4211-6 (hardback: alk. paper)
ISBN 978-1-4331-4677-0 (pbk: alk. paper) | ISBN 978-1-4331-4678-7 (ebook pdf)
ISBN 978-1-4331-4679-4 (epub) | ISBN 978-1-4331-4680-0 (mobi)
Subjects: LCSH: Communication in sports—United States.
Mass media and sports—United States.
Sports—Political aspects—United States.
Sports—Social aspects—United States.
Athletes—Political activity—United States.
Classification: LCC GV567.5 .S78 2019 | DDC 070.4/49796—dc23
LC record available at https://lccn.loc.gov/2018048532
DOI 10.3726/b14818

Bibliographic information published by **Die Deutsche Nationalbibliothek**.
Die Deutsche Nationalbibliothek lists this publication in the "Deutsche
Nationalbibliografie"; detailed bibliographic data are available
on the Internet at http://dnb.d-nb.de/.

© 2019 Peter Lang Publishing, Inc., New York
29 Broadway, 18th floor, New York, NY 10006
www.peterlang.com

Contents

Section II: Mobilizing Resistances

Section III: Confronting Stigmas

Section IV: Future Provocations

Acknowledgments

We are grateful to Mary Stuckey and Mitchell McKinney, the editors of the Frontiers in Political Communication series, for supporting this work and for creating a space for the expansion of studies in rhetoric and sport. We also appreciate the time, effort, and talent of each author who contributed to this volume. Our goal was to bring together scholars who have focused their programs of study on sport, and scholars who are leaders in areas of thought that relate centrally to sporting contexts, in order to offer the broadest sense of what a study of rhetoric and sport might include. We believe we have succeeded thanks to each author's insightful work.

The timing for this volume is fortunate, both because of current events that make plain the connections between politics and sport and because of the steady growth we have seen in the emergent field of communication and sport. It is no longer unusual for sport to be featured in communication scholarship—including within the more narrow confines of rhetorical studies—and our major disciplinary organizations now embrace the kind of work found in this volume. This was not always the case, and we offer our sincere gratitude to the scholars of this and previous generations who have legitimized the critical study of sport. Their work has made this book possible.

Dan continues to benefit from the mentoring of Ken Zagacki and Andy King. He is also grateful for the encouragement of colleagues from the Department of

Communication Studies at the University of North Carolina at Charlotte, including Margaret Quinlan, Ashli Stokes, Jon Crane, Jason Black, Cris Davis, Min Jiang, and Richard Leeman.

For Mike, work on this book overlapped with a move and a transition to a new job. He is grateful for the opportunity to have been a part of the School of Communication Studies and the Scripps College of Communication at Ohio University. Midway through the project, he left small town life in Appalachia for the big city life in Texas. He is consistently impressed by the quality of the work and the commitment of the people at the University of Texas at Austin, and he thanks all of his colleagues in the Moody College of Communication and the Department of Communication Studies.

Finally, we are thankful for our loving families, especially for the unconditional support of our partners and our children.

Contributors

Meredith M. Bagley (Ph.D., Communication Studies, University of Texas-Austin) is an associate professor of communication studies at The University of Alabama. Her research interests center on the rhetoric of protest in sport, particularly intersections of gender, race and sexuality. She is a contributor to the upcoming volume *Uniformly discussed: Sportswomen's apparel in the United States*. A former two-sport college athlete, for the past two decades Meredith has coached and played rugby.

Jeffrey A. Bennett is Associate Professor of Communication Studies at Vanderbilt University. He is the author of *Managing Diabetes: The Cultural Politics of Disease* (NYU Press) and *Banning Queer Blood: Rhetorics of Citizenship, Contagion, and Resistance* (University of Alabama Press). Jeff's work has also appeared in the *Quarterly Journal of Speech*, *Critical Studies in Media Communication*, and *Communication and Critical/Cultural Studies*, among others.

Daniel C. Brouwer is an Associate Professor in the Hugh Downs School of Human Communication at Arizona State University. His research foci include social movements, publics and counterpublics, cultural performance, genders and sexualities, and HIV and AIDS. Co-editor of the book projects *Counterpublics and the State* (2001) and *Public Modalities: Rhetoric, Culture, Media, and the Shape of*

Public Life (2010), his work has also appeared in *Quarterly Journal of Speech, Rhetoric and Public Affairs,* and *Critical Studies in Media Communication.*

Barry Brummett (Ph.D., University of Minnesota, 1978) is the Chair of the Department of Communication Studies at The University of Texas at Austin and Charles Sapp Centennial Professor in Communication. Brummett's research interests turned early to the theories of Kenneth Burke and to epistemology and rhetoric. In those studies Brummett laid the foundation for a research program that investigates the functions and manifestations of new rhetoric. Brummett's most recent, ongoing interests are in the rhetoric of popular culture. He has developed a general theoretical basis for understanding this rhetoric based largely on symbolic forms. Brummett has published a textbook, *Techniques of Close Reading,* which is entering its second edition, and a fifth edition of his popular textbook, *Rhetoric in Popular Culture.* Brummett is the author of the scholarly book monographs *A Rhetoric of Style, Rhetorical Dimensions of Popular Culture, Contemporary Apocalyptic Rhetoric, Rhetoric of Machine Aesthetics, The World and How We Describe It,* and *Rhetorical Homologies.* He has edited *Landmark Essays: Kenneth Burke, Uncovering Hidden Rhetorics, Sporting Rhetorics, Reading Rhetorical Theory, Sports and Identity, The Politics of Style and the Style of Politics,* and *The Rhetoric of Steampunk.* He is working on a variety of studies exploring the rhetoric of form in popular culture and rhetoric. Brummett is the author or coauthor of numerous scholarly essays and chapters.

Michael L. Butterworth is a Professor in the Department of Communication Studies and Director of the Center for Sports Communication & Media in the Moody College of Communication at The University of Texas at Austin. His research explores the connections between rhetoric, democracy, and sport, with particular interests in national identity, militarism, and public memory. He is the author of *Baseball and Rhetorics of Purity: The National Pastime and American Identity during the War on Terror,* co-author of *Communication and Sport: Surveying the Field,* and editor of *Sport and Militarism: Contemporary Global Perspectives.* Butterworth's essays have appeared in journals such as *Communication and Critical/Cultural Studies, Communication & Sport, Communication, Culture & Critique, Critical Studies in Media Communication,* the *International Review for the Sociology of Sport,* the *Journal of Communication,* the *Journal of Sport & Social Issues,* and the *Quarterly Journal of Speech.*

James L. Cherney (Ph.D., Indiana University) is an independent scholar living in Saline, Michigan. He has held Instructor and Assistant Professorships at Indiana University, Westminster College, Miami University, and Wayne State University. His work has appeared in such journals as the *Quarterly Journal of Speech,*

Argumentation and Advocacy, and the *Disability Studies Quarterly*. He frequently collaborates with Kurt Lindemann, and their work has appeared in several books and as lead articles in *Communication & Sport* and *Western Journal of Communication*. Among other projects, they are currently working on a book analyzing coverage of the 2018 Winter Paralympics.

Lisa M. Corrigan (Ph.D. University of Maryland) is an Associate Professor of Communication, Director of the Gender Studies Program, and Affiliate Faculty in both African & African American Studies and Latin American Studies at the University of Arkansas. Her first book, *Prison Power: How Prison Politics Influenced the Movement for Black Liberation* (University Press of Mississippi, 2016), is the recipient of the 2017 Diamond Anniversary Book Award and the 2017 African American Communication and Culture Division Outstanding Book Award both from the National Communication Association.

Daniel A. Grano (Ph.D. Louisiana State University) is a Professor in the Department of Communication Studies at the University of North Carolina at Charlotte. His research focuses on sport and politics, including issues surrounding race, labor, religion, and health. He has published in top peer-reviewed journals in communication studies, including *The Quarterly Journal of Speech, Rhetoric Society Quarterly, Rhetoric & Public Affairs*, and *Critical Studies in Media Communication*. His recent book *The Eternal Present of Sport: Rethinking Religion and Sport* (Temple University Press, 2017) won the National Communication Association Communication and Sport Division Outstanding Book Award.

Katrina N. Hanna is a doctoral student in the Hugh Downs School of Human Communication at Arizona State University (Kansas State University, M.A.). Her key area of research focuses on rhetorics of school choice within K-12 public education. Such work is informed by the intersection of critical race theory and rhetorical criticism.

Karen L. Hartman is an Associate Professor in the Department of Communication, Media, & Persuasion at Idaho State University. She earned her Ph.D. in Rhetoric from Louisiana State University and her research interests revolve largely around the role of sport in the United States and how language and public relations efforts frame athletes, organizations, and laws. She has authored numerous articles including research published in the *Journal of Communication Studies, International Journal of Sport Communication, Academic Exchange Quarterly*, and the edited volume *The ESPN Effect: Academic Studies of the Worldwide Leader in Sports*.

Abraham I. Khan holds a joint appointment as an Assistant Professor in Communication Arts and Sciences and African American Studies at Penn State University. He is a rhetorical scholar who specializes in research on civic engagement and African American politics and social life, with a particular emphasis on black athletes and the history of sports in the United States. His book, Curt Flood in the Media: Baseball, Race, and the Demise of the Activist Athlete, examines the competing models of public address at work in black political culture in the late 1960s and 1970s. Similar themes animate his work on figures such as Jackie Robinson, Michael Sam, and Richard Sherman, in essays that appear in journals such as *Communication & Sport* and *Popular Communication.*

Kyle W. Kusz is Associate Professor of Cultural Studies of Sports Media at the University of Rhode Island. His work investigates how sport media, films, celebrities, and cultures operate as political terrains that play key roles in contemporary debates about race, gender, and nationalism. He is the author of *Revolt of the White Athlete: Race, Media and the Emergence of Extreme Athletes in America* (Peter Lang, 2007).

Katherine L. Lavelle is an Associate Professor of Communication Studies at the University of Wisconsin-La Crosse, where she teaches courses in Advocacy, Public Communication, and Communication and Sport. Her previous research has explored representations of race, nationality, sex/gender, and other identity issues in sport. She has published work in a variety of communication and sport anthologies, and journals including Communication & Sport, and The Journal of Sports Media. She currently serves on the Board of Directors for IACS (International Association for Communication and Sport).

Kurt Lindemann (Ph.D., Arizona State University) is a Professor in the School of Communication at San Diego State University, where he is Director of Graduate Studies. He currently serves as Director of The Center for the Study of Media and Performance at SDSU. His research on disability, sport, and identity has appeared in a variety of scholarly outlets, including *Qualitative Inquiry, Text and Performance Quarterly, Western Journal of Communication*, and *Communication and Sport.*

Mike Milford (Ph.D., University of Kansas, 2005) is an Associate Professor in the School of Communication and Journalism at Auburn University. His research explores the ways in which popular culture, sports, and politics share ideological messages, with particular interests in collective identity, wartime public address, and national myths. Dr. Milford's research has appeared in journals such as *Rhetoric & Public Affairs, Mass Communication and Society, Rhetorica, Sport in History, Western Journal of Communication, Southern Communication Journal, Communication*

Quarterly, Communication Studies, Journal of Sports Media, Sport in Society, and the *International Journal of Sport Communication*.

Thomas P. Oates is an associate professor at the University of Iowa, where he holds a joint appointment in the Department of American Studies and the School of Journalism & Mass Communication. He is the author of *Football and Manliness: An Unauthorized Feminist Account of the NFL*.

Raymond I. Schuck is an Associate Professor of Communication in the Department of Humanities at Bowling Green State University Firelands. His research focuses on rhetorical and critical analysis of popular culture with particular emphasis on sport.

Anna M. "Amy" Young is Associate Professor and Chair of the Department of Communication at Pacific Lutheran University. Her work centers on questions of expertise and public and political life including her book, *Prophets, Gurus & Pundits: Rhetorical Styles & Public Engagement* (SIU Press, 2014). Most recently she's interested in food and wine politics, and is pursuing a second book manuscript on conservative rhetorical style. She is a lifelong athlete—a former competitive gymnast, dancer, skier, and runner, she's invested in the ways athletes can use their expertise to make political change.

Rhetoric, Sport, and the Political

An Introduction

DANIEL A. GRANO AND MICHAEL L. BUTTERWORTH

Prevailing wisdom in the United States has long held that politics and sport should not mix. Athletes are commonly told to "shut up and play," or "stick to sports," rather than express political opinions.[1] Indeed, Americans largely prefer to think of sport as a sanctuary, an arena where one can "escape" the politics and controversies that characterize life outside the ballpark or stadium. This belief shapes a narrative we might consider a "rhetorical fiction." In her study of the nation's founding narrative, Jennifer Mercieca observes, "Political fictions are narratives that political communities tell themselves about their government.... [They] both create and reflect political realities, and as such they are central to any political community."[2] If we shift our focus away from the formal institutions of government, we can find a meaningful parallel to Mercieca's description, as members of sport communities routinely tell themselves narratives that attempt to preserve the division from politics. Of course, such efforts have always been premised on the *illusion that sport is not already political*.

Even the most cursory historical review would yield powerful examples of the intersection between politics and sport in the United States. From activist-athletes such as Muhammad Ali and Billie Jean King, to invitations to the White House for championship teams, to diplomatic efforts facilitated by friendly competition, the evidence suggests that sport—like other prominent cultural institutions—both reflects and mobilizes political commitments, ideologies, and antagonisms. Yet, even if such evidence has long been available, it has been thrust to the forefront in recent years by a series of compelling and powerful expressions of political will in and through sport. Consequently, the rhetorical fiction of sport as apolitical is subject to renewed contestation. Such an effort is the focus of this book, and it is worth briefly assessing the terrain before we proceed.

Early in 2018, scandal engulfed a trio of prominent institutions—USA Gymnastics, the United States Olympic Committee (USOC), and Michigan State University (MSU). The common link between the three was Dr. Larry Nassar, an MSU faculty member and the team doctor for the nation's Olympic gymnastics team. In 2016, former gymnast Rachel Denhollander became the first of many athletes to accuse Nassar of sexual abuse; by the time Nassar was found guilty and sentenced to 175 years in prison, 156 women had delivered heartbreaking "impact statements" dramatizing the scope of his crimes.[3] To identify any of these statements as the most "important" or "influential" would be misguided—the survivors of Nassar's predatory behavior need not be categorized into some hierarchy of victimization. That said, the testimonies of particular women stood out, especially in the cases when the athletes were familiar Olympic heroes.

Based on her celebrated success as a member of the USA Gymnastics team that won a gold medal at the 2012 London Games, Aly Raisman became a primary spokesperson against Nassar. Although her fame may have provided her with initial visibility, it was her courage and intellect that expanded her influence. In one of the most widely reported impact statements, Raisman directed her testimony to Nassar in personal terms, declaring, "I am here to face you Larry, so you can see I have regained my strength—that I am no longer a victim, I am a survivor." Later, she invited Nassar (and others) to consider, "Imagine feeling like you have no power and no voice. Well, you know what, Larry, I have both power and voice, and I am only beginning to just use them."[4] Few moments were as powerful as when Raisman confronted Nassar, and her testimony exposed the political conditions that enabled his abusive behavior in the first place. In particular, she crystalized the collective voice of her fellow survivors to call into question the nation's mythic quest for Olympic glory and the institutional forms of sexism that view girls and women as objects of male dominance. Especially in the context of the emergent #MeToo movement, Raisman's example was politically powerful.[5]

Raisman is but one focal point in a much larger issue. As Nassar's trial moved toward sentencing, ESPN reported that officials in MSU's upper administration and athletics department had either dismissed or underestimated the seriousness of sexual assault allegations made against not only Nassar but also its football and men's basketball programs. The fallout led to the resignation of MSU President Lou Anna Simon and the "retirement" of Athletic Director Mark Hollis; meanwhile, the USOC compelled all members of the USA Gymnastics board to step down.[6] Such consequences are not insignificant, but they regrettably cannot dismantle all of the corruption found within university athletics programs, national Olympic committees, or international sporting bodies. Previous collegiate scandals at Penn State University and Baylor University, as well as ongoing cases of corruption within the International Olympic Committee (IOC) and Fédération Internationale de Football Association (FIFA), make clear that the institutional intersection of sport and politics is pervasive.

Shortly after the Nassar trial concluded, politics again intersected with the Olympics. Pyeongchang, South Korea hosted the 2018 Winter Games, and numerous storylines focused on the geopolitical stakes of staging the Olympics in a country embroiled in a bitter historical dispute with its neighbor to the north. These tensions were amplified by ongoing discussions—often facilitated online on Twitter—between U.S. President Donald Trump and North Korean leader Kim Jong-un. Trump did not travel to South Korea for the Games, but Vice President Mike Pence attended in his place. While the two heads of state traded in predictable efforts to leverage the symbolism of Olympic competition,[7] Pence found himself engaged in an unexpected conflict with a vocal member of Team USA.

Figure skater Adam Rippon had already made news as the first openly gay American male athlete to compete in the Winter Olympics. Throughout his years in public service, Mike Pence has established a record that is not hospitable to the LGBTQIA community. In particular, comments he made during a 2000 congressional campaign were interpreted by many as supportive of conversion therapy, a position on sexual identity that is widely discredited. Pence's comments re-entered the public conversation as Rippon became an increasingly visible and vocal member of Team USA. When asked prior to the Games about the Vice President's planned appearance, Rippon replied, "You mean Mike Pence, the same Mike Pence that funded gay conversion therapy? I'm not buying it." With respect to a potential meeting with Pence, Rippon added, "I would absolutely not go out of my way to meet with someone who I felt has gone out of their way to not only show that they aren't a friend of a gay person but that they think they're sick."[8] Although Pence's actual feelings about conversion therapy are unclear, Rippon's comments prompted a consideration of the ways athletes can be used as political props on the global stage even if they might belong to a community that remains marginalized at home.

The mediated dispute between Pence and Rippon escalated after a *USA Today* report suggested that the Vice President's office attempted to arrange a meeting between the two in Pyeongchang and that Rippon declined. Pence's press secretary insisted the accusations about conversation theory were baseless and Pence himself alleged on Twitter that *USA Today*'s Christine Brennan was guilty of "fake news."[9] Although the controversy dissipated shortly after this exchange, it disrupted the standard portrayal of American Olympians as national heroes and spotlighted the political contradictions embedded in such mythic narratives. Rippon's refusal to accept a passive definition of patriotism and team membership was juxtaposed against substantial questions about the Trump administration's diplomatic relationship with North Korea, its contempt for the mainstream media, and its loose interpretations of what counts as "fake" and "truth."

Before the Winter Olympics concluded, another controversy emerged in the United States. National Basketball Association (NBA) superstar LeBron James appeared with Kevin Durant on the digital sports network UNINTERRUPTED, where both were interviewed by ESPN's Cari Champion. James commented on several political issues, including the loss of esteem in the office of the presidency under the leadership of Donald Trump. He concluded, "At this time right now, with the president of the United States, it's at a bad time, and while we cannot change what comes out of that man's mouth, we can continue to alert the people that watch us, that listen to us, that this is not the way." Such comments directly challenge the notion that athletes should "stick to sports," but that sentiment was at the core of one especially prominent response to James. On her nightly show on FOX News, Laura Ingraham criticized James and Durant by suggesting that their relative lack of formal education and high salaries earned "to bounce a ball" made their perspectives illegitimate. "You're great players but no one voted for you. Millions elected Trump to be their coach," she said. "So keep the political commentary to yourself or, as someone once said, shut up and dribble."[10]

Few comments could better illustrate the prevailing wisdom that athletes should "shut up and play." Ingraham defiantly defended her critique when she received significant criticism of her own. For their part, James and Durant were unbowed. James responded with a hashtag on Twitter, "#wewillnotshutupanddribble," and also declared in a press conference, "We will definitely not shut up and dribble. I will definitely not do that."[11] Durant, meanwhile, noted that Ingraham's commentary contained a none-too-subtle racial subtext. He also pointed out her ignorance, noting, "I do play basketball, but I am a civilian and I am a citizen of the United States, so my voice is just as loud as hers, I think—or even louder."[12] As evidenced by the substantial support James and Durant received following the incident,[13] it is clear that the "shut up and play" mentality has limited utility. Indeed, while the entire episode may have cemented the attitudes of those on the political left, it also facilitated robust conversation among other communities about political speech in sports. That so many were quick to defend James and Durant and, by extension, other politically active athletes, demonstrates the rhetorical possibilities that lie at the intersection of politics and sport.

If Americans routinely tell themselves that politics and sport do not intersect, then the cases of Raisman, Rippon, and James and Durant work collectively to help imagine a new rhetorical fiction. More specifically, we argue in this volume that political discourses intersect in ways that make sport a unique site for rhetorical invention. As we open with these anecdotes from 2018, one might wonder why we have not yet mentioned the most obviously controversial figure of the past two years: Colin Kaepernick. For those unfamiliar with his situation, he was a back-up quarterback for the San Francisco 49ers going into the 2016 season. In the wake of numerous instances in the United States of young, African American men being killed by police officers, Kaepernick sought to draw attention to racial injustice by refusing to stand for the national anthem ceremony prior to the start of each game. In subsequent months, his protest led to accusations that he was unpatriotic, inspired others to emulate his example, prompted media to ponder the conditions for appropriate political speech, and alienated NFL owners who refused to sign him after his contract with San Francisco expired.[14]

Just as it appeared the controversy might burn out, President Donald Trump infamously reignited it with vulgar comments directed toward protesting athletes. At a campaign event in Alabama, he blustered, "Wouldn't you love to see one of these NFL owners, when somebody disrespects our flag, to say, 'Get that son of a bitch off the field right now, out, he's fired.'"[15] Trump's comments surely resonated with his supporters and many NFL viewers, but they also redirected attention to Kaepernick even as he remained out of the league. By the end of 2017, *GQ* magazine named Colin Kaepernick its "citizen of the year,"[16] and few could credibly claim that politics and sport do not mix. Later chapters in this book will address both Trump and Kaepernick so, for now, we are content to use this controversy to contextualize further our opening examples. Indeed, we want to suggest that the more we think about these incidents in conversation with one another, the more we can begin to understand sport as a rhetorical site that is constitutive of political culture. To demonstrate more clearly how this case, we turn our attention to the rhetorical tradition and the recent growth of interest in the study of sport.

SPORT/RHETORIC/POLITICS: FRAMING THE ARTICULATION

As rhetoric came of age in ancient Greece it was connected overtly with sport. Both were interrelated *agonistic* arts, practices of contest and struggle that constituted the citizenry. John Poulakos summarizes how an agonistic disposition mutually shaped sporting and civic contexts at the time, writing that athletics "shaped sophistical rhetoric in its image, making public discourse a matter of competition," while in turn "sophistical rhetoric pushed competition beyond the boundaries of the stadium and into the rhetorical forums of the court and the Assembly."[17] In her work on ancient connections between rhetoric and athletics, Debra Hawhee notes that agonism was not related simply to "outcome-driven competition." Rather, *agon* emphasized "the event of the gathering itself," an encounter between persons (athletes, judges, and spectators) and "a gathering of forces—cultural, bodily, and discursive" directed at competitive development of virtue along both physical and civic dimensions.[18] A core assumption that emerged in ancient notions of athletics and citizen-production was that a person's "nature" (e.g. temperament, character) could be produced agonistically, preparing "the mind-body complex for its role in the polis."[19]

We cannot draw a straight line from athletics in the ancient world to formalized, mediated sport today. In fact, Hawhee argues that mutually constitutive understandings of rhetoric and athletics dissolved as ancient sports became more specialized, demarcating activity around the beginnings of a mind/body split.[20] Yet the foundational belief underwriting these early sport/rhetoric articulations—that sport is a public proving ground for the intellectual and bodily virtues that constitute an ordered polity—remains powerful today. This is especially apparent in the fantasy that athletics serve as "both cause and consequence of moral virtue,"[21] an idea advanced in inspirational athlete profiles, documentary films, commemorative specials, advertising campaigns, and presidential addresses. It is also evident, though more controversially, where sportspersons and sport organizations engage in activities recognized as overtly or implicitly political.

The shared agonism of sport and rhetoric also overlapped with the emergence of democracy in ancient Greece. A democratic focus has been especially formative for contemporary rhetorical studies of sport, which have engaged sporting institutions and events as productive, contested sites of democratic culture. We are thankfully past the stage of minimizing sport's importance as a "microcosm" of society, as rhetorical studies of sport, along with decades of sociological and critical/cultural treatments, have demonstrated sport's constitutive influence over broader spheres of democratic culture. Sport fosters unique potential for resistive politics and social change. At the same time, the values upholding sport as a paragon for liberal, pluralistic democracy (inclusiveness, meritocracy) often circumscribe contestation of the very racial, gendered, religious, and nationalistic ideologies it constructs.[22] As a result, sport may be "valued as an exemplary *democratic* institution without any acknowledgment of the *political* contests that make democracy meaningful."[23]

Thus, sport's more explicitly "political" moments arise on the stage of an idealized democratic order (e.g. a level playing field, a space for transcending difference and inequity), a space that holds simultaneously open the possibilities of meaningful ruptures and hegemonic reinforcements. Mike Milford, for example, demonstrates how iconic athletes like Jesse Owens can enact "their nation's mythologies" through physical-rhetorical performances that at once dismantle white supremacist doctrine, while also affirming the goods of American liberal democracy in a way that averts consciousness of continued structural racism back home (as Owens experienced when he returned to the U.S.).[24] Similarly, Ron Von Burg and Paul Johnson illustrate how baseball's status as a uniquely powerful reserve for nostalgic memory also makes it a site where fantasies about exceptionalism, progress, and the American dream might come apart (particularly in moments of crisis such as the steroid era).[25] Both of these examples speak to a broader overlap between rhetoric of sport and public memory studies, and shared interests in how a democratic polity is imagined in relation to an idealized past, a process that always exceeds the ideological control of producers and officials.[26]

Despite these foundational linkages to agonism and democracy, sport has been until quite recently a marginal area of study among rhetorical scholars. Thomas Farrell's 1989 essay "Media Rhetoric as Social Drama" marks the first engagement with sport by a National Communication Association (NCA) affiliated rhetorician,[27] and that essay was followed by minimal similar treatment until the 2000s.[28] For the past couple decades or so, a number of rhetoricians have turned to sport figures and contexts occasionally to advance research agendas in related areas (e.g. identity, body rhetoric), and a much smaller group of scholars have focused primarily on sport as a site for criticism and articulated that site explicitly to the rhetorical tradition. Top national and regional journals within communication studies now feature rhetorical analyses of sport. This volume will add to a very short list of book-length treatments on the subject,[29] but rhetoricians covering sport can potentially place their work in any number of disciplinary and interdisciplinary book series. This is in large part because rhetoricians benefit—as do scholars in the broader area of communication and sport—from preceding work that established sport's legitimacy as an area of inquiry. To borrow from Abraham Khan, rhetoricians come to sport through the influence of interdisciplinary forces that are now decades old, as "the progeny of cognate fields within which we patiently gestated." As Khan notes, the founding document for academic studies of sport is Harry Edwards's book *Sociology of Sport* in 1973.[30] Communication studies goes back almost as far, to Michael Real's 1975 essay "Super Bowl: Mythic Spectacle,"[31] a work that preceded a broader media- and cultural studies-focused agenda for communication and sport.[32]

Rhetoric and sport studies are also upheld by several important, interrelated turns in contemporary rhetorical theory and criticism. First, rhetoric's move away from the strategic focus of neo-Aristotelian criticism and toward the demands of the "ideological turn" or a "critical rhetoric" involved through its various stages of development calls to take sides in relation to vested power—to make judgments and advocate for alternative structures and practices—across an expanded array of contexts.[33] Today the mission of a "critical rhetoric" informs scholarship across diverse sites such as food culture, environmental activism, and queer theory.[34] Rhetoric and sport scholarship has focused consistently on problems surrounding power and social change and, as such, it has performed a mission that is recognizably "critical" within the discipline. Second, efforts to open rhetoric to studies of the popular, whether in relation to popular culture[35] or cultural studies,[36] extended critiques of dominant power to cultural domains that rhetoricians may have regarded previously as too low or vernacular. These connections to the popular also open up spaces for sport scholarship, and while sport has not historically had the same status within rhetoric as, say, popular music, television, film, or advertising, this is starting to change.[37] Third, the turn toward materialist rhetoric opened the discipline to the study of bodies,[38] an especially important development considering the centrality of corporeality and movement in sport. Debra Hawhee's *Bodily Arts* is a particularly important work for advancing a bodily conception of rhetoric—across the field and particularly within sport—but rhetoric of sport studies also fit into and advance broader justifications for corporeal approaches.[39]

Rhetorical studies of sport do not ride these turns passively; rather, they contribute actively to problems, approaches, and priorities central to contemporary theory and criticism. That contribution has remained somewhat quarantined, however, due to a tendency among scholars, editors, and reviewers within our discipline to compartmentalize sport rhetoric studies as ultimately, merely *about sport*. Essays analyzing complex processes of struggle and change condensed in the case of a sport star or sporting event—e.g. whiteness, nationalism, sexuality, citizenship, commemoration—are commonly categorized as "sports" essays, and are thus published and read apart from "non-sport" essays that cover directly-related problems.[40] The practical result is that rhetorical scholars who study sport are unlikely to be cited by colleagues with parallel and overlapping interests. Just as problematic, rhetoricians who study sport only occasionally will often cite a cherry-picked list of studies (usually from sociology of sport) without engaging with directly relevant sport rhetoric scholarship published within disciplinary journals and book series. One of our hopes for this volume, then, is that it might work against reductions of scholarship focused on the complex social relations structured around and through sport as simply "about sports."[41] To that end our contributors include scholars who have focused their programs of study on sport, and scholars who are leaders in areas of thought (e.g. race, sexuality, the body, circulation, public memory, activism, public health) that relate centrally to sporting contexts. This book serves, then, as a dwelling place that illustrates how porous the lines between "sport" and "non-sport" rhetoric are, or ought to be.

This brings us to the subject of how to think about the political in relationship to sport. In general terms we find Chantal Mouffe's distinction between the terms *political* and *politics* helpful. Mouffe maintains that "the political" refers to a permanent condition in which human relations are unavoidably defined by conflict. In such a state, "politics" is a mechanism for establishing order through practices, discourses, and institutions. Politics, then, is the means by which we come to terms with conflict and construct collective identities.[42] Thinking in these broad terms allows us to appreciate *as political* a broad range of activities in sport, from explicit activism to mundane institutional processes. As Davis Houck argues, the scope one assigns to the political will focus critical attention within the broader terrain of communication and sport and align a given project with specific disciplinary influences. An essay that limits the term "political" to "a civic context in which politicians, elected and otherwise, leverage sport for rhetorical ends," for example, will contribute to our understandings of governmental spheres of influence, while also deemphasizing some of the broader power/knowledge relations examined in critical/cultural studies of sport.[43] Each essay in this volume demonstrates how attention to a specific athlete, event, mode of activism, or production process offers unique insights about the relationships between rhetoric, sport, and the political. What ties all of the chapters together is a common definition of "politics" or "the political" around issues of struggle and change—including actual, potential, and failed changes.

THE MEANINGS OF POLITICAL STRUGGLE IN SPORT: OUR EXHORTATION

So, for rhetoricians engaging sport in the 21st century the news is mostly good. We come into a disciplinary context more receptive to sport studies than ever before, supported by decades of interdisciplinary and intradisciplinary work. A rhetorical scholar coming to the subject anew is likely to understand, borrowing from Khan, that they can "talk about sport without embarrassment."[44] In our estimation rhetorical studies of sport are positioned well for a new stage of development, one aimed less at the *legitimacy* of sport as an object of study than at the *importance* of sport as political context. Here we run into sport's presumed limits as a site for political struggle and social change, a problem that rhetoricians and scholars throughout interdisciplinary sport culture studies confront alike. For a representative example of what this challenge looks like in rhetoric, consider a review of Barry Brummett's edited volume *Sporting Rhetoric* in *The Quarterly Journal of Speech*. The review is generally positive, but it ends with the following lines:

> The authors are particularly successful in challenging the romanticized notion that sport offers a site of resistance and change. Although sport has functioned in that capacity at times, the contributors demonstrate how sport more often functions to reinforce or reify dominant social values.[45]

The problem with this review—and with the broader disciplinary presumptions it projects—is that it totalizes sport as inherently repressive, an institution about which scholarship can only expose corruptions, but not locate alternative possible futures. We perceive this as a principal barrier to the fuller development of sport studies in rhetorical theory and criticism. As Ben Carrington writes, many scholars perceive sport as fundamentally incompatible with social change, a form of activity that is not just "apolitical" but "actively *anti*-political." If sport is solely complicit with "ideological manipulation" and ultimately "devoid of any counter-cultural elements," then the only point in critiquing it is to expose it as a site for false consciousness.[46]

A more expansive theoretical and practical project would involve acknowledging how sport often limits the possibilities of a progressive politics, while also understanding that sport can, "under specific circumstances, offer a space through which oppositional politics could be fought and won."[47] Neither we nor the contributors to this volume idealize or romanticize such oppositional moments. We recognize they are complex and, at times, contradictory. Moreover, the "success" of such efforts is variable and may or may not provide a model for additional political action. Nevertheless, we are intrigued by the possibilities of political struggle within and around sport and believe that our moment provides particularly important opportunities to consider more broadly what it means to be political in our contemporary age.

It is perhaps more obvious today than at any point in recent history that sport is an inherently, inescapably political institution. This has much to do with a current upsurge in athlete-activism. Until recently, scholars and popular commentators worried over the "demise" of activist athletes.[48] As the story went, sport stars whose performances threatened predominant social mores—Babe Didrikson Zaharias, Billie Jean King, Tommie Smith, John Carlos, Muhammad Ali, Jim Brown, Curt Flood, Arthur Ashe, and others—used to be willing to leverage their status as a pulpit for social change. In contrast, "modern athletes" have presumably come to view political activism as a threat to their pursuit of lucrative contracts and endorsement deals. As our opening narratives suggest, however, there has been a noteworthy intensification of activism at all levels of sport. As basketball great Kareem Abdul-Jabbar (himself a historically prominent athlete-activist) proclaimed in a 2015 *Time* magazine article, "The days of the silenced jock are long gone."[49]

Multiple news outlets have framed athlete activism from 2012 forward as a return to a 1960s- and 1970s-era *ethos* of social responsibility, long lost to base self-interest but now renewed in the face of overwhelming injustice and supercharged by social media.[50] While bridging our moment to the 60s and 70s problematically glosses decades of political activity in sport, there has, in fact, been a glut of activism in recent years. As Khan has demonstrated, athlete-activists' efforts (and more generally, athletes' efforts at antiracist or anti-homophobic resistance) are often captured by and reshaped around sport's dominant logics (e.g. respectability, neoliberalism). Yet even in failed or appropriated attempts we can extract lessons for meaningful change.[51]

In addition to activism, sport rhetoric scholars have attended to a broader range of activities that fall under the more ordinary, normalizing practices of ideological production. The studies on sport and public memory cited above are good examples. We would also cite attention to issues of identity, myth, ritual, celebrity, and body politics as illustrations of how broadly rhetoricians have considered the political within and around sport.[52] A broad view of politics and the political allows, then, for recognition of how central sport is to contemporary antagonisms over, for example, gender and sexual binarism, queer visibilities, race and labor relations, public health, domestic violence, global institutional corruption, and posthuman body politics. Rhetoricians can justify sport as politically *consequential* through attention to these antagonisms but this requires, in our estimation, a dual focus.

We cannot maintain that *sport alone* produces the political struggles we analyze in our work, as this would isolate sport from its broader social and institutional connections. In his exhortation to cultural studies critics Lawrence Grossberg calls for research based in a "radical contextualism" wherein scholars assume that "the identity, significance, and effects of any practice or event … are defined only by the complex set of relations that surround, interpenetrate, and shape it." We want to make a similar exhortation for rhetorical studies of sport, insisting that sport cannot be "isolated from it relations," but must be understood "as a condensation of multiple determinations and effects."[53] From that standpoint, it becomes essential to demonstrate how sport condenses these effects in ways that exert *unique force* across a broader structure of social relations.[54]

At the same time, we cannot insist upon sport's importance without demonstrating how relations of power take *particular shape* within, through, and around sport. If those of us who are interested in rhetorical approaches to sport look to justify sport as *yet another* site for struggles over problems that fellow rhetorical scholars already care about (race, class, sexuality, gender, nationalism, and so on) then we risk losing by way of comparison: if we can learn everything we need to know about these problems by routing through a context with more long-standing status among rhetoricians (say electoral politics, social movements, even other popular cultural forms like film, music, or reality TV) why bother with sport? Why not just leave engagements with sport to the "sport" people? The improved standing of sport rhetoric studies provides only partial assistance here. We still need to provide good reasons for spending time and labor within the context (even if that labor simply involves reading and transposing sport-specific insights to non-sport contexts), arguing not only that sport is important (or popular or influential, all of which is obvious by now), but that it is *productive*. We can make that case through critiques that demonstrate how sport offers understandings of practices or social formations or economies that scholars cannot get in quite the same way elsewhere.

OVERVIEW OF CHAPTERS

The chapters in this volume reflect both a recognition that sport enacts particular ideologies and the affirmation that sport can be a site for resisting and reframing those ideologies. As editors, we had at least two important commitments in mind. First, we wanted to assemble a set of studies that accounted for as much range as possible—we wanted to represent diverse perspectives, multiple identities, and a dialogue between historical and contemporary cases. In many ways, we believe we have accomplished this goal. That said, as much as the subjects of each chapter reflect significant diversity, our hope is that this collection will provide a platform to support even more work by people of color, women, and queer scholars. We recognize that rhetorical scholarship generally, and rhetorical studies of sport specifically, would benefit from much more diversity.[55] Second, we aimed to include established scholars whose primary focus is on sport and those with a record in rhetorical studies that would provide meaningful insights into an area they typically do not study. On this account, we are delighted by the outcome, as many of the chapters included here are authored by scholars who do not usually write about sport. We are confident the volume is strengthened by the inclusion of scholars with varied research agendas, each of whom has added unique insights to the project.

As we have noted, recent conversations about sport and politics have been prompted by the renewed energy of the "activist athlete," especially as it has been channeled toward racial injustice and violence. Given the significance of this moment, we open the book with a section called "Contextualizing Sport and Political Struggle," where we aim to reflect on both the history of athlete activism and its prospects for the future. The first chapter features Abraham Khan's engagement with the legacy of Curt Flood, the former Major League Baseball (MLB) player frequently credited with paving the way for free agency in professional sports. Journalists and other observers use memories of Flood to frame the public's understanding of free agency in terms of sport's marketplaces, often leading to discussions about contracts and salaries. Khan urges us to see in Flood's resistance a model for understanding labor mobility in sport (free agency) as the capacity to act politically (rhetorical agency). This happens, he suggests, through the lens of confrontational rhetoric, a strategy that threatens oppressive ideologies.

Flood's actions half a century ago dramatized the exploitation of *labor*, but he carefully articulated that exploitation to *race* by invoking slavery as a metaphor to describe the conditions of the professional sports marketplace. Nearly fifty years later, race remains central to athletic expressions of resistance. In chapter two, Katherine Lavelle attends to the specific context of the Women's National Basketball Association (WNBA) in 2016, where several players responded to the many instances of innocent African American men being killed by (mostly) white police officers. Lavelle centers the WNBA players as examples of democratic engagement, arguing that their actions helped shed light on the mobilization efforts of the Black Lives Matter movement. As she points out, much of the recent discussion about political activism among athletes revolves around men—in the case of the WNBA, the activism of women helps to show how feminist sensibilities can be brought to bear on challenges to hierarchy. Whereas white male athletes in 2016 remained largely silent on matters of racial justice, both African American and white players spoke out in the WNBA. Additionally, the league's players built on established connections to their local community to build support for their actions on the court. In these ways, female athletes demonstrated early on an appreciation for intersectionality and a challenge to traditional hierarchy.

Pulling the lens back up, in chapter three Karen Hartman uses the historical precedents of the 1960s and 1970s to contextualize contemporary acts of protest. While using the high-profile example of Colin Kaepernick to ground her chapter, she attends to a range of political acts in multiple sports. For Hartman, the theories of Kenneth Burke provide a vocabulary for making sense of how sport's ritualistic role in civil religion masks the politics in operation. Consequently, the public interprets actions as "political" only when they disrupt rituals we have taken for granted. Here, Hartman echoes the spirit of Khan's reference to confrontational rhetoric, revealing how contemporary athletes enact the threats to ideologies that reveal their rhetorical agency. Although constraints remain, such actions open new spaces for further political engagement.

The second part of the book is called "Mobilizing Resistances" and, in this section, we look to a range of specific contexts, texts, and discourses in order to envision other forms of political action. In other words, while protest is dramatic and highly visible, it is far from the only mode of engagement. The section opens with chapter four, in which Jeffrey Bennett revisits the legacy of Olympic diver Greg Louganis through the lens of queer memory. As an elite athlete, Louganis had suppressed his sexual identity for fear of losing sponsors, and subsequent panic over his announcement that he was HIV-positive confirmed many of those fears. Years later, in 2016, General Mills placed Louganis's image on the cover of the Wheaties cereal box as part of its "Legends Series," a move that may not have nullified his absence from the iconic box in the 1980s but nevertheless signaled a shift in the politics of representing queer athletes. As Bennett notes, a degree of liberation can be found in the marketplace, and the visibility of Louganis's Wheaties box makes it a commodity that moves images of queer identity and HIV/AIDS into mainstream spaces. Once stigmatized, Louganis now symbolizes transcendence and success.

Another once-stigmatized Olympian was Muhammad Ali, feared not for his sexuality but for his refusal to please norms of white society. In chapter five, Lisa Corrigan also considers the role of memory, this time by attending to the friendship between Ali and civil rights advocate Malcolm X. For Corrigan, their relationship was defined by what she calls "rhetorical intimacy," in which the two figures enacted a form of black male pride that helped shape the public sphere. Because sport is both a "sphere of sociality" and the most visible public site of black male intimacy, Ali and Malcolm were able to complement each other's rhetorical strengths and help establish their shared humanity in the context of significant resistance to civil rights. In particular, the photographic record of this intimacy allows for a reconsideration of how both men factor into public memory, especially in our contemporary moment that is too often defined by hostility toward African American men.

In chapter six, Mike Milford turns our attention to Native Americans in sport by focusing on the Iroquois Nationals, the only team of indigenous people competitive at an international level. The Nationals play lacrosse, a sport with elitist connotations in the United States that is actually rooted in Native American history and culture. By honoring the sport's mythic origins, their success at high-level competitions allow them to enact what Kenneth Burke would call "symbolic boasting." As Milford observes, symbolic boasting is often a strategy of appropriation, wherein the accomplishments of one party are borrowed by another in the hopes of benefitting from the spoils of success. In the case of the Nationals, however, symbolic boasting is a means for Native Americans to translate success on the field into an affirmation of community and heritage. In this way, sport provides a means of representation that is rarely available to Native American communities.

Daniel Brouwer and Katrina Hanna are also interested in identity in chapter seven, where they focus on the intersections of race and sexuality as performed in the "Honey Badger" meme. Although this meme and its voice—Randall—have had many incarnations, they argue that it became most visible once football player Tyrann Mathieu was given "honey badger" as a nickname. Brouwer and Hanna point out that Randall's vocalizations mark him obviously as "queer," a characteristic not typically articulated with the hypermasculine world of football. Yet Mathieu's own identity is complicated by his creole heritage and troubled history at Louisiana State University. For Brouwer and Hanna, the articulation of Mathieu to the "tenacity" of the honey badger allows him to fashion his own redemption while subverting common racial stereotypes. Although this disarticulates queer identity from the original meme, it also enables certain forms of oppositional politics.

The final chapter in this section features an athlete often understood for his oppositional expressions. In chapter eight, Anna Young defines NFL player Richard Sherman as a kind of public intellectual, drawing on Gramsci's notion of the organic intellectual and the religious metaphor of "witnessing." As she contends, witnessing functions as a rhetorical commonplace that calls attention to matters of justice and injustice. For Sherman, whose brash expressions have earned him the scorn of many (white) fans, his vernacular performances seek to challenge criticisms rooted in racism. Through the lens of witnessing, Young views these performances as a public modality, a means of democratic engagement. Furthermore, as a vocal African American male athlete, Sherman *embodies* this engagement in ways that allow him to reclaim his own agency.

We believe the chapters in "Mobilizing Resistances" demonstrate various forms of rhetorical agency that are crucial for envisioning future forms of political action in sport. In the next section, "Confronting Stigmas," we see some of the limitations and barriers that continue to challenge those who envision political change. These chapters are not wholly determined by ideology or oppression; nevertheless, they remind us that political struggle in sport is no less complicated as it is in other arenas. The first chapter in this section, chapter nine, is written by two scholars who have helped define our understanding of disability in sport. James Cherney and Kurt Lindemann are quick to acknowledge the importance of more visibility of disabled athletes through media productions of events such as the Paralympic Games. At the same time, however, they lament the over-emphasis on stereotypes such as the "supercrip," a construction that celebrates disabled athletes only when they achieve spectacular feats and, at the same time, minimizes the accomplishments of disabled athletes who are elite competitors. Their focus is primarily on the NBC broadcast in 2016, which used multiple human interest stories to emphasize the inspirational athletes who overcame their physical challenges. The other side of this coverage, Cherney and Lindemann argue, is that those who cannot overcome an injury or disability are perceived as failures.

Meredith Bagley examines the role of bodies in the presentation of sexuality at the annual ESPY awards in chapter ten. The ESPYs mimic more established awards shows such as the Emmys and Oscars, recognizing various athletes and teams for their accomplishments. One of the more noteworthy honors is the Arthur Ashe Courage Award, given to someone who has overcome adversity, inspired others, or contributed to society in a meaningful way. Recipients of the award in 2014 and 2015—Michael Sam and Caitlyn Jenner—demonstrate some of the ways the politics of identity have been featured in sport. Both Sam—an African American male who became the first openly gay man to be drafted by an NFL team—and Jenner—an Olympic hero as "Bruce" in 1976 who helped recast perceptions of trans identity as "Caitlyn"—embody overt challenges to perceived norms about gender and sexuality. Bagley observes the ways their presence and the awards programs queer identity by presenting gender as fluid. Nevertheless, both athletes are still celebrated through a conventional neoliberal narrative that affirms individual achievement and may elide structural concerns. And, while Bagley finds promise in the ways Sam and Jenner link athletic praxis to rhetorical agency, she also points to the limits of such expressions when they are presented in an ESPN-branded package.

The presence of Michael Sam and Caitlyn Jenner at an awards show may help reconstitute our shared ideas about gender and sexuality, therefore demonstrating how sport can assist in facilitating uncomfortable conversations. Similarly, discussions of mental health are often difficult, and sport's traditional emphasis on "mental toughness" can make them even more challenging. In chapter eleven,

Raymond Schuck examines mental health through the case of former MLB pitcher Pete Harnisch. Harnisch acknowledged struggling with depression, which landed him on the disabled list (DL) in 1997. As Schuck points out, baseball is a mentally grueling sport, and Harnisch's admission opened a new dialogue about players' well-being. In light of more recent conversations, led by athletes such as the NBA's Kevin Love and DeMar DeRozan, it seems fair to mark 1997 as an important starting point for being open about mental health. At the same time, Schuck demonstrates the ways Harnisch's own language defines his health in terms of his own personal struggles. In this way, mental health remains something for individual athletes to "overcome," as opposed to something that can be productively managed at a structural level.

Barry Brummett provides the final chapter of this section, turning his attention to athletes' coming out narratives in chapter twelve. He brings our focus back to Michael Sam and also Jason Collins, who became the first professional male athlete on a team sport in the United States to come out as gay. Brummett is interested in Kenneth Burke's notion of piety and the rhetorical norms that guide people about what is permissible to say and when. Sport provides a particularly good site to examine this notion because of its visibility and the ways intersectionality factors into identity. Both Sam and Collins are African American and gay, meaning that both are constituted by cultural and historical assumptions about those identity categories. Through the act of coming out, these athletes provide the "justification" for some observers to make comments about race and sexuality they otherwise know would be inappropriate. Thus, although coming out narratives may carry some emancipatory weight, they might also become the grounds on which rhetorical norms can be violated.

It is fair to say that all of the chapters previewed above are nuanced enough to know that sport is neither entirely emancipatory nor entirely oppressive. That said, there are moments of courage, inspiration, and observable change that provide some optimism that sport may be a productive site for political struggle. And yet, at a moment in the United States when democratic norms and practices are under siege, we are quick to urge caution. This is why the final section of the book, "Future Provocations," relies on a single chapter to issue a final call to rhetorical critics of sport. In chapter thirteen, Thomas Oates and Kyle Kusz ponder a political terrain defined by "Trumpism," and critique the president's use of sport to drive a wedge between "winners" and "losers." As they demonstrate, Trump's history with sport is freighted with commitments to white masculinity, and his associations with contemporary figures such as Bo Knight confirm his contempt for women, people of color, and the LGBTQ community. As much as *Sport, Rhetoric, and Political Struggle* is premised on viewing sport as a vehicle for meaningful social change, the damage wrought by the Trump presidency compels us to end the book with a clear note of concern. As Oates and Kusz note in their conclusion, it is incumbent upon critical scholars to identify and invent the rhetorical means for sport to bring about a better world.

NOTES

1. For more on this idea, see Dave Zirin, *A People's History of Sports in the United States: 250 Years of Politics, Protest, and Play* (New York: New Press, 2008); and Michael L. Butterworth, "The Athlete as Citizen: Rhetorical Invention and Judgement in Sport," *Sport in Society: Cultures, Commerce, Media, Politics* 17, no. 7 (2014): 867–83.

2. Jennifer R. Mercieca, *Founding Fictions* (Tuscaloosa, AL: University of Alabama Press, 2010), 27.

3. Marisa Kwiatkowski, Mark Alesia, and Tim Evans, "A Blind Eye to Sex Abuse: How USA Gymnastics Failed to Report Cases," *Indianapolis Star*, August 4, 2016, https://www.indystar.com/story/news/investigations/2016/08/04/usa-gymnastics-sex-abuse-protected-coaches/85829732/; Stephanie Wang, "'I Knew What the Cost Would Be': Why Sexual Assault Victims Stay Silent," *Indianapolis Star*, October 18, 2017, https://www.indystar.com/story/news/crime/2017/10/18/metoo-rachael-denhollander-usa-gymnastics-sexual-assault/776387001/; Tom Lutz, "Victim Impact Statements Against Larry Nassar: 'I Thought I Was Going to Die,'" *The Guardian*, January 24, 2018, https://www.theguardian.com/sport/2018/jan/24/victim-impact-statements-against-larry-nassar-i-thought-i-was-going-to-die.

4. "Full Text of Aly Raisman's Statement," *New York Times*, January 20, 2018, https://www.nytimes.com/2018/01/20/sports/full-text-of-aly-raismans-statement.html.

5. For more on the mythic quest for Olympic glory, see Dvora Meyers, "The U.S. Gymnastics System Wanted More Medals, and Created a Culture of Abuse to Get Them," *Deadspin.com*, May 1, 2017, https://deadspin.com/the-u-s-gymnastics-system-wanted-more-medals-and-crea-1794525855; For more on #MeToo, see Sophie Gilbert, "The Movement of #MeToo," *The Atlantic*, October 16, 2017, https://www.theatlantic.com/entertainment/archive/2017/10/the-movement-of-metoo/542979/.

6. Mark Tracy, "Nassar Case Topples U.S.A. Gymnastics Board and M.S.U. Athletic Director," *New York Times*, January 26, 2018, https://www.nytimes.com/2018/01/26/sports/michigan-state-mark-hollis.html.

7. For more on the political significance of the Winter Games for Kim Jong-Un, see Joshua Keating, "Kim Jong-Un Is Having a Great Olympics," *Slate.com*, February 12, 2018, https://slate.com/culture/2018/02/kim-jong-un-is-having-a-great-olympics.html.

8. Liam Stack, "Mike Pence Tangles with Olympian Adam Rippon over Gay Rights Record," *New York Times*, February 9, 2018, https://www.nytimes.com/2018/02/09/sports/pence-rippon-olympics.html.

9. Christine Brennan, "Openly Gay Figure Skater Adam Rippon Declined Chance to Speak with Vice President Pence," *USA Today*, February 7, 2018, https://www.usatoday.com/story/sports/columnist/brennan/2018/02/07/2018-winter-olympics-vice-president-mike-pence-adam-rippon-south-korea-gay-rights/314167002/.

10. Chris Chavez, "FOX News' Laura Ingraham: LeBron Should 'Shut Up and Dribble' After Criticism of President Trump," *Sports Illustrated*, February 16, 2018, https://www.si.com/nba/2018/02/16/fox-news-laura-ingraham-lebron-james-president-donald-trump-shut-dribble.

11. Jonah Engel Bromwich, "'To Me, It Was Racist': N.B.A. Players Respond to Laura Ingraham's Comments on LeBron James," *New York Times*, February 16, 2018, https://www.nytimes.com/2018/02/16/sports/basketball/lebron-laura-ingraham.html; Daniel Popper, "LeBron James Responds to Laura Ingraham: 'We Will Definitely Not Shut Up and Dribble,'" *New York Daily News*, February 18, 2018, http://www.nydailynews.com/sports/basketball/lebron-james-responds-laura-ingraham-trump-comments-article-1.3827247.

12. Sam Amick, "Kevin Durant on Laura Ingraham's Commentary: 'To Me, It Was Racist,'" *USA Today*, February 16, 2018, https://www.usatoday.com/story/sports/nba/2018/02/16/kevin-durant-lebron-james-laura-ingraham-comments/347322002/.

13. Bromwich, "'To Me, It Was Racist'"

14. For a good summary of the Kaepernick story through 2016, see John Branch, "The Awakening of Colin Kaepernick," *New York Times*, September 7, 2017, https://www.nytimes.com/2017/09/07/sports/colin-kaepernick-nfl-protests.html.

15. Ken Belson and Julie Hirschfield Davis, "Trump Attacks Warriors' Curry," *New York Times*, September 23, 2017, https://www.nytimes.com/2017/09/23/sports/football/trump-nfl-kaepernick.html?hp&clickSource=story-heading&WT.nav=top-news&_r=0&module=ArrowsNav&contentCollection=Sports&action=keypress&region=FixedLeft&pgtype=article.

16. "Colin Kaepernick Is GQ's 2017 Citizen of the Year," *GQ*, November 13, 2017, https://www.gq.com/story/colin-kaepernick-cover-men-of-the-year.

17. John Poulakos, *Sophistical Rhetoric in Classical Greece* (Columbia: University of South Carolina Press, 1995), 32–3.

18. Debra Hawhee, "Agonism and Aretê," *Philosophy and Rhetoric* 35, no. 3 (2002): 185–207; Debra Hawhee, *Bodily Arts: Rhetoric and Athletics in Ancient Greece* (Austin, TX: The University of Texas Press, 2004), 17–22.

19. Debra Hawhee, "Emergent Flesh: Phusiopoiesis and Ancient Arts of Training," *Journal of Sport and Social Issues* 25, no. 2 (2001): 149; also see Heather L. Reid, "Sport and Moral Education in Plato's Republic," *Journal of the Philosophy of Sport* 34, no. 2 (2007): 160–75.

20. Debra Hawhee, "Rhetorics, Bodies, and Everyday Life," *Rhetoric Society Quarterly* 36, no. 2 (2006): 156. Here Hawhee assigns this shift toward professionalization and dualism to the Hellenistic period.

21. Dan D. Nimmo and James E. Combs, *Mediated Political Realities* (New York: Longman, 1983), 128.

22. Michael L. Butterworth, "Militarism and Memorializing at the Pro Football Hall of Fame," *Communication and Critical/Cultural Studies* 9, no. 3 (2012): 241–58; Michael L. Butterworth, *Baseball and Rhetorics of Purity: The National Pastime and American Identity During the War on Terror* (Tuscaloosa: University of Alabama Press, 2010); Michael L. Butterworth and Stormi D. Moskal, "American Football, Flags, and 'Fun': The Bell Helicopter Armed Forces Bowl and the Rhetorical Production of Militarism," *Communication, Culture & Critique* 2, no. 4 (2009): 411–33; Michael L. Butterworth, "Purifying the Body Politic: Steroids, Rafael Palmeiro, and the Rhetorical Cleansing of Major League Baseball," *Western Journal of Communication* 72, no. 2 (2008): 145–61; Michael L. Butterworth, "The Politics of the Pitch: Claiming and Contesting Democracy Through the Iraqi National Soccer Team," *Communication and Critical/Cultural Studies* 4, no. 2 (2007): 184–203; Michael L. Butterworth, "Ritual in the 'Church of Baseball': Suppressing the Discourse of Democracy After 9/11," *Communication and Critical/Cultural Studies* 2, no. 2 (2005): 107–29.

23. Michael L. Butterworth, "Saved at Home: Christian Branding and Faith Nights in the 'Church of Baseball,'" *Quarterly Journal of Speech* 97, no. 3 (2011): 313.

24. Mike Milford, "The Olympics, Jesse Owens, Burke, and the Implications of Media Framing in Symbolic Boasting," *Mass Communication and Society* 15 (2012): 486.

25. Ron Von Burg and Paul E. Johnson, "Yearning for a Past that Never Was: Baseball, Steroids, and the Anxiety of the American Dream," *Critical Studies in Media Communication* 26, no. 4 (2009): 351–71. Also see Butterworth, *Baseball and Rhetorics of Purity* and Butterworth, "Purifying the Body Politic."

26. See for example, Daniel A. Grano, *The Eternal Present of Sport: Rethinking Sport and Religion* (Philadelphia, PA: Temple University Press, 2017); Daniel A. Grano and Kenneth S. Zagacki, "Cleansing the Superdome: The Paradox of Purity and Post-Katrina Guilt," *Quarterly Journal of Speech* 97, no. 2 (2011): 201–23; Butterworth, "Militarism"; Butterworth, *Baseball*; Victoria J. Gallagher and Margaret R. LaWare, "Sparring with Public Memory: The Rhetorical Embodiment of Race, Power, and Conflict in *The Monument to Joe Louis*," in *Places of Public Memory: The Rhetoric of Museums and Memorials*, eds. Greg Dickinson, Carole Blair, and Brian L. Ott (Tuscaloosa: University of Alabama Press, 2010), 87–112; and Roger C. Aden, "Nostalgic Communication as Temporal Escape: *When It Was A Game's* Re-Construction of a Baseball/Work Community," *Western Journal of Communication* 59 (1995): 20–38.

27. Thomas B. Farrell, "Media Rhetoric as Social Drama: The Winter Olympics of 1984," *Critical Studies in Mass Communication* 6, no. 2 (1989): 158–82. Noreen Wales Kruse published an earlier 1981 essay on sport in *The Quarterly Journal of Speech* but Farrell was the first rhetorician associated with the National Communication Association to publish on the subject. See Noreen Wales Kruse, "Apologia in Team Sport," *The Quarterly Journal of Speech* 67, no. 3 (1981): 270–83.

28. See as a lone example Barry Brummett and Margaret Carlisle Duncan, "Theorizing Without Totalizing: Specularity and Televised Sports," *Quarterly Journal of Speech* 76, no. 3 (1990): 227–46. This is not to say that sport communication essays were not published during this period. Some were, but none by rhetoricians and few very with an implicitly rhetorical focus. Nick Trujillo's work has influenced current rhetoric of sport scholarship and stands as an important exception. See Nick Trujillo, "Hegemonic Masculinity on the Mound: Media Representations of Nolan Ryan and American Sports Culture," *Critical Studies in Mass Communication* 8, no. 3 (1991): 290–308; and Nick Trujillo, "Interpreting (the Work and the Talk of) Baseball: Perspectives on Ballpark Culture," *Western Journal of Communication* 56, no. 4 (1992): 350–71.

29. See, Grano, *The Eternal Present*; Barry Brummett and Andrew Ishak, eds., *Sports and Identity: New Agendas in Communication* (New York: Routledge, 2014); Abraham Iqbal Khan, *Curt Flood in the Media: Baseball, Race and the Demise of the Activist-Athlete* (Oxford, MS: University Press of Mississippi, 2012); Butterworth, *Baseball and Rhetorics of Purity*; Barry Brummett, ed., *Sporting Rhetoric: Performance, Games and Politics* (New York: Peter Lang, 2009); and Linda K. Fuller, ed., *Sport, Rhetoric and Gender: Historical Perspectives and Media Representations* (New York: Palgrave MacMillan, 2006).

30. Abraham I. Khan, "Sport and Race: A Disciplinary History and Exhortation," in *Defining Sport Communication*, ed. Andrew C. Billings (New York: Routledge, 2017), 107–20.

31. Michael Real, "Super Bowl: Mythic Spectacle," *Journal of Communication* 25, no. 1 (1975): 31–43.

32. See, for example, Lawrence A. Wenner, "Media, Sports, and Society: The Research Agenda," in *Media, Sports, & Society*, ed. Lawrence A. Wenner (Newbury Park, CA: Sage, 1989), 13–48; and Sut Jhally, "Cultural Studies and the Sports/Media Complex," in *Media, Sports, & Society*, ed. Lawrence A. Wenner (Newbury Park, CA: Sage, 1989), 70–93. For a summary of the evolution

of communication and sport studies see Nick Trjuillo, "Introduction," in *Case Studies in Sport Communication*, eds. Robert S. Brown and Daniel J. O'Rourke III (Westport, CT: Praeger), xi–xv.

33. See, for example, Karlyn Kohrs Campbell, "'Conventional Wisdom—Traditional Form': A Rejoinder," *The Quarterly Journal of Speech* 58, no. 4 (1972): 451–54; Philip C. Wander, "The Ideological Turn in Modern Criticism," *Central States Speech Journal* 34, no. 1 (1983): 1–18; Philip C. Wander, "The Third Persona: An Ideological Turn in Rhetorical Theory," *Central States Speech Journal* 35, no. 4 (1984): 197–216; Maurice Charland, "Constitutive Rhetoric: The Case of the *Peuple Québécois*," *The Quarterly Journal of Speech* 73, no. 2 (1987): 133–50; Raymie E. McKerrow, "Critical Rhetoric: Theory and Praxis," *Communication Monographs* 56, no. 2 (1989): 91–111; Michael Calvin McGee, "Text, Context, and the Fragmentation of Contemporary Culture," *Western Journal of Speech Communication* 54, no. 3 (1990): 274–89; and Kent A. Ono and John M. Sloop, "Commitment to *Telos*—A Sustained Critical Rhetoric," *Communication Monographs* 59, no. 1 (1992): 48–60.

34. Stephanie Houston Grey, "A Growing Appetite: The Emerging Critical Rhetoric of Food Politics," *Rhetoric & Public Affairs* 19, no. 2 (2016): 307–20; Phaedra C. Pezzullo, "Unearthing the Marvelous: Environmental Imprints on Rhetorical Criticism," *Review of Communication* 16, no. 1 (2016): 25–42; Erin J. Rand, "Queer Critical Rhetoric Bites Back," *Western Journal of Communication* 77, no. 5 (2013): 533–7.

35. Barry Brummett, *Rhetorical Dimensions of Popular Culture* (Tuscaloosa: University of Alabama Press, 1991).

36. Thomas Rosteck, ed. *At the Intersection: Cultural Studies and Rhetorical Studies* (New York: The Guilford Press, 1999).

37. Butterworth, "Sport as Rhetorical Artifact," 13.

38. Sky LaRell Anderson, "The Corporeal Turn: At the Intersection of Rhetoric, Bodies, and Video Games," *Review of Communication* 17, no. 1 (2017): 18–36.

39. For the development materialist and bodily approaches to rhetoric see, Michael Calvin McGee, "A Materialist's Conception of Rhetoric," in *Explorations in Rhetoric: Studies in Honor of Douglas Ehninger*, ed. Ray E. McKerrow (Glenview, IL: Scott Foresman, 1982), 23–48; Ronald Walter Greene, "Another Materialist Rhetoric," *Critical Studies in Mass Communication* 15, no. 1 (1998): 21–7; Raymie E. McKerrow, "Corporeality and Cultural Rhetoric: A Site for Rhetoric's Future," *Southern Communication Journal* 63, no. 4 (1998): 315–28; Jack Selzer and Sharon Crowley, eds., *Rhetorical Bodies* (Madison: University of Wisconsin Press, 1999); Hawhee, *Bodily Arts*; Lawrence J. Prelli ed., *Rhetorics of Display* (Columbia: University of South Carolina Press, 2006); Debra Hawhee, *Moving Bodies: Kenneth Burke at the Edges of Language* (Columbia: University of South Carolina Press, 2009); Diana Coole and Samantha Frost, eds., *New Materialisms: Ontology, Agency, and Politics* (Durham, NC: Duke University Press, 2010); and Jeremy Packer and Stephen B. Crofts Wiley, eds., *Communication Matters: Materialist Approaches to Media, Mobility and Networks* (London: Routledge, 2012).

40. Michael L. Butterworth, "Introduction: Communication and Sport Identity Scholarship, and the Identity of Communication and Sport Scholars," in *Sports and Identity: New Agendas in Communication*, ed. Barry Brummett and Andrew Ishak (New York: Routledge, 2014), 1–3.

41. Butterworth, "Introduction," 14.

42. Chantal Mouffe, *The Democratic Paradox* (London: Verso, 2000), 101–02.

43. Davis W. Houck, "Sport and Political Communication/Political Communication and Sport: Taking the Flame," in *Defining Sport Communication*, ed. Andrew C. Billings (New York: Routledge, 2017), 81.

44. Khan, "Sport and Race," 108.

45. Bonnie J. Sierlecki, "Sporting Rhetoric: Performance, Games, and Politics," *The Quarterly Journal of Speech* 99, no. 4 (2013): 510; Barry Brummett, ed. *Sporting Rhetoric: Performance, Games, and Politics* (New York: Peter Lang, 2009).

46. Ben Carrington, "Sport Without Final Guarantees: Cultural Studies/Marxism/Sport," in *Marxism, Cultural Studies and Sport*, eds. Ben Carrington and Ian McDonald (New York: Routledge, 2009), 20–2.

47. Carrington, "Sport Without," 20–2. Also see William J. Morgan, *Leftist Theories of Sport: A Critique and Reconstruction* (Urbana: University of Illinois Press, 1994), 25.

48. See, for example, Abraham Iqbal Khan, *Curt Flood in the Media: Baseball, Race and the Demise of the Activist-Athlete* (Oxford, MS: University Press of Mississippi, 2012); and Daniel A. Grano, "Muhammad Ali versus the 'Modern Athlete': On Voice in Mediated Sports Culture," *Critical Studies in Media Communication* 26, no. 3 (2009): 191–211.

49. Kareem Abdul-Jabbar, "The Importance of Athlete Activists," *Time*, November 16, 2015, http://time.com/4114002/kareem-abdul-jabbar-athlete-activists/.

50. See, for example, Jorge Arangure, Jr., "2014: The Year of the Activist Athlete," *Vice Sports*, December 19, 2014, https://sports.vice.com/en_us/article/wn3adm/2014-the-year-of-the-activist-athlete; Dave Zirin, "The Enduring Importance of the Activist Athlete," *The Nation*, December 10, 2014, https://www.thenation.com/article/enduring-importance-activist-athlete/; Stanley Kay, "NBA Players Making Their Voices Heard as New Civil Rights Movement Rises," *Sports Illustrated*, May 25, 2015, https://www.si.com/nba/2015/05/26/nba-civil-rights-lebron-james-carmelo-anthony-trayvon-martin-eric-garner; Matt Vasilogambros, "When Athletes Take Political Stands," *The Atlantic*, July 12, 2016, https://www.theatlantic.com/news/archive/2016/07/when-athletes-take-political-stands/490967/; Mahita Gajanan, "Colin Kaepernick and A Brief History of Protest in Sports," *Time*, August 29, 2016, http://time.com/4470998/athletes-protest-colin-kaepernick/; and Hua Hsu, "The Political Athlete: Then and Now," *The New Yorker*, March 22, 2017, https://www.newyorker.com/culture/cultural-comment/the-political-athlete-then-and-now.

51. Abraham Iqbal Khan, "A Rant for Good Business: Communicative Capitalism and the Capture of Anti-Racist Resistance," *Popular Communication* 14, no. 1 (2016): 39–48; Abraham Iqbal Khan, "Michael Sam, Jackie Robinson, and the Politics of Respectability," *Communication & Sport* 5, no. 3 (2015): 331–51.

52. See for example, Kyle R. King, "Three Waves of Gay Male Coming Out Narratives," *Quarterly Journal of Speech* 103, no. 4 (2017): 372–94; Katherine L. Lavelle, "The ESPN Effect: Representation of Women in 30 for 30 Films," in *The ESPN Effect: Exploring the Worldwide Leader in Sports*, ed. John McGuire, Greg G. Armfield, and Adam Earnhardt (New York: Peter Lang, 2015), 127–38; Daniel A. Grano, "Michael Vick's 'Genuine Remorse' and Problems of Public Forgiveness," *Quarterly Journal of Speech* 100, no. 1 (2014): 81–104; James Cherney and Kurt Lindemann, "Queering Street: Homosociality, Masculinity, and Disability in *Friday Night Lights*," *Western Journal of Communication* 78, no. 1 (2014): 1–21; Michael L. Butterworth, "Public Memorializing in the Stadium: Mediated Sport, the 10th Anniversary of 9/11, and the Illusion of Democracy," *Communication & Sport* 2, no. 3 (2014): 203–24; Michael L. Butterworth, "The Passion of the Tebow: Sports Media and Heroic Language in the Tragic Frame," *Critical Studies in Media Communication* 30, no. 1 (2013): 17–33; John M. Sloop, "'This Is Not Natural': Caster Semenya's Gender Threats," *Critical Studies in Media Communication* 29, no. 2 (2012): 81–96; Rachel A. Griffin and Bernadette Marie Calafell, "Control, Discipline, and Punish: Black Masculinity and

(In)visible Whiteness in the NBA," in *Critical Rhetorics of Race*, eds. Michael G. Lacy and Kent A. Ono (New York: New York University Press, 2011), 117–36; Daniel A. Grano, "Risky Dispositions: Thick Moral Description and Character-Talk in Sports Culture," *Southern Communication Journal* 75, no. 3 (2010): 255–76; Thomas P. Oates, "The Erotic Gaze in the NFL Draft," *Communication and Critical/Cultural Studies* 4, no. 1 (2007): 74–90; Daniel A. Grano, "Ritual Disorder and the Contractual Morality of Sport: A Case Study in Race, Class, and Agreement," *Rhetoric & Public Affairs* 10, no. 3 (2007): 445–73; Michael L. Butterworth, "Race in 'The Race': Mark McGwire, Sammy Sosa, and Heroic Constructions of Whiteness," *Critical Studies in Media Communication* 24, no. 3 (2007): 228–44; Michael L. Butterworth, "Pitchers and Catchers: Mike Piazza and the Discourse of Gay Identity in the National Pastime," *Journal of Sport & Social Issues* 30, no. 2 (2006): 138–57; John M. Sloop, "Riding in Cars Between Men," *Communication and Critical/Cultural Studies* 2, no. 3 (2005): 191–213.

53. Lawrence Grossberg, *Cultural Studies in the Future Tense* (Durham, NC: Duke University Press, 2010), 20.

54. Grano, *The Eternal Present*, 2–3.

55. For more on this issue, see Paula Chakravartty et al., "#CommunicationSoWhite," *Journal of Communication* 68, no. 2 (2018): 254–66.

Section I: Contextualizing Sport and Political Struggle

CHAPTER ONE

Curt Flood, Confrontational Rhetoric, and the Radical's Constellation

ABRAHAM I. KHAN

After being traded from the St. Louis Cardinals to the Philadelphia Phillies at the end of the 1969 Major League Baseball (MLB) season, Curt Flood, who had played ten years for the Cardinals and considered St. Louis home, filed suit in federal court asking for something now taken for granted in professional sports: free agency. In a letter to Commissioner Bowie Kuhn demanding his "right to consider offers from other clubs," Flood made his motives clear: "I do not feel I am a piece of property to be bought and sold irrespective of my wishes."[1] This was only Flood's opening move in a full-throated campaign of likening baseball to slavery. His initial lawsuit in federal court claimed that the reserve clause, MLB's standard contract language which bound a player for life to the team with which he first signed, violated the 13th Amendment's prohibition of involuntary servitude.[2] That argument had little chance in court, a fact which did not stop Flood from telling Howard Cosell on national television that "a well-paid slave is nonetheless a slave."[3] With that incendiary characterization, Flood thrust himself into public consciousness, achieving a gripping stage presence in the American racial theater of the early 1970s. Flood's case would be heard by the US Supreme Court in 1972,[4] where he finally lost his struggle before disappearing into Europe as a broke and beaten man.

These details are hardly news. Beginning around 2006, when legal historian Brad Snyder published *A Well-Paid Slave*, Flood's life has come to assume a meaningful place in sport's collective memory. Prior to then, Flood's story had been trapped in something of a paradox. He was remembered frequently as someone who had been forgotten. Free agency did not begin until 1975 when a labor arbitrator eliminated the archaic reserve clause, but Flood would never reap its benefits. A year later, Murray Chass, the *New York Times*'s influential sportswriter, would call him the "forgotten man in baseball's freedom fight,"[5] initiating a line of reasoning so pervasive that it would become a genre of barroom argument. Then came Snyder's copiously researched book. A few years later, HBO produced *The Curious Case of Curt Flood*, a melancholy but detailed chronicle of Flood's life and court case. As this surge of remembrance took shape in 2012, I suggested in *Curt Flood in the Media* that "Flood may be the most remembered forgotten athlete in the history of professional American sport."[6] For my own part, I was invited in 2014 to a two-day symposium at the Negro Leagues Baseball Museum called "A Supreme Decision," where the particulars of Flood's biography and legal challenge were debated by baseball enthusiasts, scholars, and the lawyers who opposed each other in *Flood v. Kuhn* some four decades years earlier. Since the Court's legal reasoning defied sensible explanation, his case has always been a curiosity to law scholars, but Flood's broad cultural presence has caught up, generating a spike in discourse which tries to comprehend his significance. As the resurgence of interest in Flood has taken shape over approximately the last decade, however, the potential purposes to which remembrance might be put have not remained stable. Whereas ten years ago Michael Jordan and Tiger Woods remained avatars for the rise of the corporate athlete, Vice News in 2014 announced "the new dawn of athlete activism."[7] Memories of Flood fit into both stories, but after NBA stars wore t-shirts bearing the inscription "I Can't Breathe" in reference to the police killing of Eric Garner, St. Louis Rams receivers took the field in a "hands up/don't shoot" pose, and Colin Kaepernick precipitated a wave of athletes kneeling or raising fists in protest of police violence, we would be wise to locate our memory of Flood within the emergent recognition that athletes offer something meaningful to American political culture.

Flood's story may now be fairly well known, but the memories which narrate it exist largely within social imaginaries that valorize his loneliness and celebrate the economic effect he had on sports. Such strategies of public memory have their merit, especially considering the islands—one figurative, the other literal—on which Flood found himself. Not one fellow ballplayer testified on his behalf in federal court in 1970. Jackie Robinson, white-haired and hobbled, took the stand, as did Bill Veeck, the notorious renegade who once owned the Cleveland Indians, but Flood's colleagues, fearful of the backlash Flood would soon endure, stayed far away from lawyers and courtrooms. Baseball owners were monolithic in their recalcitrance; they infamously warned that an end to the reserve clause would mean "the end of baseball as we know it."[8] After exiting baseball for good,

Flood fled the country and ran a bar on Majorca, showing Cardinals games on TV to ex-pats while descending into alcoholism. Three years before his death from throat cancer in 1997, he was recognized in a ceremony organized by the players union, and just before the beginning of the 2014 season, the league itself seemed to have finally come around. In a brief article on MLB.com (effectively a propaganda instrument), Terence Moore placed Flood within baseball's most revered company: "Babe Ruth. Kenesaw Mountain Landis. Jackie Robinson. You can make the case that, when it comes to the most influential persons in baseball history, those are the only folks who rank higher than Curt Flood." For someone of Flood's ignominious demise at MLB's hands, Moore seemed to work with an unusual metric for "influence," but he clarified Flood's cash value. "Free agency was born," he wrote, "and so were the gigantic salaries for players and the eternal legacy of Flood's courage."[9]

MLB's attempt to affix Flood's courage (eternally, no less) to baseball's salary explosion is nakedly self-serving. Moore offers little account of how the economic modernization of sport benefited owners through increased revenues and franchise expansion, and he is awfully late to the celebration; his claim is how those barroom arguments have been won for decades. The central problem is that Flood offers us better things to celebrate, more useful things to remember than sporting wage-labor's procession into the neoliberal paradise of mobility and wealth. In this essay, I want to refigure our memory of Curt Flood by shifting our backward glance away from the outlines of his purported heroism and toward the remarkable quality of his public address. By looking primarily at his 1970 autobiographical book *The Way It Is*, I argue that Flood's attempt to achieve free agency provides a compelling warrant for revisiting "confrontational rhetoric," a theory of oppositional discourse whose utility abated upon rhetoric's disciplinary focus on social movements in the 1970s, but whose revival offers to recover a memory of Flood that might liberate him from a triumphant capitalist narrative and lend his symbolic weight to struggles for social justice. Moreover, in reconsidering confrontational rhetoric through Flood, we might identify sport not simply as another cultural space suitable for rhetorical inquiry, but as a generative site for rhetorical invention. In other words, it is not simply that rhetorical scholarship can teach us something about Flood, but that Flood can teach us something about rhetorical criticism, namely that confrontation possesses enduring interpretive value, especially as we observe the revival of athletic activism. Through Flood, we might observe sport's ability to serve as an organic source of the theory required for its own explication.

Remembering Flood as a martyr to the wealth that contemporary athletes command seems to work as a retroactive atonement for the widespread failure to appreciate the righteousness of his cause in the 1970s. After all, Flood did not create free agency, he never exercised the right of free agency, and every attempt he made to secure that right was a failure. He could not persuade fellow players to join his lawsuit or testify in court, the owners were altogether immune to per-suasion, and the courts kept siding with the owners. Flood's link to the story of free agency, then, has less to do with a stirring climax than with his indirect effect. He made free agency thinkable by emboldening the players union, dramatizing baseball's injustices, and nudging the needle of public opinion. In a 2005 essay on Flood, Jonathan Leshanski wrote that Flood "opened the door to the modern era of free agency."[10] A year later, Bill Fletcher wrote that Flood "threw himself on barbed wire" so that others "could jump over the restrictions imposed by the reserve clause."[11] And in 2007, Carl Bialik delivered the same point with the inev-itable pun, writing that Flood "opened the floodgates for free agency and today's economic structure" in sports.[12] Flood is not responsible for free agency but, we are asked to remember, he is responsible for its *plausibility*. Marvin Miller was the legendary labor executive who oversaw the creation of MLB's players union in the 1970s, the visionary who stewarded the formation of free agency. As Allen Barra put it in *The Atlantic* in 2011, "if Curt Flood had not existed, not even Marvin Miller could have invented him."[13]

There is a rotten core to this mode of remembrance to which I will return shortly, but we should recognize here exactly what makes Flood's story so salient for rhetorical criticism. Karlyn Kohrs Campbell asserts that "whatever else it may be, rhetorical agency refers to the capacity to act, that is, to have the competence to speak or write in a way that will be recognized or heeded by others in one's community."[14] At first glance, Campbell provides a reason for regarding Flood's fight for economic agency as a simultaneous struggle for rhetorical agency. Flood was in fact desperate to be recognized and heeded. Campbell also allows us to observe the relationship between rhetorical agency and public memory; Flood was eventually recognized and heeded by both his baseball community and sport's broader public once the years wore on, even as contentious debate rages over his Hall of Fame credentials. By scratching past this surface, however, we might also notice a homology between the manner in which Flood is remembered and the very notion of rhetorical agency itself. Campbell's formulation performs a deft sleight-of-hand: the distinction between speech and action, which many rhetorical scholars reject, is invoked in the phrase "capacity to act" and then collapsed as the action implied in "agency" refers to speaking and writing. As she clarifies, "such competency permits entry into ongoing cultural conversations and is the *sine qua non* of public participation."[15] There are a few ways to read Campbell's point, but if we emphasize public participation, we might think of rhetorical agency as the capacity to alter the symbolic environment, to change not necessarily what is, but to change what is possible. Therein lies Curt Flood's significance. Never a free agent himself, Flood intervened successfully in public discourse by reshaping the conditions for social and political change. Perhaps a football metaphor offers more insight: Flood was a fullback who led ball carriers into daylight.

Flood's most dramatic rhetorical act was to call himself a "well-paid slave" in front of a national television audience. He referenced the nation's founding sin, evoked the language of Black Power, and undermined MLB from the very moral ground on which baseball had built its meritocratic racial mythos. Baseball might be plodding and pastoral, but it had, after all, given us Jackie Robinson. Moreover, the 13th Amendment claim had dubious chances in court, but did important symbolic work by shifting the terms of public debate and inviting a new way of seeing Flood and other ballplayers in his circumstances. Running implicitly through every public statement he made, Flood's slave metaphor was an extraordinary rhetorical resource. It condensed arguments about economic self-determination and dehumanization into a complex imagery and polarized his audiences in response. It also amplified his risks and ensured the loneliness of his sacrifice. *The Way It Is*, written (with coauthor Richard Carter) in the summer of 1970 just before trial in federal court, captures his isolation and forlornness. In one early passage, Flood recalls having received a racist letter in the mail and guesses what might have motivated its writer, whom he calls "the animal":

> I probably had spoiled the animal's breakfast. I might even have ruined his day. No doubt it had started splendidly, with a front page full of grand news about undesirable elements being bombed, shot, incinerated, beaten, arrested, suspended, expelled, drafted, and otherwise coped with here and abroad. Then he must have turned to the sporting page, where horror confronted him. Curt Flood had sued baseball on constitutional grounds.[16]

As Flood positioned himself as a desolate rebel, abandoned by allies and left at the mercy of a racist legal system, Flood's slave metaphor centered an elaborate public performance staged in his book, in the press, and on television. He even likened himself to Dred Scott.[17] At Flood's own suggestion, we might label this performance a rhetoric of confrontation.

As a theory of rhetoric, confrontation owes its origin to a 1969 essay by Robert L. Scott and Donald K. Smith in the *Quarterly Journal of Speech*. Endeavoring to study the kind of artifacts scholars in the field had generally ignored—"marches, sit-ins, demonstrations, and discourse featuring disruption, obscenity and threats"[18]—Scott and Smith began with a simple empirical observation: "Confrontation crackles menacingly from every issue in our country."[19] What followed was an exegesis of radical speech characteristic of the 1960s, striking for the efficiency of its trip through the contemporaneous discursive environment. Covering a grand total of eight pages, Scott and Smith proposed that the rhetoric of confrontation communicates a speaker's radical division from the social order, enacts "the rite of the kill" in an attempt to achieve the enemy's "symbolic annihilation," and can be used as a totalistic strategy which willingly risks a speaker's self-abnegation or as a limited tactic in pursuit of practical goals. Scott and Smith concluded by challenging rhetoric's disciplinary orthodoxy, insisting that "a rhetorical theory suitable to our age must take into account the charge that civility and decorum serve as masks for the preservation of injustice."[20]

A comprehensive account of confrontational rhetoric's disciplinary legacy is well beyond the scope of this essay, but Scott and Smith's piece was foundational, especially in reconstituting the field's object domain and orienting rhetorical studies to the asymmetrical power relations civility and decorum often instantiate. In the 1970s, Scott and Smith incited a debate about the difference between persuasion and coercion,[21] engendered an elucidation of "establishment" rhetoric,[22] and precipitated the field's turn to the study of social movements.[23] In 1978, Robert Cathcart offered the most lucid refinement of confrontational rhetoric which, he argued, is a "consummatory form essential to a movement."[24] What makes a social movement a "real threat," Cathcart claimed, is that "confrontational rhetoric occurs only in special and limited circumstances, such as periods of societal breakdown or when moral underpinnings are called into question."[25] By contrast, "managerial rhetoric," a category into which "the great bulk of communication in any society must of necessity fall," works to "uphold and reinforce the established order or system," acquiring a reformist logic complicit with "a *modus vivendi* with those in power."[26] Cathcart captured confrontational rhetoric's oppositional relationship to the social order, but as he and others harnessed confrontation to the study of movements, it lost its status as a first-order theory and would in the 1980s disappear from critical practice. As Cox and Faust put it, "the search for sweeping accounts of the rhetoric of social movements ceased by the end of [the 1970s]."[27] Perhaps, then, if we extract confrontational rhetoric from its disciplinary genealogy, we might rediscover its critical appeal. Put differently, we do not need a theory of the social movement to avail ourselves of the insights confrontational rhetoric can provide.

For my purposes, Scott and Smith's original account requires little modification, but deserves a point of clarification. They waste little effort defining confrontation explicitly, calling it "a simple enough verb meant to stand or to come in front of," observing that confrontation's "strongest" meaning "is the sense of standing in front of as a barrier or threat." The "threat" posed by confrontational rhetoric, I suggest, consists in exposing the truth, in revealing that which mystifies a clear understanding of the order of things. In other words, I also want to consider the sense of confrontation implied in "facing the facts," or "being confronted with reality." This is not to say that truth, facts, or reality are self-evident or objectively discernible, but that confrontational speech attempts to show us something that those whom it opposes would prefer to remain hidden. Confrontational speech can occasion exposure either directly or indirectly, and Curt Flood illustrates both.

First, as Flood continued his description of "the Animal" who authors hate-mail, Flood evaluated the way his case was being covered in the press, as if to summarize the rhetorical environment in which the imaginary letter writer must have found himself: "If the newspaper was typical, it lied that a victory for Flood would mean the collapse of our national pastime. God profaned! Flag desecrated! Motherhood defiled! Apple pie blasphemed!"[28] God, the flag, motherhood, and apple pie held together a romantic imagery that sustained baseball's power, but Flood did not simply announce that baseball was a powerful ideological institution. He parodied baseball's mystifying language, bathed it in acid, and together with his slave metaphor delivered a threat to baseball's very legitimacy by identifying a repugnant corruption at its heart. Flood confronted baseball with an ugliness so shameful that the league might be exposed as the expression of an unjust social order. Working directly like this, confrontational rhetoric is a kind of anti-ideology, a tool of de-interpellation.

Second, Cathcart reminds us that confrontational rhetoric is marked by "the reciprocating rhetorical acts which came forth from all levels of the existing system." Individuals and institutions invested in the status quo, in other words, deliver force to confrontation by being provoked. Joe Cronin and Chub Feeney, presidents of the National and American Leagues respectively, issued a statement in response to Flood's lawsuit reported widely in the press. "The chaotic results that would be created without the reserve clause should be obvious," they said. What followed was an enumerated list of dystopian phrases, including, "totally destroy league competition," "the integrity of the game would be threatened," "a game the public would refuse to accept," and the last, which read like an exclamation point: "Professional baseball would simply cease to exist."[29] The league dug in, Flood faced "demonization, denigration, and denunciation"[30] from owners and reporters, and the only thing which ever ceased to exist was Flood's baseball career. Working indirectly, confrontational rhetoric "causes the establishment to reveal itself for what it is."[31] Flood got baseball to show itself, to expose its fragility in the face of a five foot-nine inch, 165 pound centerfielder as an institution so frightened it would fire cannonballs at mosquitoes.

Flood's humiliating exit from baseball reveals confrontation's perils, but we should also focus on its promise, particularly as it relates to the way we remember him. His detractors, like St. Louis baseball writer Bob Broeg, rolled their eyes at the "well-paid slave" while pointing to his $90,000 salary. Broeg patronizingly dismissed Flood's assertion that race might have factored into the league's visceral overreaction.[32] The 13th Amendment claim never even made it into his Supreme Court arguments. Supporters softened the edges of the slave metaphor and simply urged baseball to reform. Other supporters (though they were few) pointed to the possibility that white and black athletes seem to be treated differently, but pined for baseball's commitment to colorblind meritocracy. These were managerial rhetorics, and to fully appreciate what confrontational rhetoric offers public memory, we should not think of Flood's slave metaphor as containing a particular argument, but as drawing attention to a constellation of social forces and public statements which, in their totality, could be regarded as morally problematic. The shapes formed by stars depends on how one maps the sky, and the importance of remembering Flood consists in how he drew his map. If we remember his confrontation, Flood illuminates a position from which to view the problems of our present, a place to rearrange our understanding of the social order.

Flood is often tasked with helping us notice that athletes have become rich. Here we arrive at the rotten core of remembrance when we pull the fruit of memory from the tree of wealth. In the mid-2000s, when it appeared that activists had disappeared from sport forever, Flood worked as a cudgel with which disillusioned critics berated black athletes. As legendary *New York Times* Sportswriter Bill Rhoden wrote, "contemporary black athletes have abdicated their responsibility to their community with treasonous vigor."[33] The genre is well-worn: *Selfish, overpaid, black athletes have no use for history. Woe unto those who forget the sacrifices of Curt Flood, the well-paid slave!* Even Harry Edwards, the mastermind of the 1968 Olympic protests, once pointed his finger at black athletes and uttered the phrase "militantly ignorant."[34] To be fair, other athletes did this genre's heavy lifting. Jackie Robinson, Muhammad Ali, Kareem Abdul-Jabbar, John Carlos and Tommie Smith—these are the conscientious radicals the wealthy generation ignored. When Flood found his way into this genre, however, its cantankerous, paternalistic reasoning conveniently elided an ugly irony. Consider these two passages in Shaun Powell's *Souled Out*: (1) "Activism by Curt Flood and John Mackey, pioneers in free agency, made baseball and football players rich."[35] (2) "Highly paid black athletes are too busy hiding behind their precious public profiles and endorsement deals to lend a voice to activism, which means they've Souled Out in the worship of the almighty dollar."[36] So, we can blame Flood for the demise of black athletes as a collective political force or we can upbraid contemporary athletes for their failure to follow a narrative that they never really helped to write.

Snyder writes that "Robinson started the revolution by putting on a uniform. Flood finished it by taking his uniform off. Robinson fought for racial justice. Flood fought the less-sympathetic fight for economic justice."[37] This grasps an important difference, but if our revolutionary train starts at the station of racial inclusion and leads us no place else than the junction of exceptional wealth, it is vicious to take cheap shots at black athletes for buying themselves first class airfare instead of traveling by rail like their forefathers. And now that the renaissance of the activist athlete is upon us, our deliverance achieved in figures like Colin Kaepernick, Michael Bennett, and the WNBA's Minnesota Lynx,[38] whose emergent consciousness addresses the brutal realities of police violence and systemic racism, are we to suppose that they got woke because they read about Flood? It's worth remembering that as confrontationally as he approached MLB, he never expressed anger or frustration at his colleagues for fleeing his side. In 1976, just a few years removed from his court case, he told Murray Chass, "the things I did,

I did it for myself."[39] We should take him at his word. His significance to our memory consists less in the idea that he made athletes rich than in the idea that he presented American political culture with a novel map for the relationships between sport and society. Flood's loneliness revealed to him a radical's constellation which, I believe, finds a familiar pattern today in college sports, the broader image of labor, and the NCAA.

In *The Way It Is*, Flood puts sarcasm to a variety of productive uses. As he critiques baseball mythology, he engages the rhetoric of confrontation with poisonous artistry:

> These dedicated men [baseball owners] are custodians of a great tradition, the slightest neglect of which would plunge the entire United States into degradation. Their gravest concern is the Good of the Game. With this in mind, they maintain constant vigil over the integrity of the game—its competitive honesty and fairness. Everyone in baseball plays a structured role in the promotional rites that emphasize the integrity, enhance the Image and consolidate the Good of the Game. On camera or within earshot of working reporters, the behaved player is an actor who projects blissful contentment, inexhaustible optimism and abiding attitude. "I'll sweep out the clubhouse to stay here," he says. "I love the game. I owe everything to baseball. I am thankful to this grand organization for giving me my big chance. I'm in love with this town and its wonderful fans."[40]

Flood had exposed a secret: baseball's romantic image was built on lies about fairness which everyone involved in baseball had learned to tell. Cathcart distinguished between confrontational rhetoric and managerial rhetoric by claiming that the former "reveals persons who have become so alienated that they reject 'the mystery' and cease to identify with the existing hierarchy," and that the latter finds voice in rhetors who "maintain the mystery; i.e., keep the secret that the existing order is a true order." "The good of the game," which owners used to justify the existence of the reserve clause, like the American flag and apple pie, both misunderstood the indignities of baseball peonage and structured a ritually enacted public image no more authentic than a Broadway play. It was all artifice, Flood saw, and the path to a new social order in baseball, perhaps even at the expense of the game itself, pressed sarcasm into service as a means of revealing the secrets responsible for holding the old order together.

In 2014, a regional office of the National Labor Relations Board ruled that college football players at Northwestern University qualify as employees, and thus had the right to form a union to collectively bargain for their working conditions (including, possibly, wages). In what can only be described as an epic cop out, the NLRB reversed the lower board's ruling, contending that the Northwestern case applied too narrowly to work as precedent. Between rulings, however, the NCAA issued an official statement reading, in part, "We strongly disagree with the notion that student-athletes are employees. We frequently hear from student-athletes, across all sports, that they participate to enhance their overall college experience and for the love of their sport, not to be paid."[41] The spectral presence of Flood's sarcastic laughter is audible between these lines, as "love of their sport" echoes forth perfidiously like "the good of the game."

Taylor Branch, the civil rights historian who wrote a lengthy article for *The Atlantic* in 2011 titled "The Shame of College Sports," perhaps did the most damage to the term "student-athlete" when he called it a "legal confection," drummed up by NCAA attorneys seeking to retain all the privileges of scholarship athletics while shielding schools from inconveniences like workers compensation claims.[42] Everything about college sports has been professionalized, according to Branch, except the labor status of the athletes. *Everyone in college sports is paid*, except for the athletes without whom there would be no college sports. Following the regional labor board's ruling in the players' favor, Tennessee Senator Lamar Alexander, the senior Republican on the Senate Labor Committee told the press, "This is an absurd decision that will destroy intercollegiate athletics as we know it."[43] Not since Cronin and Feeney issued their reply to Flood's lawsuit had such dystopian bluster issued forth from sport's power matrix. The ideological investment in intercollegiate athletics is showing itself.

Measured critics argue that unionized athletes present insuperable complexities. Will they ask for wages? What will happen to non-revenue sports? What about athletic departments that operate in the red? Answers to these questions are not easily found, but armed with a confrontational rhetoric, we might bear Flood in mind. Addressing the idea that baseball could not sustain the revenues necessary to handle the payroll consequences of free agency, Flood wrote, "The whole spiel is sheer humbug, of course. It seems to me that subsidies should come not from the employees but from the suffering owner's fellow monopolists. Let them pass the hat. Unless I misread history, we have passed the stage when indentured servitude was justifiable on grounds that the employer could not afford the cost of normal labor."[44] The principle for which Flood claimed to stand was that wealth founded on an abomination is no less abominable when the wealth it generates is abundant. That baseball owners could not figure their way to riches without exploiting its labor did not mean that such exploitation was somehow rendered morally irrelevant. Perhaps the best account of this principle came from a sports columnist in the *Chicago Defender*, a black newspaper, named William Lloyd Hogan, who in 1970 said, "There are howls that baseball is dead if Flood wins his suit. That's tough, because if making the Lords obey one of the basic tenets upon which a democracy is built will kill baseball, it's time it was dead anyway. So, Curt Flood, stay cold. Stick it to the Man, elbow deep—and twist it. If you kill baseball—it needs to die anyway."[45] This is what made the slavery metaphor so powerful, not that it accurately analogized an economic relation, but that it confronted economic rationality with the corrosive moral foundation upon which it rested. The slave metaphor was an essential rhetorical tool for tearing down the precarious symbolic edifice baseball had built for itself.

In 2014, the athletic director of Ohio State University triggered receipt of an $18,000 bonus when one of the school's wrestlers, a white athlete, won a national championship.[46] The sporting plantation need not be racialized, but we ignore its racial dimensions at our moral peril. Dave Zirin reminds us that "the population of the United States that is most desperate for an escape out of poverty is the population that has gotten the rawest possible deal from an NCAA, which is actively benefiting from this state of affairs."[47] Sadly, Flood never found the racial solidarity he needed to win his case, a sad result we should not romanticize as virtue in remembering his sacrifice and courage. Instead, we should remember the spirit of his critique, the sublime moral clarity delivered by confrontational rhetoric.

As we observe the revival of the activist athlete, it is difficult not to notice that confrontation once again crackles menacingly from every issue in our society. Around the time of this writing, Donald Trump called for athletes protesting racial injustice at NFL games to be fired before directing a repulsive, misogynistic epithet at them. But Trump is not confrontational. He is obnoxious. He reveals no truth, he obscures it. He does not provoke power, he wields it. Athletes like Colin Kaepernick practice a confrontational rhetoric, clarifying the social divisions that impede our moral progress, inviting us into a view of exploitation and injustice. In a defense of Kaepernick, Jesse Jackson placed him within the tradition of activist athletes, name checking Robinson, Ali, and "Curt Flood," who, "refused to be bought and sold 'like a slave.' His protest and litigation cost him much of his career, but it broke open the owners' control of players, opened the way to free agency and transformed baseball."[48] Perhaps in a different context, this would return us to the triumphant capitalist narrative that grinds its gears on ironic vituperation, but Jackson alters memory's inflection. Jackson's point is about power and who is allowed to use it, not money and who is allowed to spend it. Jackson's point affirms Kaepernick's confrontational gesture toward the systemic racism concealed in vapid appeals to patriotism.

When I first read *The Way It Is*, it occurred to me that Flood was more than a symbol of baseball's hypocrisy, more than a tragic figure in a long-forgotten fight. He was a marvelous thinker whose challenge to baseball's reserve clause contained the stuff of which the best criticism is made. If we measure the weight of a historical figure's legacy according to their enduring symbolic significance, then Flood need not be invoked by name in order to for us to notice his presence in our collective imagination. If we want to make use of our memories of Curt Flood, we would be wise to avoid simplistic analogies, and avoid using his selflessness as a means of condemning the selfish. Instead, we should remember how to plot the stars like a radical, with an unflinching willingness to confront powerful individuals and institutions with the truths which much be concealed for their power to be sustained. We should chart the constellation of dehumanizing, exploitive practices that burned through the darkness of Flood's night skies, because that constellation is there, waiting to be seen, with justice blazing for our remembrance.

NOTES

1. Curt Flood, "Curt Flood's Letter to Bowie Kuhn," *MLB.com*, March 15, 2007, http://m.mlb.com/news/article/1844945/.
2. Flood v. Kuhn, F. Supp 275–76 (SDNY 1970).
3. Brad Snyder, *A Well-Paid Slave: Curt Flood's Fight for Free Agency in Professional Sports* (New York: Viking, 2006), 104.
4. Flood v. Kuhn, 407 U.S. 258 (1972).
5. Murray Chass, "Curt Flood, Forgotten Man in Baseball Freedom Fight, Lives in Self-Imposed Exile," *New York Times*, September 9, 1976.
6. Abraham Iqbal Khan, *Curt Flood in the Media: Baseball, Race, and the Demise of the Activist Athlete* (Jackson, MS: University Press of Mississippi, 2012), 169.
7. Jorge Arangure, Jr., "2014: The Year of the Activist Athlete," *Vice Sports*, December 19, 2014, https://sports.vice.com/en_us/article/wn3adm/2014-the-year-of-the-activist-athlete.
8. Charles Korr, *The End of Baseball As We Knew It: The Players Union, 1960–81* (Champaign, IL: University of Illinois Press, 2005).
9. Terence Moore, "Flood's Impact on Baseball's Evolution Undeniable." *MLB.com*, March 25, 2014, http://m.mlb.com/news/article/70114070/terence-moore-curt-floods-impact-on-baseballs-evolution-undeniable/.
10. Jonathan Leshanski, "The Curt Flood Case Part 1 (of 4)," *The Glory of Baseball*, January 27, 2005, https://thegloryofbaseball.blogspot.com/2005/01/?m=0.
11. Bill Fletcher, "Curt Flood: 10 Years Later and No Closer to the Hall of Fame," *The Berkeley Daily Planet*, December 19, 2006, http://www.berkeleydailyplanet.com/issue/2006-12-19/article/25904?headline=Curt-Flood-10-Years-Later-and-No-Closer-To-the-Hall-of-Fame--By-Bill-Fletcher-Jr.-New-America-Media.
12. Carl Bialik, "Curt Flood's Tragic Fight," *Gelf Magazine*, December 4, 2006, http://www.gelfmagazine.com/archives/curt_floods_tragic_fight.php.
13. Allen Barra, "How Curt Flood Changed Baseball and Killed His Career in the Process," *The Atlantic*, July 12, 2011, https://www.theatlantic.com/entertainment/archive/2011/07/how-curt-flood-changed-baseball-and-killed-his-career-in-the-process/241783/.
14. Karlyn Kohrs Campbell, "Agency: Promiscuous and Protean," *Communication and Critical/Cultural Studies* 2, no. 1 (2005): 3.
15. Kohrs Campbell, "Agency," 3.
16. Curt Flood and Richard Carter, *The Way It Is* (New York: Trident Press, 1970), 38.
17. Flood and Carter, *The Way*, 13–14.
18. Robert L. Scott and Donald K. Smith, "The Rhetoric of Confrontation," *Quarterly Journal of Speech* 55, no. 1 (1969): 1–8.
19. Scott and Smith, "The Rhetoric," 2.
20. Scott and Smith, 8.

21. See, for example, James R. Andrews, "Confrontation and Columbia: A Case Study in Coercive Rhetoric," *Quarterly Journal of Speech* 55, no. 1 (1969): 9–16.
22. See, for example, David Zarefsky, "President Johnson's War on Poverty: The Rhetoric of Three 'Establishment' Movements," *Communication Monographs* 44, no. 4 (1977): 352–73.
23. See, for example, Robert S. Cathcart, "Movements: Confrontation as Rhetorical Form," *Southern Speech Communication Journal* 43, no. 3 (1978): 233–47.
24. Cathcart, "Movements," 235.
25. Cathcart, 236.
26. Cathcart, 237.
27. Robert Cox and Christina R. Foust, "Social Movement Rhetoric," in *The Sage Handbook of Rhetorical Studies*, eds. Andrea A. Lunsford, Kirt H. Wilson, and Rosa A. Eberly (Thousand Oaks: Sage, 2009), 609.
28. Flood and Carter, *The Way It Is*, 38.
29. Leonard Koppett, "Baseball Chiefs Attack Flood's Suit," *New York Times*, January 31, 1970.
30. David J. Leonard, "'Death is a Slave's Freedom': His Fight Against Baseball, History, and White Supremacy," in *Reconstructing Fame: Sport, Race, and Evolving Reputations*, ed. David C. Ogden and Joel Nathan Rosen (Jackson, MS: University Press of Mississippi, 2008), 33.
31. Cathcart, "Movements," 245.
32. Bob Broeg, "Does 'Principal' or 'Principle' Motivate Flood?," *St. Louis Post-Dispatch*, January 25, 1970.
33. William C. Rhoden, *Forty Million Dollar Slaves* (New York: Crown, 2006), 8.
34. David Leonard, "What Happened to the Revolt of the Black Athlete?" *ColorLines*, June 10, 1998, https://www.colorlines.com/articles/what-happened-revolt-black-athlete.
35. Shaun Powell, *Souled Out? How Blacks Are Winning and Losing in Sports* (Champaign, IL: Human Kinetics, 2008), 28.
36. Powell, *Souled Out?*, xix.
37. Snyder, *A Well-Paid Slave*, 352.
38. Christina Cauterucci, "The WNBA's Black Lives Matter Protest Has Set a New Standard for Sports Activism," *Slate*, July 25, 2016, http://www.slate.com/blogs/xx_factor/2016/07/25/the_wnba_s_black_lives_matter_protest_has_set_new_standard_for_sports_activism.html.
39. Chass, "Curt Flood."
40. Flood and Carter, *The Way It Is*, 49–50.
41. NCAA press release, "NCAA Disagrees with Union Decision," March 26, 2014, http://www.ncaa.org/about/resources/media-center/press-releases/ncaa-disagrees-union-decision.
42. Taylor Branch, "The Shame of College Sports," *The Atlantic Monthly*, October 2011, http://www.theatlantic.com/ magazine/archive/2011/10/the-shame-of-college-sports/308643/.
43. "Reaction to Ruling on College Athletes' Union," *Washington Post*, March 26, 2014.
44. Flood and Carter, *The Way It Is*, 139.
45. William Lloyd Hogan, "Now's the Time!," *Chicago Defender*, November 18, 1969.
46. Dan Wetzel, "Wrestler Wins NCAA Title, Athletic Director Gets $18,000 Bonus," *Yahoo Sports*, March 25, 2014, http://sports.yahoo.com/news/college-wrestler-wins-title--athletic-director-gets--18-000-bonus-210331816.html.
47. Dave Zirin, "It's the Racism, Stupid: Meet the Press's Epic NCAA Fail," *The Nation*, March 23, 2014, http:// www.thenation.com/blog/178969/its-racism-stupid-meet-presss-epic-ncaa-fail#.
48. Jesse L. Jackson, Sr., "Kaepernick's Protest is Part of a Patriotic Tradition," *Charleston Chronicle*, September 5, 2017.

CHAPTER TWO

"Change Starts with Us"

Intersectionality and Citizenship in the 2016 WNBA

KATHERINE L. LAVELLE

In the summer of 2016, there were several high-profile police officer-involved killings of African American men in the United States, including Alton Sterling in Baton Rouge, LA on July 5 and Philando Castile in St. Paul, MN on July 6.[1] On July 7 during a peaceful protest about these killings, five Dallas police officers were ambushed and killed.[2] These deaths helped elevate discourse about gun violence and policing practices in the U.S. Starting with the 2012 shooting death of unarmed black teenager Trayvon Martin, the role of officer-initiated shootings has been increasingly scrutinized.[3] One of the leaders of this conversation is Black Lives Matter, a political movement critical of the persistence of police brutality during the Obama administration (an era imprudently declared to be "post-racial" by some observers).[4] While criticisms of police are not new, social media posts of police killings and the perceived lack of accountability has increased their profile.[5]

Beginning in 2016, professional athletes participated in these protests. Notably, NFL Quarterback Colin Kaepernick inspired numerous athletes to protest after sitting and then kneeling during the performance of the National Anthem. "No athlete lately has caused more commotion than Kaepernick," and "at least 42 players from 17 NFL teams" participated in similar protests and "at least 134 protests [occurred] at professional, college, and high school sporting events."[6] NBA players had been involved in these protests since 2012: critical of the Trayvon Martin shooting, Miami Heat players wore hoodies and posted a picture on Instagram.[7]

Players such as LeBron James and Derrick Rose wore "I Can't Breathe" shirts after the 2014 death of Eric Garner in New York, and James, Dwyane Wade, Carmelo Anthony, and Chris Paul made a statement about gun violence before the 2016 ESPYs.[8] Previously, scholars have posited that most athletes refrained from social justice activism, and those who did were criticized because of their wealth and perceived position in society.[9] However, since 2012, more athletes have taken public, progressive stances on officer-initiated shootings.[10]

Female athletes were also involved in social justice issues. In July of 2016, WNBA (Women's National Basketball Association) players used social media and press availability to discuss policing practices and gun violence in America.[11] On July 9, the Minnesota Lynx held a press conference with its four captains wearing black t-shirts honoring Sterling, Castile, and the Dallas 5, and bearing the phrase "Change Starts with Us."[12] The next day, the New York Liberty, Seattle Storm, and Phoenix Mercury wore black Adidas t-shirts with the phrases "#BlackLivesMatter" and "#Dallas5."[13] Sometime between July 18 and 20, the WNBA sent a memo asking players to stop wearing these shirts. As a compromise, several teams wore black Adidas shirts to promote discussion about gun violence while supporting sponsors.[14] On July 21, the WNBA announced fines for violating the dress code policy, ranging from $500 for individual players to $5000 for the team.[15] Players were punished for "not complying with uniform guidelines."[16] In context, WNBA rookies make $40,000 per year, meaning that the fines were 1/80th of their salary.[17] Uniform fines are usually $200 instead of $500.[18] That same day, the Indiana Fever and New York Liberty played at 11am EST. Players from both teams refused to talk to the media about anything but officer-initiated shootings and gun violence.[19] Before the game, the Liberty's Tina Charles received her Player of the Month Award on court, wearing her warm up shirt inside out and wrote a response to the league fines on Instagram.[20]

While these fines were quickly rescinded, the WNBA provides a unique space for exploring how sports figures function as political figures. Previous scholarship notes that WNBA players have less agency than male athletes. For instance, players' efforts to position themselves as legitimate athletes are often ignored or mocked and the WNBA is often stereotyped as a lesbian space.[21] Descriptions of the league often reinscribe dominant cultural beliefs about the inferiority of female athletes.[22] Despite these conditions, WNBA players engaged in substantive and sustained protests at the risk of their jobs.[23] Consequently, the WNBA protests provide a place for "*hearing* these marginalized voices."[24] By examining these events through the lens of citizenship and intersectionality, I argue that the 2016 WNBA protests opened a unique political space for evaluating public discussion of gun violence and policing practices.

CITIZENSHIP AND ATHLETES

Before examining these protests, it is critical to conceptualize a few terms. Here, citizenship is what Robert Asen calls a "mode of public engagement" which stems from an individual's "agency," as opposed to a government or institution.[25] Citizenship is developed from an individual's own definition of engagement, such as involvement with their community because "democracy is not confined to a set of institutions or specific acts, but as a guiding spirit that informs human interaction."[26] WNBA players' protests functioned in this way because "they embody a conception of citizenship that is active, engaged, and constitutive."[27] Particularly for black athletes, they "embody a unique place in sports as activists, especially since sports have integrated faster than the rest of society."[28] However, these places are not uniform. For instance, black athletes are often discouraged from speaking their minds outside of culturally accepted norms on race.[29] Because of these constraints, Asen's conceptualization of citizenship may be "an ideal marker for tracking processes of race formation and the potential for change as reflected in popular moral thought."[30] While discussing citizenship, it is critical to understand how protest operates in sports, especially when studying black women. They are often silenced in political discussions and as American media figures.[31]

A lens that can help explain how citizenship operates for black women in the WNBA is intersectionality. Intersectionality identifies power relationships beyond sex differences.[32] Crenshaw argues that the unique impacts of racism are often ignored by focusing on a single demographic characteristic because it creates a false perception that there are "mutually exclusive categories of experience and analysis."[33] Understanding how identity issues intersect and influence each other is critical. Intersectionality allows scholars to analyze how interactions operate along interlocking structures, as opposed to additive qualities.[34] For this study, I explore how WNBA players are positioned as advocates for victims of gun violence and police brutality.[35]

Using intersectionality as a critical tool is key to understanding "differential policing for minority and poor communities … and the militarization of police."[36] One of Collins and Bilge's case studies in their intersectionality book examines the unique position for black women involved in Black Lives Matter. They argue that the expansion of police powers combined with the perpetuation of stereotypes about black women creates inequalities.[37] In sport scholarship, numerous scholars have used intersectionality as a lens in their research.[38] For instance, in communication studies research, Emily Deering Crosby notes that US track star Lolo Jones was constrained by intersectional double binds because of her gender, race, sexuality and class, which limited how her public discourse was interpreted, especially when she did not meet competitive expectations at the 2012 Olympics.[39] The application of intersectionality to the construction of a political platform by

WNBA players is helpful because they recognized their visible role as professional athletes, which allowed them to be heard on social justice issues. For this present study, exploring how intersectionality and citizenship operate as a theoretical tool helps explain how WNBA players participated in dialogue about policing practices and gun violence during the Summer of 2016.

THE WNBA AS A SITE OF PROTEST

The involvement of WNBA players in protest is critical to study for several reasons. First, women are essential to Black Lives Matter because they create space for black women to fight for justice."[40] Like black and Latino men, black women have died in the hands of police custody (such as high profile cases like Sandra Bland in Texas), but much of the national focus is on male victims.[41] In addition, women involved in Black Lives Matter are committed and engaged, working on a variety of social justice issues related to structural inequality.[42] This framework allows for multiple community leaders (like WNBA players) to emerge.[43] As Chatelain notes, "Black Lives Matter is feminist in its interrogation of state power and its critique of structural inequality. It is also forcing a conversation about gender and racial politics that we need to have."[44] This structure provides opportunities for women to shape discussion about issues of gun violence and policing practices that are nuanced and reflect the complexities inherent in this movement.

Second, the WNBA protests in 2016 included white athletes. Their presence did not legitimize the protests, but instead demonstrated support for them. In 2016, white male athletes were absent from this conversation in professional sports. High profile athletes such as Kevin Love (LeBron James' teammate) and Aaron Rodgers (involved in a variety of civic issues) refrained from public engagement, despite the work of teammates and fellow players.[45] white WNBA players, such as Sue Bird, Stephanie Dolson, and Lindsey Whalen, actively participated in protests, wearing t-shirts, posting on social media, and speaking to journalists about gun violence and policing issues.[46]

Third, WNBA players see themselves as community advocates.[47] New York Liberty player Swin Cash described WNBA players as "strong women in those communities" who are connected "with politicians or people or some of the civil rights activists."[48] Her teammate Tina Charles noted that participation in dialogue "shows that there's more to us than putting a ball in a basket. We are women. We have a voice. Often times, women are forced to be silent, and that's why I think it's really a beautiful thing that we were able to do, very resilient of us to say, 'No, this time we are not going to be silent.'"[49] Charles discussed the practice of women being ignored and demonstrated the importance of "discourse practices" as accessible and powerful everyday enactments of citizenship.[50] In the case of the WNBA, one of the reasons that Tina Charles and other players wanted to participate in dialogue around games was because of their schedules.[51] Most WNBA players play overseas during the off-season and do not have the free time to participate in traditional protests.[52]

DIALOGUE FROM THE WNBA

This involvement reflects "community accountability as a normative practice" where WNBA players participated in dialogue on issues that were identity based.[53] Tanisha Wright discussed the importance of her identity as an African American woman who had a responsibility to "make other people aware of the social injustices that are happening the different levels that are unfair in our society."[54] For Wright, these forces were critical. Tina Charles noted that all eleven WNBA teams were united in their response and her description exemplifies "cultural citizenship" because a group of marginalized people reach a "common identity, establish solidarity, and defines a common set of interests."[55] WNBA players emphasized the importance of a broad, shared platform, which could operate as "impactful[ly and] as positively as we could" in promoting peaceful dialogue.[56]

This notion of "platform" was critical to players. For instance, players encouraged dialogue through apparel. Players wore Black Lives Matter t-shirts traveling to and from games to inspire media coverage, and Seattle Storm players posted of the team wearing them.[57] These decisions were examples of "creative participation," and an opportunity to use social media tools for advocacy and embody ways to enact citizenship as a means of engagement outside of typical norms and practices.[58] These efforts allow athletes to involve themselves in political activism because "they embody a conception of citizenship that is active, engaged, and constitutive."[59] Using their personal experiences and opportunities to speak to the media about policing practices and gun violence meant that players could facilitate dialogue as a way to enact citizenship.

WNBA players participated in protests for a variety of reasons. Players frequently cited specific experiences with violence and were upset by the shootings.[60] Tanisha Wright describes the Liberty's "boiling" point surfacing after Alton Sterling and Philando Castile were shot in early July.[61] The Lynx players felt compelled to respond after Castile was shot in St. Paul, literally miles from their home arena.[62] Maya Moore described the Dallas killings as "senseless" and teammate Rebekah Brunson noted that the "divide is way too big between our community and those who have vowed to protect and serve us."[63] These politically conscious reactions responded to racism.[64] The Lynx players talked with Coach Cheryl Reeves about their experiences growing up as black women in the United States.[65] As Reeves noted, this discussion "forc[ed] a conversation about gender and racial politics we need to have," especially in the case of Black Lives Matter.[66] As a child, Brunson encountered police with weapons drawn when playing in an apartment complex.[67] Her German grandmother resisted the Nazis during World War II, and then moved to the United States and married a black man. Brunson declared: "I've never been taught to be just silent."[68] Brunson's experiences exemplify how black women's stories are often underrepresented in social justice movements.[69] Mainstream media conversations often focus on direct encounters with police, as opposed to the fear that exists in communities with heightened police control and surveillance.[70] Like Brunson, Swin Cash was inspired by her grandmother who lived through the Civil Rights era in the United States, noting, "It's like the boogeyman's come back out of the closet and those things that used to be are now being brought to this forefront once again, and that's what really scares me."[71] Cash's "discursive engagement" is an opportunity to "call attention to the subject of civil rights and to the denial of these rights to some citizens and their unfair and unjust application to others."[72] By connecting Black Lives Matter in 2016 to previous social justice movements, these players helped reinforce and amplify the significance of the movement.

Additionally, players talked about concerns for their families as a justification for involvement. Rebekah Brunson expressed fear for "my brothers and sisters, my nieces and nephews, my future son or daughter."[73] Tanisha Wright was worried about her three nephews that "I love to death, and if something was to ever happen to them, I would be devastated."[74] These comments are examples of what Chatelin describes as issues unique to communities of color.[75] Police brutality happens to actual people, it is not just a news headline. On Twitter, the Connecticut Sun's Chiney Ogwumike reinforced this connection by describing it as an issue that affected 70% of the league.[76] (Sixty-eight percent of players self-identify as African American).[77] Ogwumike's comments echo those made by Ta-Nehesi Coates, who argues that black people in the US live in fear of police and have markedly different experiences than white people because law enforcement upholds systematic inequalities.[78]

Players framed their protests as part of community experience. Tanisha Wright "underst[ood] the poverty and the disenchantment and racial injustice that happened just in my neighborhood," which moved her to speak out.[79] Childhood experience can help people develop a sense of purpose and identity, which can translate later into activism.[80] Tina Charles talked about the connection players felt to the movement, especially since they had "family, we have close friends, relatives that are affected by everything that is going on."[81] In addition to their personal concerns, players worried about "systematic" problems, and the importance of addressing larger structural issues.[82] Swin Cash was concerned because "we cannot sit here and act like there is not a problem in America."[83] These players felt connected because the Black Lives Matter movement provides a "space for black women to fight for justice."[84] WNBA players' collective experiences help explain why participating in the movement was so important to them.

In addition to these connections, WNBA players defended Black Lives Matter. Tanisha Wright framed Black Lives Matter as inclusive and recognized the complex issues involved with gun violence in the US.[85] Swin Cash noted that the Dallas 5 shootings took place when police officers were "trying to protect a peaceful movement."[86] In their support of Black Lives Matter, Cash and Wright allude to Daniel Grano's discussion of citizenship as a "potential for change as reflected in popular moral thought."[87] By acknowledging and supporting the concerns of protestors, these players offered the perspective that the movement was peaceful.

LEAGUE RESPONSE AND FINES

In contrast, the league office was not fully supportive of this movement. NBA Commissioner Adam Silver recommended that players protest outside of game obligations.[88] WNBA Commissioner Lisa Borders described the black Adidas shirts as "not regulation" and told ESPN's Cari Champion that players violated league guidelines by wearing them on the court.[89] Instead, black Adidas shirts were worn as a compromise by players who wanted to avoid backlash from sponsors.[90] When asked by Cari Champion why the WNBA still issued fines, Borders responded, "When we came to this decision most recently, we recognized that this is a very complex issue. There is no right way to deal with it."[91] These fines demonstrate an example of "risk" because players were (briefly) punished for enacting their citizenship.[92]

When the fines were issued, there was swift reaction. Many criticized the league describing the fines as inconsistent with active discussion between the players and the league office.[93] Player representative Mistie Bass found the league response and punishment "disheartening" after Lisa Borders talked about the "incredible stage and platform [we have] to take a stance on social issues."[94] On Twitter, Bass used the hashtags #notpuppets and #cutthestings to criticize the league office.[95] Bass used social media to "engag[e] with wider publics to develop more just and inclusive political and social processes and outcomes."[96] Ivory Letta of the Washington Mystics was critical of the league because "you [the WNBA] penalize us for our speaking and showing our action" when they were encouraged to use their platform.[97] Players noted that the fines were not expected, especially since the league had been publicly supportive of the players just days earlier.[98]

To respond, several players and teams used social media to criticize the fines, an example of "public speech."[99] For instance, Seattle Storm veteran Sue Bird tweeted out an image of the team wearing black shirts with a Martin Luther King

Jr. quote: "There comes a time when silence is betrayal."[100] WNBA players' use of digital media reflected an increasingly popular and effective tool for social justice advocates to organize.[101]

One of the most high-profile criticisms came from Tina Charles, who received the Player of the Month award during the July 21, 2016 Liberty-Fever game.[102] Charles was not known for taking public stances on political issues, but after seeing Floridian Charles Kinsey shot by the police when he was trying to protect an autistic man in his care, Charles felt compelled to act.[103] She posted on Instagram a picture of herself with her warm ups inside out and the statement: "Today, I decided not to be silent in the wake of the WNBA fines. My teammates and I will continue to use our platform and raise awareness for Black Lives Matter movement until the WNBA gives it support as it does for breast cancer awareness, Pride, and other subject matters."[104] Charles' statement embodies "cultural visibility in sports" because her statement could "be mobilized against the social status quo and its value system" and it helped contextualize her argument to a broader audience.[105] WNBA players can participate in this type of discourse because they are connected to their communities and receive some national and digital news coverage. As Mechelle Voepel observed in her *Outside the Lines* interview on July 21, "These are players [WNBA], who are for the most part, who are all college graduates, they've traveled the world ... and they have passionate views on social issues."[106] Unlike professional women's soccer, nearly 70% of the WNBA identifies as African American—there is no other women's league with this type of diversity and experience.[107] The WNBA media was willing to cover these comments and gave players a platform to discuss social justice issues. As evident from their comments, WNBA players are aware of their position and use it to speak out for social justice issues.

Charles' post identified a common WNBA player criticism of the fines. Players were frustrated because the WNBA had responded to other crises with greater speed and clarity. For instance, in June 2016, one of the worst mass shootings in US history occurred in an Orlando LGBT night club.[108] After these shootings, the league distributed t-shirts to players "within a day or two" according to Vice President of the Players Union, Tamika Catchings.[109] Players across the league supported Orlando by raising money and holding blood drives.[110] Orlando native and Liberty guard Shavonte Zellous wrote "LGBT" and "Orlando strong" on her game sneakers.[111] In response to player criticisms about differential treatment, Lisa Borders made the distinction that Orlando was "an attack on our homeland" to justify the quick response in comparison.[112] Countering Borders, WNBA Players Association Director of Operations Terri Jackson noted, "Our players sought only to demonstrate in a constructive way that was consistent with reactions to social issues by NBA players and with earlier league initiatives, including the recent tragedy affecting the LGBTQ community in Orlando."[113] By fining players and asking them to wear league appropriate clothing without responding to criticisms, the WNBA sent the message that police shootings and gun violence were not as significant as other tragedies. This inconsistency was frustrating for players. Tanisha Wright noted, "They [the WNBA] also can't pick and choose what initiatives to support and what not to support just because it doesn't push their agenda."[114] WNBA players wanted to support the Orlando survivors, but felt that the league "did not recognize how strongly they felt about this issue [Black Lives Matter]."[115] Even though individual incidents of police violence do not kill as many people as the Orlando shooting did in one night, 963 people were killed in police involved shootings in 2016.[116] Wright emphasized, "This not just a black problem, no, this is an American problem, we're all going to be affected by this in some shape or form."[117] Asen's discussion of risk is important here because he argues that part of citizenship is risking being wrong in one's beliefs or creating unintended instability by speaking out on controversial issues.[118] By redefining Black Lives Matter as addressing a problem beyond individual shootings, players emphasized the importance of their advocacy and therefore put themselves out there to be criticized and to have their cause potentially minimized.[119]

Additionally, players were angry with how the league enforced fines. Players wore noncompliant shirts for four games before fines were issued. Tanisha Wright argued, "If you're going to do something, stand strong on it…do it from the beginning."[120] The league suggested, "OK, we'll look the other way for a little . . . but then we'll take action."[121] Players were upset because there was a series of negotiations and discussions between the league and players, and many of the players felt like they were, according to Wright, "strong armed" by fines.[122] The fines ended negotiations without reaching compromise between players and the league.[123] Here, the league reinforced authority over players. This is an example of how "power, privilege, and resources all inform people's abilities to join with others to construct publics, to articulate the needs and interests of publics, and to engage and hold accountable other publics and societal institutions."[124] Players were concerned that they might have been suspended, a decision with more ramifications than a fine.[125] These suspensions did not materialize, but the fines reinforced the WNBA's place in a long and conflicted history about women and sport.[126] Sports leagues rely on sponsors averse to potentially polarizing political statements.[127] The WNBA has struggled financially, which could limit how much players can voice their opinions. The league office tried to eliminate the players' ability to co-construct their narrative by punishing players. By both supporting protest, and attempting to control it, the WNBA leadership sent a conflicted message about the importance of dialogue about police brutality and gun violence. Much like the NFL has struggled with responding to on field player protests, professional sports must balance political discourse with other responsibilities.

Despite this stance from the league, media coverage was favorable for players. Reporters from national news outlets, such as *ESPN/ESPNW* and *USA Today* wrote about the players' call for dialogue. Players were asked about their reasons for protesting, and print stories included pictures of players in Black Lives Matter shirts (such as Washington Wizards' Stefanie Dolson in *USA Today*).[128] Tanisha Wright thanked the WNBA media, noting that when players would only discuss Black Lives Matter and gun violence, reporters asked them even more questions than they normally did.[129] This reporting demonstrates the importance of framing in media coverage. If the players were framed as selfish or distracting in their protests, it would have changed the perception of their protests. Instead, players were described as "erudite" and "worldly," and reporters asked them substantive questions about their advocacy.[130] These "affective, embodied rhetorical acts" were opportunities for "engagement with other citizens."[131] The acts themselves articulate these athletes as both citizens and athletes. By participating in a larger public conversation about gun violence and policing practices as part of their identity WNBA athletes embody Asen's discussion of citizenship. Consequently, the WNBA engagement was not described as a reactionary or isolated act; instead, it was part of a larger national conversation about police brutality and gun violence because players brought attention to an issue that was not being discussed in other forums.

This coverage and pressure were effective. One day after the fines were issued, the WNBA rescinded them.[132] Borders credited the month long Olympic break as an opportunity to discuss the concerns of the players.[133] On July 22, 2016 via Twitter, Borders wrote, "Appreciate our players expressing themselves on matters important to them. Rescinding imposed fines to show them even more support."[134] While this decision muted the media story between the league and players, the fact that players were fined was critical.

IMPLICATIONS

In July of 2016, WNBA players advocated for dialogue about gun violence and police brutality. Their activities amplified the work of Black Lives Matter and are important to study as a political formation in sports because they involved an underrepresented population (black women and/or female athletes), as well as support from allies who had not been outspoken in other sports. WNBA players were willing to take risky political stands because they recognized the importance of their leadership in their communities and on a national stage.

Player representative Mistie Bass provides some insight to why WNBA players felt so strongly about speaking out. "We have a platform that we may never have again."[135] When WNBA players retire or play outside of the U.S., they rarely have the spotlight to speak outside of their own fan base. Even though they may not get as much coverage as other female athletes, the fact that the players operated as a collective and used a variety of media strategies embodies the discursive notion of citizenship.[136] For critical/rhetorical sport scholars, the WNBA protests provide an opportunity to explore how a league not routinely part of the national conversation on social justice issues used their agency and platform at a critical time in U.S. culture. The WNBA is comprised predominately by educated African American women who have been visible sport media figures since college. Their support of the Black Lives Matter movement contextualized a platform that involved a variety of connected and engaged individuals. Future scholars should continue to trace and explore these issues, especially as athletes speak out on gun violence and policing. These conversations are critical to evaluate at the intersection of politics and sports, especially as this intersection continues to evolve through digital platforms and athletes, willingness to lend their voices to these issues.

NOTES

1. Richard Fausset, Richard Pérez-Peña, and Campbell Robertson, "Alton Sterling Shooting in Baton Rouge Prompts Justice Dept. Investigation," *The New York Times*, July 6, 2016; Christina Capecchi and Mitch Smith, "Officer Who Shot Philando Castile Is Charged with Manslaughter," *The New York Times*, November 16, 2016.

2. Faith Karimi, Catherine E. Shoichet, and Ralph Ellis, "Dallas Sniper Attack: 5 Officers Killed, Suspect Identified," *CNN.com*, July 9, 2016, http://www.cnn.com/2016/07/08/us/philando-castile-alton-sterling-protests/index.html.

3. Cathy J. Cohen and Sarah J. Jackson, "Ask a Feminist: A Conversation with Cathy J. Cohen on Black Lives Matter, Feminism, and Contemporary Activism," *Signs: Journal of Women in Culture and Society* 41, no. 4 (2016): 775–92.

4. Jelani Cobb, "The Matter of Black Lives," *The New Yorker*, March 14, 2016, http://www.newyorker.com/magazine/2016/03/14/where-is-black-lives-matter-headed.

5. Wesley Lowery, *They Can't Kill Us All: Ferguson, Baltimore, and a New Era in America's Racial Justice Movement* (Boston: Little, Brown and Company, 2016).

6. John Eligon and Scott Cacciola, "As Colin Kaepernick's Gesture Spreads, a Spirit Long Dormant Is Revived," *The New York Times*, September 12, 2016; Tom Junod, "The Anthem: Six Voices on the Song that Everyone Hears Differently," *ESPN.com*, January 31, 2017, http://www.espn.com/espn/feature/story/_/id/18519123/the-national-anthem-experience.

7. Eligon and Cacciola, "As Colin Kaepernick's."

8. Eligon and Cacciola, "As Colin;" "WNBA Issues Fines for T-shirts but Affirms 'Passionate Advocacy,'" ESPN.com, July 25, 2016, http://espn.go.com/wnba/story/_/id/17117125/wnba-fines-teams-players-black-warm-t-shirts; Cari Champion, *SportsCenter*, ESPN, July 25, 2016.

9. Michael Butterworth, "The Athlete as Citizen: Judgement and Rhetorical Invention in Sport" *Sport in Society: Cultures, Commerce, Media, Politics* 17, no.7 (2014): 867–83; Sarah J. Jackson, *Black Celebrity, Racial Politics, and the Press: Framing Dissent* (New York, NY: Routledge, 2014);

Peter Kaufman, "Boos, Bans, and Other Backlash: The Consequences of Being an Activist Athlete," *Humanity & Society* 32, no. 3 (2008): 215–237; Cohen and Jackson, "Ask a Feminist."

10. Wesley Lowery, "The Activist Minds," *Sports Illustrated*, December 19, 2016.

11. Swin Cash, interview with Jane McManus, Sarah Spain, and Kate Fagan, The Trifecta, ESPN.com, podcast audio, July 23, 2016, http://www.espn.com/espnradio/podcast/archive/_/id/12273641.

12. Matt Vasilogambros, "The Cost of Athletes Taking Political Stands," *The Atlantic*, July 21, 2016, http://www.theatlantic.com/news/archive/2016/07/wnba-politics-fines/492431/?utm_source=atltw.

13. Vasilogambros, "The Cost of Athletes."

14. Stefan Fatsis, Josh Levin, and Mike Pesca, *Hang Up and Listen: The Granny Shot Edition*, Podcast Audio, July 25, 2016, http://www.slate.com/articles/podcasts/hang_up_and_listen/2016/07/hang_up_and_listen_on_russians_in_rio_wnba_and_free_throws.html.

15. Vasilogambros, "The Cost of Athletes."

16. Victor Mather, "Players Criticize W.N.B.A. For Fines Over Shirts Worn to Underscore Shootings," *The New York Times*, July 21, 2016.

17. "WNBA Issues Fines."

18. Christina Cauterucci, "The WNBA's Black Lives Matter Protest Has Set a New Standard for Sports Activism," *Slate.com*, July 25, 2016, http://www.slate.com/blogs/xx_factor/2016/07/25/the_wnba_s_black_lives_matter_protest_has_set_new_standard_for_sports_activism.html.

19. Cauterucci, "The WNBA's Black Lives Matter."

20. Cauterucci, "The WNBA's Black Lives."

21. Tiffany Muller, "'Lesbian Community' in Women's National Basketball Association (WNBA) Spaces," *Social & Cultural Geography* 8, no. 1, (2007): 9–28; Sarah Banet-Weiser, "Hoop Dreams: Professional Basketball and the Politics of Race and Gender," *Journal of Sport and Social Issues* 23, no. 4 (1999): 403–20.

22. John Lisec and Mary G. McDonald, "Gender Inequality in the New Millennium: An Analysis of WNBA Representations in Sport Blogs," *Journal of Sports Media* 7, no. 2 (2012): 153–78.

23. Cauterucci, "The WNBA's."

24. Darrell Wanzer, "Delinking Rhetoric, or Revisiting McGee's Fragmentation Thesis through Decoloniality," *Rhetoric & Public Affairs* 15, no. 4 (2012): 652.

25. Robert Asen, "A Discourse Theory of Citizenship," *Quarterly Journal of Speech* 90, no. 2 (2004): 189–211.

26. Asen, "A Discourse Theory," 196.

27. Butterworth, "The Athlete as Citizen," 13.

28. Abraham Iqbal Khan, *Curt Flood in the Media: Baseball, Race, and the Demise of the Activist-Athlete* (Jackson, MS: University Press of Mississippi, 2012), 183.

29. Jackson, *Black Celebrity*.

30. Khan, *Curt Flood*, 273.

31. Sumi Cho, Kimberlé Williams Crenshaw, and Leslie McCall, "Toward a Field of Intersectionality Studies: Theory, Applications, and Praxis," *Signs: Journal of Women in Culture and Society* 38, no. 4 (2013): 785–810; Cathy J. Cohen, *Democracy Remixed: Black Youth, and the Future of American Politics* (Oxford, UK: Oxford University Press, 2010).

32. Kimberlé Williams Crenshaw, "Intersectionality, Identity Politics, and Violence Against Women of Color," *Stanford Law Review* 43, no. 6 (1991): 1241–99.

33. Crenshaw, "Intersectionality"; Suriya Nayak, *Race, Gender and the Activism of Black Feminist Theory* (New York, NY: Routledge, 2015) , 16.

34. Crenshaw, "Intersectionality."

35. Patricia Hill Collins and Sirma Bilge, *Intersectionality* (Hoboken, NJ: Wiley, 2016), 27.

36. Collins and Bilge, *Intersectionality*, 149.

37. Collins and Bilge, *Intersectionality*.

38. Nicolas Apostolis and Audrey R. Giles, "Portrayals of Women Golfers in the 2008 Issues of *Golf Digest*," *Sociology of Sport Journal* 28, no. 2 (2011): 226–38; Megan Chawansky, "Be Who You Are Be Proud: Britney Griner, Intersectional Invisibility and Digital Possibilities for Lesbian Sporting Celebrity," *Leisure Studies* 35, no. 6 (2016): 1–12; Chelsea Marie Elise Johnson, "Just Because I Dance like a Ho, I'm Not a Ho," *Sociology of Sport Journal* 32, no. 4 (2015): 377–94; Montserrat Martin, "Assessing the Sociology of Sport: On Gender Identities in Motion and how to Deessentialize Difference(s)," *International Review for the Sociology of Sport* 50, no. 4–5 (2015): 542–6; Jennifer McGovern, "The Boundaries of Latino Sport Leadership: How Skin Tone, Ethnicity, and Nationality Construct Baseball's Color Line," *Sociological Inquiry* 87, no. 1 (2017): 49–74; Kristin Skare Orgeret, "The Unexpected Body: From Sara Baartman to Caster Semenya," *Journal of African Media Studies* 8, no. 3 (2016): 281–94; Philip E. Wagner, "Bulking Up (Identities): A Communication Framework for Male Fitness Industry," *Communication Quarterly* 65, no. 5 (2017): 580–602.

39. Emily Deering Crosby, "Chased by the Double Bind: Intersectionality and the Disciplining of Lolo Jones," *Women's Studies in Communication* 39, no. 2 (2016): 228–48.

40. Marcia Chatelain and Kaavya Asoka, "Women and Black Lives Matter: An Interview with Marcia Chatelain," *Dissent* (2015): 61.

41. Cohen and Jackson, "Ask a Feminist."

42. Chatelain and Asoka, "Women and Black Lives Matter."

43. Chatelain and Asoka, "Women and Black Lives."

44. Chatelain and Asoka, "Women," 57.

45. Dave Zirin, "Do #BlackLivesMatter to White Athletes? Let's Ask Them," *The Nation*, November 25, 2014, https://www.thenation.com/article/do-blacklivesmatter-white-athletes-lets-ask-them/.

46. Nina Mandell, "Protest against WNBA Fine Grows as Washington Mystics Refuse to Take Questions about Basketball," *ESPN.com*, July 22, 2016, http://www.espn.com/wnba/story/_/id/17131967/wnba-withdraws-fines-regarding-anti-violence-shirts; Nina Mandell, "WNBA Players Stage Media Blackout after Being Fined for Wearing Black Lives Matter T-shirts," *USA Today*, July 21, 2016, http://ftw.usatoday.com/2016/07/liberty-protest-wnba; Mechelle Voepel and Kate Fagan, *Outside the Lines*, Television Program, *ESPN*, July 21, 2016.

47. Voepel and Fagan *Outside the Lines*.

48. Cash , *The Trifecta*.

49. Seth Berkman, "Quiet Protest Helped Tina Charles Find the Voice of Her Conscience," *The New York Times*, July 31, 2016.

50. Cohen and Jackson, "Ask a Feminist;" Asen, "A Discourse Theory," 207.

51. "New York Liberty's Black Lives Matter T-shirts Lose Their Hashtags," *ESPN.com*, July 13, 2016, http://espn.go.com/wnba/story/_/id/17058431/new-york-liberty-black-lives-matter-t-shirts-lose-hashtags.

52. Voepel and Fagan, *Outside the Lines;* "New York Liberty's."

53. Collins and Bilge, *Intersectionality*, 158.

54. Collins and Bilge, *Intersectionality*, 158.

55. Rina Benmayor and Rosa Torruellas, "Education, Cultural Rights, and Citizenship," in *Women Transforming Politics: An alternative Reader*, eds. Cathy J. Cohen, Kathleen B. Jones, and Joan C. Tronto (New York, NY: New York University Press, 1997), 189; Benmayor and Torruellas define cultural citizenship as "a process through which a subordinated group of people arrives at a common identity, establishes solidarity, and defines a common set of interests that binds the group together in collective action," 189. This interpretation is distinct from Toby Miller, who defines cultural citizenship as "the maintenance and development of cultural lineage through education, custom, language, and religion and the positive acknowledgment of difference in and by the mainstream;" Toby Miller, "Introducing…Cultural Citizenship," *Social Text* 19, no. 4 (2001): 2.

56. "WNBA Issues Fines"; Fatsis et al., *Hang Up.*

57. Fatsis et al., *Hang Up.*

58. Asen, "A Discourse Theory."

59. Butterworth, "The Athlete as Citizen," 13.

60. Pat Borzi, "Rebekkah Brunson: 'The Important Thing Is, We're Talking about It,'" *espnw.com*, July 15, 2016, http://espn.go.com/wnba/story/_/id/17080585/minnesota-lynx-create-dialogue-look-keep-conversation-going.

61. Fatsis et al., *Hang Up.*

62. Pat Borzi, "Lynx and Liberty 'Take a Stand and Raise our Voices' Against Tragedy," *espnw.com*, July 11, 2016, http://espn.go.com/wnba/story/_/id/16984816/minnesota-lynx-new-york-liberty-speak-support-black-lives-matter-dallas-police-officers.

63. Barry Petchesky, "Minneapolis Cops Walk off Job during WNBA Game after Lynx Players Speak out against Violence," *Deadspin.com*, July 12, 2016, http://deadspin.com/minneapolis-cops-walk-off-job-at-wnba-game-after-lynx-p-1783505588; Lindsay Gibbs, "WNBA Players Fined for Honoring 'Black Lives Matter' and Slain Dallas Officers," *ThinkProgress.org*, July 21, 2016, http://thinkprogress.org/sports/2016/07/21/3800577/wnba-fines-players-black-lives-matter/.

64. Kwame Agyemang, John Singer, and Joshua DeLorme, "An Exploratory Study of Black Male College Athletes' Perception on Race and Athlete Activism," *International review for the Sociology of sport* 45, no. 4 (2010): 419–35.

65. Borzi, "Lynx and Liberty."

66. Chatelain and Asoka, "Women and Black Lives Matter," 57.

67. Borzi, "Lynx and Liberty."

68. Borzi, "Lynx."

69. Crenshaw "Intersectionality".

70. Collins and Bilge, *Intersectionality.*

71. Seth Berkman, "Liberty Shows Solidarity with Black Lives Matter in Rare Public Stance," *New York Times*, July 10, 2016, http://www.nytimes.com/2016/07/11/sports/basketball/liberty-show-solidarity-with-black-lives-matter-in-rare-public-stance.html.

72. Asen, "A Discourse Theory," 204.

73. Catherine E. Shoichet and Jill Martin, "Off-duty Cops Walk Out over WNBA Players' Black Lives Matter Shirts" *CNN.com*, July 12, 2016, para. 21, http://www.cnn.com/2016/07/12/us/wnba-minnesota-lynx-black-lives-matter-shirts/index.html.

74. Fatsis et al., *Hang Up.*

75. Chatelain and Asoka, "Women and Black Lives."

76. Rob Wile, "WNBA Players Staged an Incredible Boycott after Being Fined for Wearing Black Lives Matter Shirts," *Indianapolis Recorder*, July 22, 2016, http://www.indianapolisrecorder.com/news/article_0762e426-507b-11e6-9513-37a9b2e129b0.html.

77. Richard Lapchick, "The 2016 Women's National Basketball Association Race and Gender Report Card," *TIDES*, November 2, 2016, http://nebula.wsimg.com/75d5182d7b10f789ad38bc8e9f188ed4?AccessKeyId=DAC3A56D8FB782449D2A&disposition=0&alloworigin=1.

78. Ta-Nehisi Coates, *Between the World and Me* (New York, NY: Spiegel & Grau, 2015).

79. Fatsis et al., *Hang Up*.

80. Collins and Bilge, *Intersectionality*,.

81. Borzi, "Lynx."

82. Mechelle Voepel, "Can WNBA players really count on the league's support?", ESPNW, July 22, 2016, http://www.espn.com/wnba/story/_/id/17119599/can-wnba-players-really-count-league-support-comes-being-social-advocates; Berkman, "Liberty Shows Solidarity."

83. Berkman, "Liberty Shows."

84. Chatelain and Asoka, "Women," 61.

85. Wile "WNBA Players."

86. Berkman, "Liberty Shows."

87. Daniel Grano, "Risky Dispositions: Thick Moral Description and Character-Talk in Sports Culture," *Southern Communication Journal* 75, no.3 (2010): 273.

88. Mather "Players Criticize W.N.B.A."

89. Doug Feinberg, "WNBA Withdraws Fines for Teams that Wore Black Warmup Shirts," *San Diego Union Tribune*, July 23, 2016, http://www.sandiegouniontribune.com/sdut-wnba-with-darws-fines-for-player-protests-2016jul23-story.html; Champion *SportsCenter*.

90. Mandell, "WNBA Players Stage."

91. Champion *SportsCenter*.

92. Asen. "A Discourse Theory."

93. Cash, *The Trifecta*.

94. Voepel, "Can WNBA players."

95. Voepel, "Can WNBA."

96. Robert Asen, "Communication is the Public," *Communication and the Public* 1, no. 1 (2016): 5.

97. Feinberg, "WNBA Withdraws."

98. Gibbs "WNBA Players Fined."

99. Asen, "Communication is the Public."

100. Gibbs "WNBA Players Fined."

101. Collins and Bilge, *Intersectionality*.

102. Berkman," "Quiet Protest Helped."

103. Berkman, "Quiet Protest."

104. Mather "Players Criticize W.N.B.A."

105. Douglas Hartmann, "Activism, Organizing, and the Symbolic Power of Sport," *Journal for the Study of Sports and Athletes in Education* 3, no. 2 (2009): 191.

106. Voepel and Fagan *Outside the Lines*.

107. Lapchick ""The 2016 Women's."

108. Feinberg "WNBA Withdraws."

109. Voepel and Fagan, *Outside the Lines*.

110. "New York Liberty's"

111. Berkman, "Liberty Shows."

112. Champion, *SportsCenter*.
113. Howard Megdal, "WNBA Players Speak Out Over Fines for Protest Warm-up Shirts," *Excelle Sports*, July 21, 2016, http://www.excellesports.com/news/wnba-fines-players-teams/.
114. "Carmelo Anthony Supports WNBA Players Upset by T-shirt Fines," *ESPN.com*, July 21, 2016, http://espn.go.com/wnba/story/_/id/17117125/carmelo-anthony-backs-wnba-players-upset-t-shirt-fines.
115. Voepel, "Can WNBA players."
116. "Fatal Force," *The Washington Post*, 2016, https://www.washingtonpost.com/graphics/national/police-shootings-2016/.
117. Fatsis et al., *Hang Up*.
118. Asen "A Discourse Theory."
119. Asen, "A Discourse."
120. Mandell, "WNBA Players Stage."
121. Voepel, "Can WNBA players."
122. Fatsis et al., *Hang Up*.
123. Cash *The Trifecta*.
124. Asen, ""Communication is the Public," 5.
125. Fatsis et al., *Hang Up*.
126. Banet-Weiser "Hoop Dreams."
127. Mandell, "WNBA Players."
128. Mandell, "WNBA."
129. Fatsis et al., *Hang Up*.
130. Voepel and Fagan, *Outside the Lines*.
131. Butterworth, "The Athlete as Citizen," 3.
132. Nick Eilerson, "WNBA Withdraws Penalties for Players Black Lives Matter Protests," The Washington Post, July 23, 2016, https://www.washingtonpost.com/news/early-lead/wp/2016/07/23/wnba-withdraws-penalties-for-players-black-lives-matter-protests/?utm_term=.4bd2aebf751.
133. "Carmelo Anthony Supports."
134. Cauterucci "The WNBA's."
135. Voepel and Fagan, Outside the Lines.
136. Asen, "A Discourse Theory."

CHAPTER THREE

The New Rhetorical Space for Political Activism

KAREN L. HARTMAN

Political activism is nothing new in the world of sport. In 1967 Muhammad Ali had his heavyweight title stripped and was banned from boxing for three years after refusing to be inducted into the armed forces during the Vietnam War. Tommie Smith and John Carlos were sent home from the 1968 Olympics and ostracized after raising their fists to protest racial inequality. Athletes have often sacrificed their opportunities, their stature, even their livelihoods in speaking out for social justice. More recently, Colin Kaepernick's kneeling protest during the National Football League's pregame performance of the national anthem arguably led to ownership collusion that terminated his career.[1]

Yet Kaepernick's commitment—among other athletes in recent years who have chosen to exercise their First Amendment rights to peaceful assembly and petition—has opened up a rhetorical space wherein those affiliated with sport are more willing to engage broadly in social activism. Changes to the sports media complex, combined with the rise of social media, have emboldened some athletes to express political points of view.[2]

Several examples that marked effective change or a rising level of social consciousness of sport political activism have recently appeared in both sport and national news headlines. For example, during televised games in 2013, players from Georgia and Georgia Tech wore "APU" on their wrist tape. The letters stood for All Players United and served as "an act of protest against the NCAA's treatment of athletes."[3] Also in 2013, football players at Northwestern University took the first steps to unionizing.[4] In 2014, professional athletes, such as LeBron James, wore "I Can't Breathe" t-shirts during pre-game warm ups in response to Eric Garner's death. In 2015, members of the University of Missouri football team boycotted football activities until a graduate student, Jonathan Butler, ended a hunger strike in response to racial unrest at the university. Their protest was one element that lead to the university's president and chancellor resigning within the first 72 hours of the team's public statements.[5] In 2016, professional basketball players Carmelo Anthony, LeBron James, Chris Paul, and Dwyane Wade delivered a high-profile speech at the ESPY Awards on racism, gun violence, and injustice. And, in 2016 and 2017, San Francisco 49ers football player Colin Kaepernick made international headlines by kneeling during the national anthem, spurring other athletes to protest as well. While these protests differed in public reaction and impact, and critics might question the role of business and money in contemporary forms of athlete activism, they demonstrate a growing willingness for some athletes to be politically vocal.[6] According to former professional basketball player and long-time activist Kareem Abdul-Jabbar, the "genie is out of the locker" now that more athletes are using their status as a platform.[7]

In this chapter I argue that athlete political activism, a risky endeavor that can alienate athletes or eliminate them from the playing field, can be rethought as more athletes participate in political activities. This increased political activity, particularly during and after Kaepernick's protest, leads to a potential renegotiation of what Burke refers to as hierarchy and opens a new rhetorical space for athletes to participate in ways they historically have been unable, or unwilling, to. When athletes participate in civic change they function as an active public committed to facilitating justice, however uncomfortable their acts may be, leading to a new type of ethos for athletes. While athlete activism has transitioned over the twentieth century from an era of athletes largely adhering to the motives of the civil rights movement to an era of athletes whose interests were dominated by capitalist motives, contemporary athlete political involvement suggests a return to activism with a civic purpose that aligns with democratic ideals. Ultimately, the chapter hopes to explore the competing tensions between sport as a site for political activism and as a realm of ideological power and constraint, while positioning current athlete activism in terms of a renewed civic ethos and as a way to interrogate unsettled areas of First Amendment constitutional law.

SPORTING RITUALS AND POLITICS

The relationship between sport and politics is tenuous. Sport and politics, colloquially understood as two separate realms, are intertwined in such a way that, for most fans, it is difficult to ascertain where and if they are actually different things. According to Michael Butterworth, "it is impossible to separate sport from the field of politics. Nevertheless, fans and media alike continue to insist that sport remains divorced from the political and social terrain."[8] Media and sporting rituals have had a significant impact on neutralizing and making unrecognizable the political element of sport. The NFL, in particular, wraps its branding into the military and patriotism. From 2011–2014 the U.S. Department of Defense paid $5.4 million to 14 NFL teams to host on-field ceremonies and veteran tributes.[9] Beyond professional football, the NCAA held the Carrier Classic from 2011–2012, holding basketball games on the deck of Navy ships, and NCAA football teams occasionally wear alternate uniforms featuring the American flag or camouflage. Teams and sporting organizations frequently highlight the military and their actions, framing them as patriotic and valuable, but then resist being characterized as political organizations. Politics, however, are ingrained into the sporting realm and sporting rituals contribute to their enduring inclusion.

The rituals of sport, and the political ideologies that flow from ritual participation, create powerful forces that impact communities.[10] Ritual participation allows societies, or fan bases, to regulate, maintain, and pass down from generation to generation values and opinions that the fabric of society depends upon.[11] Rituals work to promote communal activity, identification, and unity and this can be demonstrated among fans. Susan Birrell notes that sport is "an important societal phenomenon because of its ritualistic overtones,"[12] and sport has a long list of rituals including the national anthem, singing specific songs, chanting cheers, and baseball's seventh inning stretch, among many others.

The need for ritual order provides a seemingly quasi-religious experience for fans. In 1967, Robert N. Bellah suggested that America had developed a "civil religion" as a means for political leaders to advance moral causes. Bellah argued that ceremonial speaking and rituals promulgate deeply held values and commitments not expressed in everyday life. Ceremonial speaking and rituals can advance moral causes and commitments and secular religion runs deep in American traditions spanning generations.[13] Baseball, in particular, with its overly romanticized link between the game and concepts of Americana provides values and a social order conveniently packaged as political ideology.[14]

The role of media in American culture only serves to amplify the power of ritual. As demonstrated in the United States' financial investment in the NFL, national governments invest in televised sport due to the efficacy of how sport contributes to nation building.[15] Lawrence Wenner notes that "[m]ediated sports culture is an inescapable reality, forming part of the context of every American's life" and as television and social media have developed, millions of people are exposed to rituals through television and the internet.[16] While media amplifies the power of ritual, however, it can also help dramatize and highlight when rituals are violated.

As rituals can initiate new members or keep current members part of a collective, not participating can have a range of responses. In general, not participating identifies one as an outsider and vulnerable to the consequences of being separated from the community. As Joseph Campbell reminds us, anyone standing in "exile from the community is a nothing."[17] In the sporting arena, not participating in rituals has a significant level of risk due to the political nature of some sporting rituals. Not only does ritual dissent exile or separate one from a community, but it also threatens larger political norms about what it means to be American. Dan Nimmo and James Combs illuminate the duality of rituals and politics by arguing: "Ritual dissent threatens the credibility of fantasies of national affirmation, but ritual affirmation confirms patriotic feelings."[18] Sports are inherently political, but media, fans, and athletes often see only ruptures, rather than the everyday practice of sport, as political.

RUPTURES IN THE RITUALS

James Ettema notes that "[a] social drama begins when someone who intends to trigger a confrontation publicly breaches a norm governing social relations."[19] One of the most visible rituals in sport that governs social and political relations is the playing of, and standing for, the national anthem. In 1916, by executive order, President Wilson designated "The Star Spangled Banner" as the national anthem to help rally Americans around the country's entrance into World War I. While the anthem played at sporting events as far back as 1862, it was not consistently played until game one of the 1918 World Series during the seventh-inning stretch. Players from the Cubs and Red Sox, accustomed to military drilling, faced the flag and many in the crowd sang along and cheered. When the song was ratified as the national anthem in 1931, credit was given to the public's familiarity with the song at baseball games.[20] For decades most fans and players have not questioned standing for the national anthem and it has melded itself into the routine of attending sporting events.

A few athletes, however, have disrupted the anthem ritual and have used it as a form of protest. One of the most iconic sporting images in American history comes from the 1968 Olympics in Mexico City when United States track runners Tommie Smith and John Carlos raised their fists to protest racial inequality while the national anthem played during the medal ceremony. Smith and Carlos were immediately sent home from the games and were widely lambasted by media outlets. For example, writer and commentator Brent Musburger wrote an article after their protest that referred to them as "black-skinned storm troopers" and their protest as "juvenile" and "ignoble."[21] In 1996, National Basketball Association (NBA) player Mahmoud Abdul-Rauf refused to stand for religious reasons, and after being fined and briefly suspended, he compromised with NBA officials and agreed to stand and pray with his eyes closed as the anthem played.[22] More recently in 2003, Toni Smith, a women's basketball player at Manhattanville College turned her back on the flag during the anthem to protest the Iraq War. In 2014, Knox College basketball player Ariyana Smith walked in front of the flag during the anthem with her hands in the "hands up, don't shoot" gesture in response to the Ferguson protests and Michael Brown's death. She lay on the ground for four and half minutes postponing the start of the game and, afterwards, the university suspended her from the team.[23]

An additional athlete who further helped catapult the political nature of sport into mainstream America, arguably presenting one of the most widely reported and complex political statements in American sports history, is Colin Kaepernick. Reacting to increasing news stories of police killing black men and the rise of the Black Lives Matter movement, Kaepernick made international news on August 26, 2016 when he refused to stand for the national anthem. His protest began with him sitting, but in response to an open-letter request from a veteran, Kaepernick changed to kneeling during the anthem.[24] While Kaepernick started for the rest of the 2016 season, he opted out of his contract with the 49ers and was unsigned for the 2017 season. Finally, Eric Reid, the first player to kneel beside Kaepernick, was a free agent who eventually filed a collusion grievance against the NFL after remaining unsigned going into the 2018 season. All of these examples demonstrate ruptures in the ritual of the national anthem and illustrate how deviating or questioning the ritual can exile one from the collective.

Ruptures in rituals do not only occur in terms of anthem protests, but have been represented in other ways. For example, the 2004 "basket-brawl" involving players from the National Basketball Association's Detroit Pistons, Indiana Pacers, and several fans represented a "crisis of ritual order" as players broke the physical boundary of the playing space—and consequently the rhetorically constructed boundary between ritual order and disorder—by going into the stands and fighting with fans.[25] In an example less fraught with violence, not wearing team colors to a watch party can mark the participant as an outsider and violate the norms of how to "view" sport.[26]

These examples demonstrate a large continuum between public response and notions of violation when rituals are disrupted. While the participant at the watch party most likely can easily "survive" not wearing the right team colors, political ritual violations disrupt the ideological underpinnings of what the national anthem, flag, and country mean in the sporting context. These ideologies as communicated through ritual, narrative, and myth emphasize the violation, but traditional boundaries of ideological constraint can stretch and be renegotiated as symbolic norms are resignified in a new era of political and athlete activism.

NARRATIVE AND REDEMPTION

Walter Fisher's assessment of the narrative paradigm posits humans are story-telling people and that symbolic language communicated in the form of stories gives "order to human experience."[27] Fisher's narrative paradigm is not so much concerned with individual stories such as anecdotes, depictions, or characterizations, but instead focuses on how narratives "are constitutive of people, community, and the world."[28] Effective rhetoric in the narrative paradigm relies on narrative probability that can be achieved through coherence and fidelity. Coherence refers to whether the credibility of the story and the style of delivery creates a story structure that makes sense to the audience. Narrative fidelity refers to the values of the story and if they are consistent with audience experience. Fidelity would want to ensure that the narrative transcends a mere story, and instead persuades the audience to exercise judgment.[29]

Narratives that uphold fidelity and coherence in sport often deal with frames of equality, hard work, and succeeding. According to Leah Vande Berg and Nick Trujillo, success is the dominant value emphasized in American sport and journalists are the main purveyors of "dramatic narratives that recount the successes and failures of sporting events, participants, and organizations."[30] When narratives fail to uphold sport's ideals, the collective can purge its guilt and seek redemption. Kenneth Burke posits that guilt, purification, and redemption are representative of the effects of accepting or rejecting a hierarchy.[31] In order to deal with rejection, society purifies guilt through mortification and/or victimage. Mortification involves a personal sacrifice by the guilty, while victimage involves the purging of guilt through a scapegoat that symbolizes the guilt or through shifting the blame.[32] During the redemption part of the cycle, the act of purification must be appropriate to the sin of the guilty for the drama to succeed as an act of redemption.

Figures in sport have successfully utilized narratives in defenses and attempts at redemption. For example, former basketball coach, Bobby Knight, upon being fired from Indiana University after a 29-year coaching career, framed his defensive narrative through interviews, press conferences, and speeches that invoked themes of helping others, family, and hard work.[33] Knight's messaging maintained narrative fidelity and coherence and, arguably, was one element that lead to him being hired at another university to continue his career. The commissioner of the National Basketball Association (NBA), Adam Silver, maintained narrative coherence and fidelity in his comments following racist comments the former owner of the Los Angeles Clippers, Donald Sterling, made about African-Americans. Silver connected his narrative, delivered in a major press conference and in interviews, to the history of diversity in the NBA, expressing sympathy and personal outrage, and outlining the specifics of the NBA's investigation to prove the comments were from Sterling.[34] Silver banned Sterling for life and fined him $2.5 million, and received "pretty much universal appreciation" and favorable responses from several teams in the NBA.[35]

But what about athletes and sporting figures that violate political norms? The Knight and Silver examples demonstrate the successful utilization of narrative to help redeem individuals or a league, but can narratives function the same way and uphold the mythical buttresses of sport when ideological assumptions of sport are violated? Scholars in communication and sport wrestle with the notion that sport is incompatible with social change and that it is often portrayed as non-political. Recent examples of political activism, however, suggest that there might be a way.

RENEGOTIATING BOUNDARIES AND HIERARCHICAL CHANGE

Burke's concept of hierarchy is not a static concept, and relationships and events can strengthen or weaken it.[36] If weakened, hierarchies can be rebuilt or reimagined, having implications for societal change. James Klumpp analyzes the challenges of language and power in achieving a just and productive society in the twenty-first century. Klumpp outlines Burke's merger of the linguistic power and the social power of hierarchy and focuses on how the historical situation can impact culture's social hierarchy. He believes there is a role for the critic in upending the social hierarchy and opening up hierarchies to the possibility of change:

> Burke's treatment of hierarchy in *Rhetoric of Motives* suggests an intermediate approach to criticism between the story of the culture organizing human action hierarchically and the individual nestled within hierarchy. This construction views the rhetorical act as fundamentally about hierarchy. The interior of social hierarchy becomes the stage for the rhetorical drama [...] Critics may study the ways in which the rhetoric of the motive conserves the motive and strengthens it, opens up the possibility of change by reversing hierarchies or altering focus, the ways in which single hierarchies contain both the seeds of their power and the seeds of their destruction.[37]

While Klumpp acknowledges the complexity of language and its ability to perpetuate oppression, he opens up the role of the individual critic to use the power of rhetoric to upend the hierarchy and work toward social justice.

Colin Kaepernick's protest just might provide an example of how to create a space where oppositional politics can be played out in the sporting realm. Polls suggest that Kaepernick's protest was largely rejected by whites and people with Republican political leanings, while African Americans and Democrats were widely receptive to the protest.[38] This illuminates a gap between two groups— one that largely rejects him and one that believes his protest was appropriate and acceptable within the sporting realm. It also demonstrates a departure from historical experiences of athletes who protest the anthem. For example, Tommie

Smith and John Carlos in 1968 were largely ostracized and the nation's largest newspapers and commentators wrote scathing remarks about their actions. Mahmoud Abdul-Rauf's refusal in 1996 to stand for the anthem, he believes, "caused irreparable damage to his professional basketball career, making it difficult for him to find a job and eventually sending him overseas."[39] Toni Smith faced extreme levels of pushback and violent threats. Ariyana Smith was suspended and did not return to play with her team. While it can be argued that Kaepernick was scapegoated for his activism as he was unsigned for the 2017 NFL season, there are still differences between how previous players were treated compared to Kaepernick. In addition to starting the remaining 2016 season, Kaepernick received positive press by donating $1 million to community charities, appeared on the cover of *Time* magazine, was named *GQ* magazine's Citizen of the Year, received the 2017 *Sports Illustrated* Muhammad Ali Legacy Award, and his jersey became the NFL's top seller.[40] The ability to start and have positive press, arguably, hints at a change in sports activism that has not necessarily existed in past player political protests. While challenges clearly remain with athlete activism, it can be argued that the positive press and reactions Kaepernick received represent a space where politics were fought and, on some level, were successful among specific groups.

Since Kaepernick's protest there have been additional moments of athlete activism, marking additional moments of success. Beyond the examples of athletes kneeling or raising a fist during the anthem, players like Stephen Curry publicly disputed comments by Under Armor's CEO that praised President Trump's business policies. Curry threatened to leave the company as one of its most recognizable endorsers and the CEO responded with a statement distancing himself and the company from the president. Curry's coach, Steve Kerr, publicly supported his comments and has stated that he is proud of his players for taking stands on political and social issues.[41] NBA coach Gregg Popovich has been vocal about dissatisfaction with President Trump's policies and actions. NFL players, such as Chris Long and Michael Bennett, have also established themselves as politically active. Bennett opposed an Israeli government sponsored trip to Israel for players and convinced eight of the 13 players not to go.[42] Long made comments against the white supremacist march in Charlottesville in August 2017 and publicly responded to counter Fox News commentator Laura Ingraham's comments that LeBron James should "shut up and dribble."[43] Since 2015 LeBron James has made comments about gun control, which he made again in wake of the February 2018 mass shooting at a high school in Parkland, Fla. that killed 17 people, spurring Ingraham's comments.[44]

Although these examples are not comprehensive of every political statement people in sport have made, and do not cover every criticism media and fans express they do suggest a growing willingness for athletes and coaches to embrace activism on some level. These examples combine with other events, such as those

mentioned at the beginning of the chapter like the A.P.U. activism, college athletes attempting to unionize, and players threatening to boycott and pressuring
university representatives to resign, to constitute a growing collective identity for
athlete activists. Maurice Charland's concept of constitutive rhetoric suggests that
individuals identify through language, symbols, and narratives to create a collective
identity:

> The distinct acts and events in a narrative become linked through identification arising
> from the narrative form. Narratives lead us to construct and fill in coherent unified subjects
> out of temporally and spatially separate events. This renders the site of action and experi-
> ence stable. The locus of yesterday's acts becomes that of today's. Consequently, narratives
> offer a world in which human agency is possible and acts can be meaningful.[45]

Acts of athlete activism work together to constitute larger narratives and a
collective identity that suggests a hierarchical change is afoot. This hierarchical
renegotiation has implications for athlete activism as it becomes more socially
acceptable to participate.

IMPLICATIONS

Public narratives about athlete activism and the new space opened by Kaepernick suggest a public good that sport can facilitate democratic ideals in a realm
that historically has punished political activism. Kaepernick's actions help clear a
space that helps normalize activism, as recently witnessed in the public communication of sporting figures such as Stephen Curry, LeBron James, Chris Long,
and Michael Bennett. Current athlete activism points to two major implications
specifically related to civic ethos and the First Amendment.

First, this new rhetorical space could harken a new type of civic ethos for
athletes and contribute to larger national cultural movements. According to Khan,
civic ethos is a "form of political activity" made possible by public address and acts
of protest.[46] Civic ethos was inherent to athlete activism during the mid to late
twentieth century and corresponded to Muhammad Ali, Tommie Smith, John
Carlos, and Curt Flood who characterized an era of activism spirited by selflessness. Their acts of protest spoke to democratic ideals and functioned as part of
the larger civil rights movement. The civic ethos of athletes during this era is
contrasted with athletes in the late twentieth century and critics of contemporary
athletes often accuse them of shifting athlete activism from the selfless to the
selfish with a rise in business opportunities that drove athletes to avoid activism
in favor of endorsements and pay checks.[47] Athlete activists today, while still very
much-engaged in capitalist constructs of sport, might be able to better balance
business with social justice issues. Their actions fit into larger cultural movements

of progress, such as the Millennial Generation, who are likely to reshape American values with their civic idealism.[48] And the Trump presidency has sparked citizen action as demonstrated through the Women's march, the March for Science, packed congressional town hall meetings, and a rise in first time political candidates running for office. Athletes, it can be argued, are now an additional prong in national movements for civic ethos as their activism becomes more prominent, and their actions also usher in a new activist era that helps to balance democratic ideals with the capitalist realities of American sport.

Contemporary athlete activism also suggests a way to interrogate unsettled areas of First Amendment constitutional concepts. Activist athletes are ultimately citizens exercising their First Amendment rights when they come under question for voicing political views or kneeling, and protesting gets to the heart of American democracy and freedom of expression. A March 2017 Pew Research Center poll found that 79% of respondents believe in the right to nonviolent protest and 74% view protecting the rights of people with unpopular views as an important element of a strong democracy. These findings are consistent with past polls.[49] In terms of sport protests, the American public seems a bit more conflicted, but a majority of Americans think athletes should be allowed to kneel and players should not be fired for failing to stand.[50] Beyond perceptions of First Amendment rights, enforcing the First Amendment becomes thorny. All teams of the four major sports leagues, except the Green Bay Packers, are privately owned and operated but most play in publicly funded facilities and receive subsidies. According to Nick DeSiato, "The combination of privately owned professional sports clubs and publicly funded facilities creates a unique professional sports private-public hybrid that remains legally complex and largely unsettled amongst courts."[51] Depending on how hard athletes push, they could push themselves, and sport, into new frontiers of First Amendment law due to the private and public combination that is not typical of other American institutions.[52]

While recent political expression has opened a new rhetorical space for athlete activism, the strength of ritual and ideology in sport cannot, and should not, be dismissed or downplayed. These competing tensions—sport as a site for political activism compared to its ideological strength in communicating and perpetuating democratic norms—will continue to complicate significant political progress made by athletes. This renegotiation also does not suggest that allowances for activism are consistent or automatic. It is possible that athletes can push the boundaries of myth and ideology and narratives cannot support these over extensions. However, with Kaepernick and other athletes who are willing to take some level of risk, there is now an advantage that is new to sport and can add to larger national conversations about civic ethos and First Amendment rights.

Athlete activism presents a complex site of competing tensions that exposes national anxieties related to a number of issues including capitalism, entertainment, social justice, race, patriotism, police rights, victim rights, and individual rights, among others. When athletes are politically vocal they become complex symbols that media outlets and national publics are unable to package or understand neatly. This complexity leads to a level of discomfort not necessarily felt in other arenas of protest. A politician expressing dissatisfaction with issues related to his/her constituents, a victim of a shooting expressing an opinion on gun violence, or members of differing racial groups expressing their views on inequality tend to have an underlying logic that audiences can understand even if viewers disagree with their protest. But seeing highly paid athletes taking a political stand in a perceived entertainment venue creates a dissonance that, for many, is too big to reconcile. Athletes who expose national anxieties become powerful subjects for national dialogue due to the level of discomfort they offer when rupturing rituals. This suggests the rhetorical might of athlete activists who can navigate the discomfort and find ways to expose the dissonance when possible.

For critics, a continued interrogation of the tension inherent to sport and athlete activism is needed. Continued research analyzing how athlete activism impacts public discourse and democratic ideals is appropriate, but specifically analyzing how athlete activism provides a level of national discomfort that other cultural areas does not permit can help identify the ways sport functions uniquely within protest and rhetorical studies.

NOTES

1. Ken Belson, "Kaepernick vs. the N.F.L.: A Primer on His Collusion Case," *NewYorkTimes.com*, last modified December 8, 2017, https://www.nytimes.com/2017/12/08/sports/kaepernick-coll usion.html.

2. For explanation of the term "Sports Media Complex" see, Sut Jhally, "The Spectacle of Accumulation: Material and Cultural Factors in the Evolution of the Sports/Media Complex," *Critical Sociology* 12, no. 3 (1984): 41–57.

3. Chip Patterson, "All Players United Campaign Launched with 'APU' on Wrist Tape." *CBSsports. com*, September 21, 2013, http://www.cbssports.com/college-football/news/all-players-united-campaign-launched-with-apu-on-wrist-tape/.

4. The National Labor Relations Board dismissed the petition in 2015, effectively ending the Northwestern University football players' claim and their ability to collectively bargain.

5. "One Year After Protest Rocked Missouri, the Effects on the Football Team and University Remain Tangible," *SportsIllustrated.com*, November 8, 2016, http://www.si.com/college-foot ball/2016/11/08/how-missouri-football-has-changed-1-year-after-boycott.

6. For more on the role of money in athlete activism, see, Abraham Iqbal Khan, *Curt Flood in the Media: Baseball, Race, and the Demise of the Activist-Athlete* (Jackson, MS: University Press of Mississippi, 2012).

7. Kareem Abdul-Jabbar, "Kareem Abdul-Jabbar: The Importance of Athlete Activists," *Time.com*, November 18, 2015, http://time.com/4114002/kareem-abdul-jabbar-athlete-activists/.

8. Michael L. Butterworth, "Purifying the Body Politic: Steroids, Rafael Palmeiro, and the Rhetorical Cleansing of Major League Baseball," *Western Journal of Communication* 72, no. 2 (2008): 147.

9. Darren Rovell, "NFL Returning $723K for Sponsored Military Tributes," *ESPN.com*, May 19, 2016, http://www.espn.com/nfl/story/_/id/15611052/nfl-returning-723000-taxpayers-paid-military-tributes.

10. See, for example, Butterworth, "Purifying," 145–61; Daniel A. Grano, "Ritual Disorder and the Contractual Morality of Sport: A Case Study in Race, Class, and Agreement," *Rhetoric & Public Affairs* 10, no. 3 (2007): 445–73; Michael Real, *Mass-Mediated Culture* (Englewood Cliffs, NJ: Prentice Hall, 1977); Susan Birrell, "Sport as Ritual: Interpretations from Durkheim to Goffman," *Social Forces* 60, no. 2 (1981): 354–76.

11. Alfred Radcliffe-Brown, "Religion and Society," in *Religion, Culture and Society*, ed. Louis Schneider (New York: Wiley, 1964), 66.

12. Birrell, "Sport as Ritual," 354.

13. Robert Bellah, "Civil Religion in America," *Daedalus* 96, no. 1 (1967): 1–21.

14. Michael L. Butterworth, "Ritual in the 'Church of Baseball': Suppressing the Discourse of Democracy After 9/11," *Communication and Critical/Cultural Studies* 2, no. 2 (2005): 107–29.

15. David Rowe, *Sport, Culture, and the Media: The Unruly Trinity* (Buckingham, UK: Open University Press, 1999).

16. Lawrence A. Wenner, "Media, Sports, and Society: The Research Agenda," in *Media, Sport, & Society*, ed. Lawrence A. Wenner (Newbury Park, CA: Sage, 1989), 16.

17. Joseph Campbell, *The Hero with a Thousand Faces*, commemorative ed. (Princeton, NJ: Princeton University Press, 2004), 356.

18. Dan Nimmo and James E. Combs, *Mediated Political Realities*, 2nd ed. (New York: Longman, 1990), 142.

19. James Stewart Ettema, "Press Rites and Race Relations: A Study of Mass-Mediated Ritual," *Critical Studies in Mass Communication* 7, no. 4 (1990): 309–31.

20. Robert Elias, *The Empire Strikes Out* (New York: The New Press, 2010), 94–5.

21. Dave Zirin, "After Forty-Four Years, It's Time Brent Musburger Apologized to John Carlos and Tommie Smith," *TheNation.com*, June 4, 2012, https://www.thenation.com/article/after-forty-four-years-its-time-brent-musburger-apologized-john-carlos-and-tommie-smith/.

22. Rick Maese, "Mahmoud Adbul-Rauf on Kaepernick Controversy: 'It's a Duplicate Pretty Much,'" *Washingtonpost.com*, August 24, 2017, https://www.washingtonpost.com/sports/mahmoud-abdul-rauf-on-kaepernick-controversy-its-a-duplicate-pretty-much/2017/08/24/cac9496e-890a-11e7-a94f-3139abce39f5_story.html?utm_term=.8ab358f86232.

23. Dave Zirin, "Interview with Ariyana Smith: The First Athlete Activist of #BlackLivesMatter," *TheNation.com*, last modified December 19, 2014, https://www.thenation.com/article/interview-ariyana-smith-first-athlete-activist-blacklivesmatter/.

24. Will Brinson, "Here's How Nate Boyer Got Colin Kaepernick to Go From Sitting to Kneeling," *CBSSports.com*, September 27, 2016, https://www.cbssports.com/nfl/news/heres-how-nate-boyer-got-colin-kaepernick-to-go-from-sitting-to-kneeling/.

25. Grano, "Ritual Disorder," 453.

26. Roger C. Aden, Timothy A. Borchers, Amy Grim Buxbaum, Kirstin Cronn- Mills, Shannon Davis, Natalie J. Dollar, Innes Mitchell, and Alena Amato Ruggerio, "Communities of Cornhuskers: The Generation of Place Through Sports Fans' Rituals," *Qualitative Research Reports in Communication* 10, no. 1 (2009): 26-37.

27. Walter Fisher, "Narration as a Human Communication Paradigm: The Case of Public Moral Argument," *Communication Monographs* 51, no. 1 (1984): 4.

28. Walter Fisher, "Clarifying the Narrative Paradigm," *Communication Monographs* 56, no. 1 (1989): 56.

29. Walter Fisher, *Human Communication as a Narration: Toward a Philosophy of Reason, Value, and Action* (Columbia, SC: University of South Carolina Press, 1987).

30. Leah R. Vande Berg and Nick Trujillo, "The Rhetoric of Winning and Losing: The American Dream and America's Team," in *Media, Sports, & Society*, ed. Lawrence A. Wenner (Newbury Park, CA: Sage, 1989), 205.

31. Kenneth Burke, *Permanence and Change* (Los Angeles: University of California Press, 1965).

32. Robert Lee Scott and Bernard L. Brock, *Methods of Rhetorical Criticism* (New York: Harper & Row, 1972).

33. Karen L. Hartman, "Intertextuality and Apologia: Rhetorical Efficacy Through Shared Values as Illustrated Through the Firing of Coach Bobby Knight," *Speaker & Gavel* 45, no. 1 (2008): 19–35.

34. James R. DiSanza, Karen L. Hartman, Nancy J. Legge, and Zac Gershberg, "Crisis 'Narrative Management' in Sport," in *Reputational Challenges in Sport*, ed. Andrew Billings, W. Timothy Coombs, and Kenon Brown (New York: Routledge, 2017).

35. Royce Young, "Reactions to the NBA's Lifetime Ban of Donald Sterling," *CBSsports.com*, April 29, 2014, https://www.cbssports.com/nba/news/reactions-to-the-nbas-lifetime-ban-of-donald-sterling/.

36. Jim A. Kuypers and Ashley Gellert, "The Story of King/Drew Hospital: Guilt and Deferred Purification," *K.B. Journal* 8, no. 1 (2012), http://www.kbjournal.org/kuypers_gellert_king_drew_hospital.

37. James F. Klumpp, "Burkean Social Hierarchy and the Ironic Investment of Martin Luther King," in *Kenneth Burke and the 21st Century*, ed. Bernard L. Brock (Albany, NY: State University of New York Press, 1999), 221–2.

38. Kathryn Casteel, "How Do Americans Feel About the NFL Protests? It Depends on How You Ask," *FiveThirtyEight.com*, last modified October 9, 2017. https://fivethirtyeight.com/features/how-do-americans-feel-about-the-nfl-protests-it-depends-on-how-you-ask/.

39. Rick Maese, "Mahmoud Adbul-Rauf."

40. Ahiza Garcia, "Colin Kaepernick's Jersey Is Top Seller After Protest," *Money.cnn.com*, September 6, 2016, http://money.cnn.com/2016/09/06/news/companies/colin-kaepernick-jersey-nfl/.

41. Jack Williams, "Stephen Curry Takes Issue With Under Armour Leader on Trump," *NewYork-Times.com*, February 8, 2017, https://www.nytimes.com/2017/02/08/sports/basketball/stephen-curry-under-armour-donald-trump-warriors.html.

42. Michael Bennett, Interview by Amy Goodman and Dave Zirin, *DemocracyNow!*, February 24, 2018. https://www.democracynow.org/2017/2/24/nfl_star_michael_bennett_on_refusing.

43. Enrico Campitelli, "Chris Long Defends LeBron James After Attack from Fox News Host," *NBCsports.com*, February 16, 2018, http://www.nbcsports.com/philadelphia/the700level/chris-long-defends-lebron-james-after-attack-fox-news-host.

44. Rohan Nadkarni, "What's the Next Step for the NBA's Political Awakening?" *SportsIllustrated.com*, February 17, 2018, https://www.si.com/nba/2018/02/17/lebron-james-steve-kerr-gun-control-donald-trump-all-star-weekend.

45. Maurice Charland, "Constitutive Rhetoric: The Case of the *Peuple Québécois*," *The Quarterly Journal of Speech* 73, no. 2 (1987): 139.

46. Khan, *Curt Flood*, 5.

47. See, for example, Shaun Powell, *Souled Out? How Blacks Are Winning and Losing in Sports* (Champaign, IL: Human Kinetics, 2008); William C. Rhoden, *Forty Million Dollar Slaves* (New York, NY: Three Rivers Press, 2006).

48. Morley Winograd and Michael D. Hais, *Millennial Momentum* (New Brunswick, NJ: Rutgers University Press, 2011).

49. "Large Majorities See Checks and Balances, Right to Protest as Essential for Democracy," *people-press.org*, March 2, 2017, http://www.people-press.org/2017/03/02/large-majorities-see-checks-and-balances-right-to-protest-as-essential-for-democracy/.

50. Kathryn Casteel, "How Do Americans Feel About the NFL Protests?."

51. Nick DeSiato, "Silencing the Crowd: Regulating Free Speech in Professional Sports Facilities," *Marquette Sports Law Review* 20, no. 2 (2010), http://scholarship.law.marquette.edu/cgi/viewcontent.cgi?article=1485&context=sportslaw.

52. For more explanation of First Amendment and labor law issues as related to NFL player anthem protests, please see, Michael McCann, "Can an NFL Owner Legally 'Fire' a Player for Protesting?" *SportsIllustrated.com*, September 23, 2017, https://www.si.com/nfl/2017/09/23/donald-trump-fired-roger-goodell-player-protest.

Section II: Mobilizing Resistances

CHAPTER FOUR

Diving into the Past

Greg Louganis, Queer Memory, and the Politics of HIV Management

JEFFREY A. BENNETT

In 1988 Greg Louganis was one of the most celebrated athletes in the world. He left the Seoul Olympics with two gold medals, just as he had four years earlier in Los Angeles, making him only one of two Olympians ever to win consecutive medals in both platform and springboard diving. His accomplishments were especially noteworthy because Louganis swept the events after hitting his head on the diving board during a qualifying round. At the time, he was also the only diver in Olympic history to score over 700 points in a single competition. By the time the San Diego native retired he had collected an unprecedented 47 national titles and 13 world championships. For all these reasons, Louganis is frequently described as "quite possibly the greatest ever at his sport."[1] He retired a national hero at the top of his game.

But for all of that glory, Louganis was also an HIV-positive gay man who was often received with undisguised animus in the years following his departure from the sport. Like many athletes, Louganis shied away from discussions of his sexuality during his diving career but rumors about his private life had swirled for years. These ruinous whispers had a significant impact on his ability to attract sponsors and sustain himself after he stepped away from the pool. Whereas stars such as Mary Lou Retton garnered over one million dollars in sponsorships after the 1984 Olympics, Louganis was unable to land significant endorsement deals.[2] Companies such as General Mills elected not to lionize him on the Wheaties cereal box because he did not appeal to their "wholesome demographics."[3] The mere conjecture of being gay in Reagan's America was enough to sideline Louganis's popularity and stunt opportunities to be politically visible or economically prosperous.

In 2016 General Mills reversed course and announced that Louganis would be featured on the coveted Wheaties box as part of their so-called "Legends Series." Wheaties, the self-proclaimed "breakfast of champions," has been an iconic cultural site for acclaimed athletes and professional sports teams since the 1930s. It has long extolled those competitors coming off the wake of meaningful victories and memorable personal achievements. The decision to profile Louganis on the box was unusual, then, because his record-setting accomplishment of winning four gold medals in Olympic diving had happened decades earlier. General Mills may have once found the association between an HIV-positive gay man and their quintessentially American product to be taboo but halfway into the second decade of the new millennium this stigma appeared to recede. Louganis's placement on the box provided an expedient means to market the Wheaties brand and attract consumers.

This essay explores the queer memory politics of lauding Louganis decades after his triumphs. I argue that his presence highlights an ongoing tension in rhetorics that focus on LGBTQ people and those who are HIV-positive. On the one hand, the Wheaties box spotlights the ways queers continue to be a lucrative consumer base for expanding corporate profits and generating revenue. On the other hand, Louganis's image performs significant cultural work in an age where representations of, and conversations about, HIV-positive people are increasingly rare. HIV has morphed into a chronic condition for those with access to life-saving medications and such advancements have had the perverse effect of quelling exchanges about its social and medical complexities. Louganis's appearance on the Wheaties box animates a sliver of HIV's history, one that moves us from the dire calamity of the 1980s into the present-day stabilization of the crisis, even as this visual rhetoric is negotiated within the parameters of his carefully curated biography. Contrary to many contemporary memory projects, including a number of recent high profile documentaries about AIDS activism, Louganis embodies not the vivaciousness and precarity that underwrote HIV for so many years, but a meticulous image of control, bodily maintenance, and personal transcendence. Louganis is the perfect representation of management, hard work, and luck. The sporting world, which has long been steeped in homophobia and heterosexism, acts as the contextual backdrop to this stalled tribute, accentuating the calculated nature of this memory text and the intersecting impulses of celebrity, economic opportunism, and public health. To further investigate this unusual, if otherwise banal, cultural artifact I first look to scholarship that engages the politics of memory, especially as it relates to HIV/AIDS activism, in order to contextualize the period in which the Wheaties box emerged. I then contemplate how Louganis is both a reflection of, and ultimately resistant to, neoliberal discourses by looking to his status as an out athlete and his continued efforts to combat HIV.

PUBLIC MEMORY: BREAKING THE SURFACE

Scholars of public memory have long maintained that glancing backward into the past is an exercise in rhetorical invention. Far from a naturally occurring phenomenon or experiential process, memory is discursively constructed by those invested in the past and habitually suited to the needs of a politically-fraught present.[4] Kendall Phillips observes that the "ways memories attain meaning, compel others to accept them, and are themselves contested, subverted, and supplanted by other memories are essentially rhetorical."[5] Public memory is, according to Charles Morris, "a purposeful engagement with the past," an exercise that is "forged symbolically, profoundly constitutive of identity, community, and moral vision, inherently consequential in its ideological implications, and very often the fodder of political conflagration."[6] Who gets to stand in as representative of a community's past, who is permitted to be heralded a regional and national hero, and who is rhapsodized in cultural locations both sacred and profane is deliberately crafted and often decidedly partisan.

Public memory's circuitous and fragmentary character draws attention to the symbolic contestation waged over historical events, revered figures, and consecrated grounds. The attachments that civic actors forge to particular memory sites are guided by personal affinities and cultural narratives much more than they are a recitation of historical facts. The recent debates over confederate monuments, for example, illustrates the ways vital contextual matters can be jettisoned by those making appeals to abstractions such as "heritage" when it is well known that the statues were erected during integration and not following the Civil War. Laura Doan contends that memory "seeks an affective connection with a past already known to fulfill political aspirations in the present."[7] In this way, collective memory is enacted through everyday performative repertoires and encounters with the past. It is an "active political practice" that is essentially constitutive in nature.[8]

Despite the entrenched character of communal narratives, memory's affective possibilities are more polysemous than unidirectional. Memories can be dispiritingly hegemonic, yes, but their rhetorical composition guarantees that both negotiated and oppositional readings are always possible. The mythos constituted by memory can serve the needs of the status quo but can also provide the fodder to "disrupt and transform conditions that make survival necessary."[9] The inclusion of previously maligned and marginalized groups into memory narratives can simultaneously perpetuate hegemonic logics and present the means to disrupt dominant histories. Chronicling the lives of queer athletes can yield fuller accounts of the past and furnish the rhetorical resources for addressing structural heterosexism.

Sport provides a "common archive" of public memories and proffers insight into a culture's desired image of the past.[10] Stephen Wieting and Judy Polumbaum remind us that which sport "icons, relics, and events are selected from the past for retrieval, how they are packaged to serve the present collective ends, and what use the elements and package will have in the future are all contested grounds."[11] The presence of LGBTQ people complicates such ephemeral repositories, in part because that which is marked as "queer" has frequently been antithetical to that which is conventionally desirable. The normative force of sport and memory invariably calls attention to the violent erasures of LGBTQ people, even if such recollections sometimes attempt to hegemonically incorporate queer communities into narratives emphasizing nationalism, exceptionalism, and individual fortitude. As Michael Butterworth rightly notes, memory texts derived from sport "are not innocent references" to moments in the past.[12] They are imbued with affective attachments, ideological impulses, and unassimilable remainders.

Of course, amorphous power structures such as heterosexism and nationalism are sustained through memory practices and are not easily subverted. Scholars have warned that the political scaffolding that organizes public memory presents countless opportunities to co-opt its rhetorical contours. Marita Sturken cautions that the "changeabilty of memory raises important concerns about how the past can be verified, understood, and given meaning."[13] J. Jack Halberstam likewise expresses concern about the commodification of memory and the ways it can be used to reinforce draconian normativities.[14] The potential to polish over troublesome and oppressive histories becomes especially complicated when corporate interests articulate their bottom line to past injustices.[15] It is in the economic interest of brands to assert their dedication to inclusion, to forward (sometimes specious) arguments about diversity, and to highlight how they have made amends with a troubled past. Sport is no exception to these logics, particularly in light of the assumed LGBTQ consumer demographic, which is thought to be in the hundreds of billions of dollars.[16]

Although many scholars are wary of corporate articulations to public memory, some have exalted the gains to be made by closely aligning movement goals to the market. Arguing against broad charges of homonormativity, these thinkers find the secular possibilities of neoliberalism to be at least partially empowering. Deirdre McCloskey, for example, has argued that many of the strides made by LGBTQ people have come about because of the influence of corporate enterprises. She writes, "the market is not the enemy of queers. The restaurants and bars from which the drag queens exploded in political action in the 1960s in San Francisco then in New York were after all profit making-entities."[17] McCloskey concludes that the "enemies were the gender cops, not the owners of coffee houses."[18] In the desire to attract and retain consumers, brands have often embraced LGBTQ people and, to a lesser extent, their tumultuous histories.[19]

The LGBTQ community has repeatedly struggled over the best practices for remembering the past. In many LGBTQ enclaves, there remains a tendency to overlook people of color in queer histories, a habit of erasing trans bodies, and a bias toward centralizing the voices of cis white men. Debates over how to represent the Stonewall uprising, for example, have been waged over screenplays, monuments at the location of the bar, the political commitment of pride parades, and in the pages of LGBTQ genealogies. In this vein, a spate of memory work has attempted to capture the early years of the AIDS crisis and the struggle of activists to hold bureaucrats accountable for institutionally sanctioned queer genocide. Numerous documentaries about ACT-UP, for example, have steadily been released over the last decade. Films including *United in Anger, How to Survive a Plague, We Were Here,* and *Vito* all venture to narrate the history of HIV/AIDS and its devastating ramifications on queer communities. These mnemoscapes also include productions such as HBO's adaptation of Larry Kramer's play *The Normal Heart* and the network miniseries *When We Rise.* This is to say nothing of the rich collection of scholarship that documents the rise of groups such as ACT-UP, Queer Nation, and the Lesbian Avengers.

The Louganis box appeared on shelves in the midst of this memory work, not as a politically charged artifact that equips interlocutors to mourn or reflect, but as a mundane product whose representation of Louganis illustrates physical strength, discipline, and tenacity. Louganis himself is perhaps best remembered for his accomplishments *despite* the fact that he hit his head during that qualifying round in Seoul. That visceral scene, with its affective transmission of mediated pain and fear of contaminated blood, lingers in the collective consciousness, reiterating both risk and triumph, health and illness, nationalism and its discontents. In this vein, the box speaks to a politically finessed past, a contained vision of HIV in the present, and a future brimming with possibility.

THE NARRATIVE OF CHAMPIONS

Louganis is no stranger to the power of narrative and the politics of collective memory. The diver was the subject of the Emmy-nominated documentary *Back on Board* in 2014, a narrative that hues closely to his 1995 autobiography. This film garnered Louganis an unusual amount of media attention by juxtaposing his storied career against his sometimes turbulent personal life. The production revealed that Louganis was in dire financial straits and showed him auctioning off many of his possessions to retain his California home. Unlike the image of triumph and accomplishment that audiences are accustomed to seeing, Louganis is situated as a person with an extraordinary past, but whose problems are familiar to those who lived through the worst of the so-called "great recession." At the time, Louganis even discussed the prospects of living in an RV should he be forced from his residence. A pivotal scene in *Back on Board* contrasts Louganis's financial plight to his earlier fame, explicitly tackling the homophobia that prevented him from profiting off of his accomplishments. Viewers find Louganis at the International Swimming Hall of Fame, looking at memorabilia, and taking stock of the athletes who had appeared on the Wheaties box. He is not among them. An online petition was filed by fans shortly thereafter and executives at General Mills took notice.

The attention brought by *Back on Board* and the Wheaties box landed Louganis a spread in *ESPN The Magazine's* 2016 "body issue." This annual special issue features an array of athletes posing nude to accentuate their athletic dexterity. Louganis was 56-years-old when he appeared in the buff. His body is sculpted and trim, indicating that he has continued to monitor his health and exercise regularly. The photos harken back to the days when Louganis sat for a now iconic photoshoot with Herb Ritts, as well as the time he donned a strategically placed sheet for *Playgirl* in 1987. Despite his misfortunes and serostatus he is situated as a study in health and athleticism in middle age. Louganis openly discusses being HIV-positive with ESPN and reiterates, as he has countless times over the years, that the diagnosis left him feeling isolated and clinically depressed. The dual themes of managing HIV and modeling health continue to shape his persona three decades after he announced his serostatus. Thirty years on and Louganis is still publicly fused to his diagnosis. HIV is more than a medical condition, it's central to Louganis's identity.

The Wheaties box is the chronological centerpiece of these recent memoryscapes, connecting Louganis's highly visible past to a contemporary political context. *Back on Board,* the cereal box, and the magazine spread all revisit Louganis's achievements to highlight his continued discipline and celebrity. But it is the Wheaties box that is most fascinating because of its nostalgic flair. It extols Louganis's athletic accomplishments while allowing audiences to articulate personal knowledge of Louganis, including his notoriety in the LGBTQ community, to their consumptive habits. It would be easy to castigate the box as apolitical or economically opportunistic, especially considering the steep decline in Wheaties sales in recent years, but its potential to reach diverse audiences through different emotional registers also suggests that this banal product is not detached from political life.[20] The familiarity that consumers bring with them to the box is couched in affective notions such as victory, perseverance, and survival. These fragments of knowledge are also distant enough from the political malfeasance of the 1980s that an understanding of HIV as individually managed, and not a product of institutional mendacity, can be conjured by consumers.

The photo on the front of the box shows Louganis performing an inward pike dive that was taken while he was preparing for the 1984 Olympics. His form is characteristically symmetrical and the black and white contrast outlines his muscular physique. Louganis hit his head attempting a reverse 2 ½ pike and the semiotic remainder of that event invariably informs the visual rhetoric adorning the box. The front of the box also bears his name and lists the gold medals he won in 1984 and 1988. The back of the box applauds his many accomplishments outside the Olympics and features inspirational quotations for "becoming a champion."

Louganis has insisted that he was not overtly political for much of his life, but mentions in *Back on Board* that he has come to realize the inevitable connection between sport and politics. Louganis's biography, *Breaking the Surface*, suggests that he has been politically inclined for much of his career, even if inadvertently. At the Montreal games in 1976 he helped an athlete from the former Soviet Union defect to Canada.[21] After the 1984 games Louganis was part of the effort to allow Olympic athletes to attract sponsors while maintaining their amateur status.[22] His speech to the US Olympic Committee during their planning of the Atlanta games is nothing short of revelatory. He argued that an anti-LGBTQ ordinance in Cobb County, GA should disqualify that municipality from hosting any part of the games.[23] The committee agreed. In 1995, the year his memoire was published, he condemned the Olympic committee for not directly addressing the issue of HIV.

The political tendencies of athletes, especially in the context of product endorsement and advertising, are frequently and unsurprisingly more subtle than overt. The image of the pro-athlete metonymically represents exceptionalism and the latitude they are given to transgress from the norm is often directly correlated to their celebrity or ability. But not always. Muhammad Ali, for example, was not put on the Wheaties box until 1999. General Mills shied away from the boxer's outspoken politics, which they believed would not resonate with their (presumably white) consumer-base.[24] Louganis was never as politically controversial as Ali so his omission came about not because of his political orientation (which is assuredly racialized in Ali's case) but because of speculation about his sexuality. Still, in both instances it is impossible to completely erase the remainder of their political legacies and the attachments consumers bring to the kitchen table. Louganis's politics may be sanitized as "safe" for resale but that positioning depends on the expectation that audiences will bracket all that they know about him. His sexuality and HIV status, once used as mechanisms of stigmatization, have become symbols of transcendence, success, and status.[25] In this way Louganis's migration from margin to center mirrors the movement of LGBTQ people from social periphery to political prominence.

General Mills offered discrepant explanations for eschewing Louganis in the 1980s after the petition to put him on the Wheaties box began to circulate. One spokesperson commented that no person from the 1980s involved in the decision-making process remained at the company.[26] Another representative remarked, "There's so many great athletes and so much competition to get on the box. In 1984 and 1988 we had Mary Lou Retton, America's sweetheart, and Michael Jordan—who were both very deserving. We stand by our choices back then."[27] The patronizing label of Retton as an object of affection, what Toby Miller calls a "white American darling," and not an athlete (she is regarded by General Mills as the first woman to appear on the Wheaties box) hints both at the troubling frames used to maintain the image of profit-making athletes and the purity rules that underlined the corporation's deliberations.[28] Louganis has stated that he now finds General Mills to be an inclusive brand but the above statements indicate a rhetoric familiar to LGBTQ people, one that places them in a hierarchical relation to heterosexuality that is celebrated by virtue of its structural ubiquity. LGBTQ people are instructed to simply wait their turn. This is to say nothing of the economic disparities between LGBTQ people and their heterosexual peers, which is also highlighted by the occasion.

Louganis's Wheaties box may be indicative of LGBTQ "progress" but it also underscores the continued perils of the closet in professional sports.[29] We know that Louganis is queer and HIV-positive by virtue of his widely-circulated biography and the ways his life struggles were exacerbated by his career as a professional athlete. His persona is made intelligible in part by the attachments consumers bring to his story, not simply by the encoding performed by the manufacturer. This semiotic wink energizes a familiar rhetorical form, one in which publics read the sexualities and gender identities of athletes retrospectively, regularly applauding their talents and bravery after they depart the sporting world. Caitlyn Jenner, Jason Collins, John Amaechi, Billy Bean, Glenn Burke, Wade Davis, and Esera Tuaolo all declared their sexuality or gender identities after they had left their respective sports. The cereal box reminds us how athletes are encouraged not to reveal facets of their identity in order to protect their livelihood. It is worth remembering that Martina Navratilova lost $12 million in endorsement deals after she came out in 1981; Billie Jean King lost them all.[30] This is likely the reason there is currently no out athlete among the four major sports in the United States, just as there were none in 1988 when Louganis was competing. The branding tendencies of high profile athletes in the context of neo-liberalism is a carefully calculated matrix of risk, profitability, and public image. Despite this absence, a number of out athletes compete in American sports such as soccer, volleyball, softball, track and field, cycling, boxing, and diving.

The Louganis story is, in many respects, a series of deferred spectacles that invite continual reassessment of his past. Even with all that we know about

Louganis there has been a repeated necessity for audiences to reinterpret his public persona. Louganis has been rhetorically reconfigured at least three times following major events in his life. The first of these retrospective interpretations found audiences revisiting his life in sports after he came out. Fans again reacquainted themselves with his celebrity after he revealed he was HIV-positive. Finally, a more inspiring narrative about his accomplishments that did not require the whitewashing of his sexual orientation or HIV status has emerged at the exact moment that we are on the brink of containing the HIV epidemic. Notably, this reiteration of Louganis's persona has evolved as our understandings of sexual orientation and HIV have matured.

Louganis's coming out in 1994 illustrates the complexities of navigating the treachery of a heterosexual imaginary, one in which being queer and HIV-positive compromises quotidian life, including the job security and requisite income required to stay alive. The Olympian did not publicly come out until the Gay Games when he appeared, via a pre-recorded message, to wish participants well. Even then, Louganis only indirectly announced his sexual orientation. He concluded his well-wishes by stating "Welcome to the games! It's great to be out and proud!" Louganis has been criticized for not coming out earlier in his career, something he has openly discussed.[31] The diver has defended his actions, noting that the few sponsors he managed to attract had morals clauses in their contracts and he could have been fired for being gay.[32] He also admits that he was afraid to be open about his sexuality because the press might have discovered that he was HIV-positive. Louganis was so concerned about being outed as HIV-positive that he did not use health insurance to purchase medication, yet another way sexuality and economics converge in this case study.

When Eve Sedgwick published *Epistemology of the Closet* she described in great detail the conundrum that confronted LGBTQ people in the 1980s. According to Sedgwick, gay people could never be in the closet completely because someone, somewhere, might have knowledge that they are queer.[33] Conversely, even after a person comes out, someone could claim they always already knew about their sexuality. This epistemological privilege is not easily relinquished, a fact too many queers have learned firsthand. Louganis occupies this liminal space and makes no secret of the fact that he has always been read as gay, and in other ways non-normatively queer. As a child, for example, Louganis was adopted, struggled with a learning disability, and was taunted with racial epithets because he is Samoan. His outsider status is revisited constantly in *Breaking the Surface*, resisting easy castigations of homonormativity or unreflective assimilation. It was certainly no secret to the diving community that Louganis was gay and his achievements always drew disproportionate attention to his personal life. As is the case for many queer athletes, success is often the catalyst for scrutiny.[34] Still, Louganis had been involved with men at least since 1976 when he was 16. Prior to coming out he had a stint in the Broadway production of Paul Rudnick's play *Jeffrey*, a gay comedy about living with HIV. His subtle statements about intergenerational love and critiques of age of consent laws are also noteworthy. Louganis has been reinvented with each biographical turn. But there are few issues fused to Louganis like that of HIV.

BLOOD IN THE WATER

Louganis's image is publicly conjoined to both his HIV-diagnosis and the visceral image of his head striking the diving board in 1988. Even his own autobiography, which is otherwise narrated chronologically, opens with that fateful dive. Louganis realized that someone was going to profit off of his life story and decided it would be him. As a result, he took pains to control how his sexuality and his serostatus were unveiled. He revealed his HIV-status with the release of *Breaking the Surface* and through a series of interviews with Barbara Walters, *People* magazine, and Oprah Winfrey. The response to Louganis's announcement instigated panicked speculation that he may have exposed other athletes to HIV when he hit his head on the board. Transmitting HIV in an Olympic-sized pool filled with chlorine is virtually impossible. Scientific logic, though, did not dissuade many media outlets from ginning up a scandal. Louganis had to repeatedly dismiss accusations that he posed a threat and has gone as far as asserting that he "never bled in the pool."[35] As a one reporter put it: "If it had been almost any other disease, everyone would be talking about his courage. But it was the AIDS virus. And it was the dive Louganis missed on his way to that medal that everyone is talking about now."[36] Some also criticized him for not warning the doctor who examined his wound in Seoul, something Louganis regrets. Notably, this stood in sharp contrast to the treatment given to Magic Johnson after he came forward with his HIV-status four years earlier. Reporters consistently, and rightfully, assured their readers that the odds of HIV-transmission on the basketball court were almost non-existent. Louganis received no such sympathy from the press.[37]

Louganis confronted a series of unthoughtful and reckless attacks after he went public with his serostatus. In the mid-1990s an irrational fear of people with HIV/AIDS loomed and Louganis consistently managed uncomfortable exchanges with grace. Barbara Walters for example, pressed Louganis about whether he had AIDS. From a medical perspective, based on his t-cell count, Louganis did in fact have AIDS. He fully admitted as such to millions of viewers to educate the viewing public (and perhaps sell a few books). Louganis was also disciplined by the politics of respectability on more than one occasion. Take this invasive line of questioning on *Larry King Live*:

King:	"How would a smart guy like you practice unsafe sex?"
Louganis:	"I'm not following."
King:	"How did you get AIDS?"
Louganis:	"I'm sure I was probably exposed before they knew about unsafe sex."
King:	"So you're pretty sure about that?"[38]

The efforts Louganis put forth to combat such stigma highlights an ordinary, though exceptionally visible, political disposition that worked slowly to combat aspersions directed at people who were living with HIV/AIDS. To be sure, I am not suggesting that the public recalls every bit of activism that Louganis performed when they are confronted with his image on a cereal box— most of us do not. Rather, I want to draw attention to the fact that Louganis's persona is publicly wedded to HIV and these many instances have coalesced as a part of his appeal.

In this way, the Wheaties box is politically purposeful and is not simply a product of unreflective neoliberalism. Morris rightly notes that the "tragedy of AIDS is in an important sense a tragedy of public memory," one marked by "a lost generation of memory agents who serve as markers of a gay male past."[39] Louganis is a notable exception to such claims, being a bridge to a time underscored by paranoia, stigma, and hopelessness. The placement of the box in public arenas such as grocery stores and private enclaves like people's homes continues needed conversations about HIV and its labyrinthine memory politics.

In an age where HIV has largely fallen out of sight, Louganis's presence performs significant work in keeping it visible. The Olympian has contended that, for this reason, the Wheaties box means more to him now than it would have in the past. As he relayed, "Getting it now means people will see me as a whole person— a flawed person who is gay, HIV-positive, with all the other things I've been through."[40] Indeed, Louganis refuses to separate his HIV-status from the image of himself on the Wheaties box. NPR commentator Ari Shapiro asked Louganis what he intended the Wheaties box to communicate to a new generation that might not know him. Louganis answered:

> In a word, hope because when I was diagnosed back in 1988, I was 28. Six months prior to the Olympic Games, I didn't expect to see the age of 30. And here I am today at 56 and really living and thriving— that HIV isn't a death sentence. Also the important factor, too, is that I share my experience with my HIV meds. It hasn't been easy. I wouldn't wish my drug regimen on anyone, so prevention, prevention, prevention, education, education, education. You know, those are the kinds of things that I try to convey to the younger generation that— you know, that's coming up.[41]

In an era of PrEP technologies, one in which the tide of the epidemic may at long last be turning, the obtrusively colored Wheaties box feels almost nostalgic: it marks a time gone by, where the specter of AIDS felt like a death sentence and the possibilities of living into middle-age were grim. At the same time, it potentially propels exchanges about HIV in the present, highlighting the long road that people with HIV have taken and our collective journey toward a cure. Perhaps that is the contemporary exigence served by this memory project. Louganis has become emblematic of a renewed hope, rather than a tragic ending. His muscular physique, his optimistic attitude, and his personal endurance is now metonymically connected to the dawn of the end of AIDS. Doan rightfully notes that collective memory "confirms and consolidates, distills and simplifies" and the Wheaties box could fortify such unreflective impulses.[42] At the same time, its circulation holds the potential to initiate dialogue among a generation that might finally witness the eclipse of AIDS.

MAKING A SPLASH

Louganis has mentioned in passing that fans often approached him with Wheaties boxes that had his picture pasted on them for years before the "Legends" series was released.[43] With few options for publicly expressing the gratitude they felt for Louganis coming out as both gay and HIV-positive, his followers made due with the options that were available to them. Their efforts highlight the symbolic significance of tributes like the Wheaties box and the extent to which participatory cultures can generate memories essential to the survival of queer communities. Even as Louganis strove to remain apolitical as a diver, his life was, to some extent, always politically meaningful.

Narratives about queer athletes are not only about figures who had to overcome homophobia to clinch victory, but also about audiences who have had to transcend the obstacles put forth by heterosexism in order to incorporate LGBTQ people into the mythos of American sport. Consumption allows one perverse form of participation, one that permits people to express this evolution, even if such performances are often private, non-spectacular, and potentially even apolitical.

When Australian Olympian Ji Wallace came out as HIV-positive in 2012, he credited Greg Louganis as blazing a trail for people like himself. The ongoing reverberations of Louganis's life herald a legacy that was at once necessary and of its time. Even with the confines of commercial enterprises like the Wheaties box, Louganis's biography gives space to a multitude of issues that continue to challenge LGBTQ and HIV-positive people. Like others before him, Louganis has admitted to struggling with depression and suicide attempts and was a survivor of sexual and emotional abuse from a former partner. These aspects of Louganis's life story are overlooked, but their memory could inspire hope in countless queers who consistently confront such issues. If only we remember them.

NOTES

1. Richard Sandomir, "Movement Builds to Honor Greg Louganis on Wheaties Box," *New York Times*, August 23, 2015, https://www.nytimes.com/2015/08/23/sports/olympics/movement-builds-to-honor-greg-louganis-on-a-wheaties-box.html?_r=0.
2. He did manage to secure endorsements from American Express and Speedo. See Greg Louganis, *Breaking the Surface* (Naperville, IL: Sourcebooks, 1995), 146.
3. Elizabeth Daley, "Greg Louganis Will Finally Get His Wheaties Box," *Advocate.com*, April 5, 2016, http://www.advocate.com/sports/2016/4/05/greg-louganis-will-finally-get-his-wheaties-box.
4. Christopher Castiglia and Christopher Reed, *If Memory Serves: Gay Men, AIDS, and the Promise of the Queer Past* (Minneapolis: University of Minnesota Press, 2011), 12.
5. Kendall R. Phillips, *Framing Public Memory* (Tuscaloosa, AL: University of Alabama Press, 2004), 2–3.
6. Charles E. Morris III, "My Old Kentucky Homo: Lincoln and the Politics of Queer Public Memory," in *Framing Public Memory*, ed. Kendall R. Phillips (Tuscaloosa, AL: University of Alabama Press, 2004), 94.
7. Laura Doan, "Queer History/Queer Memory: The Case of Alan Turing," *GLQ* 23, no. 1 (2017): 122.
8. Diana Taylor, *The Archive and the Repertoire: Performing Cultural Memory in the Americas* (Durham: Duke University Press, 2003), 180.
9. Castiglia and Reed, *If Memory Serves*, 12.
10. Stephen Wieting and Jody Polumbaum, "Prologue," in *Sport and Memory in North America*, ed. Stephen Wieting (Portland: Frank Cass Publishing, 2001), 4, 10. See also, Ron Von Burg and Paul E. Johnson, "Yearning for a Past that Never Was: Baseball, Steroids, and the Anxiety of the American Dream," *Critical Studies in Media Communication* 26, no. 4 (2009): 351–71; Michael L. Butterworth, "Militarism and Memorializing at the Pro Football Hall of Fame," *Communication and Critical/Cultural Studies* 9, no. 3 (2012): 241–58.
11. Wieting and Polumbaum, "Prologue," 10.
12. Butterworth, "Militarism and Memorializing," 253.
13. Marita Sturken, *Tangled Memories: The Vietnam War, the AIDS Epidemic, and the Politics of Remembering* (Berkeley, CA: University of California Press, 1997), 2.
14. J. Jack Halberstam, *In a Queer Time and Place: Transgender Bodies, Subcultural Lives* (New York: New York University Press, 2005), 47–8.
15. Doan, "Queer History," 123.
16. See Abraham Iqbal Khan, "Michael Sam, Jackie Robinson, and the Politics of Respectability," *Communication and Sport* 5, no. 3 (2017): 331–51.
17. Deirdre McCloskey, "Introduction, Queer Markets," in *Media Queered: Visibility and its Discontents*, ed. Kevin Barnhurst (New York: Peter Lang, 2007), 86.
18. McCloskey, "Introduction," 86.
19. See Khan, "Michael Sam"; Abraham Iqbal Khan, "A Rant Good for Business: Communicative Capitalism and the Capture of Anti-Racist Resistance," *Popular Communication* 14, no. 1 (2016): 39–48.
20. Paul R. La Monica, "Does Anybody Eat Cereal for Breakfast Anymore?" *CNN.com*, March 21, 2017, http://money.cnn.com/2017/03/21/investing/general-mills-cereal-sales-down/index.html.

21. Louganis, *Breaking the Surface,* 65.
22. Louganis, *Breaking,* 130.
23. Louganis, *Breaking,* 277.
24. Richard Sandomir, "After Petition, Greg Louganis Gets His Wheaties Box," *New York Times,* April 4, 2016, https://www.nytimes.com/2016/04/05/sports/greg-louganis-wheaties-box-petition-general-mills.html.
25. For more on the progression of Louganis's identity, see Faye Linda Wachs and Shari Lee Dworkin, "'There's No Such Thing as a Gay Hero': Sexual Identity and Media Framing of HIV-Positive Athletes," *Journal of Sport and Social Issues* 21, no. 4 (1997): 327–47; Shari Lee Dworkin and Faye Linda Wachs, "'Disciplining the Body': HIV-Positive Male Athletes, Media Surveillance, and the Policing of Sexuality," *Sociology of Sport Journal* 15, no. 1 (1998): 1–20.
26. Sandomir, "Movement Builds."
27. Rose Minutaglio, "Olympic Diver Greg Louganis to Appear on Wheaties Box Decades After Winning Gold: 'It Means More Today than it Would Have Back Then,'" *People.com,* April 15, 2016, http://people.com/sports/greg-louganis-makes-wheaties-box-debut/.
28. Toby Miller, *Sportsex* (Philadelphia: Temple University Press, 2001), 107–08.
29. See John M. Sloop and Isaac West, "Heroism's Contexts: Robbie Rogers and the Ghost of Justin Fashanu," *QED: A Journal in GLBTQ Worldmaking* 3, no. 3 (2016): 1–28.
30. Tom Lamont, "Five Reasons to Stay in the Closet," *The Guardian,* February 3, 2008, https://www.theguardian.com/sport/2008/feb/03/features.sportmonthly10.
31. Louganis, *Breaking the Surface,* 274.
32. Louganis, *Breaking,* 225.
33. Eve Kosofsky Sedgwick, *The Epistemology of the Closet* (Berkeley: University of California Press, 1990), 67–75.
34. John M. Sloop, "'This Is Not Natural': Caster Semenya's Gender Threats," *Critical Studies in Media Communication* 29, no. 2 (2012): 85.
35. Louganis, *Breaking the Surface,* 287.
36. *Back on Board: Greg Louganis.*
37. See Samantha King, "The Politics of the Body and the Body Politic: Magic Johnson and the Ideology of AIDS," *Sociology of Sport Journal* 10, no. 3 (1993): 270–85.
38. See *Back on Board: Greg Louganis.*
39. Charles E. Morris, "Introduction," in *Remembering the AIDS Quilt,* ed. Charles E. Morris (Lansing, MI: Michigan State University Press, 2011), xl; Morris, "My Old Kentucky Homo," 95.
40. Melissa Chan, "Olympic Diver Greg Louganis will Get His Own Wheaties Box After Petition," *Time.com,* April 5, 2016, at http://time.com/4282908/greg-louganis-wheaties/.
41. Ari Shapiro, "Better Late Than Never: Olympic Champion Greg Louganis Gets His Wheaties Box," *NPR,* April 5, 2016, http://www.npr.org/templates/transcript/transcript.php?storyId=473107455.
42. Laura Doan, "Queer History," 118.
43. Shapiro, "Better Late Than Never."

CHAPTER FIVE

Touching Ali

Rhetorical Intimacy and Black Masculinity

LISA M. CORRIGAN

In their award-winning book *Blood Brothers: The Fatal Friendship Between Muham-mad Ali and Malcolm X*, Randy Roberts and Johnny Smith provide the first full-length account of the friendship between the Greatest of All Time and the fiery black Muslim orator. Writing about the similarities between the two men, Roberts and Smith note, "Malcolm X and Cassius Clay seemed the product of the same DNA. Both thrived on center stage surrounded by an audience. Standing beneath the spotlight—at Malcolm's pulpit or in Clay's ring—they responded to the thundering sound of applause and the deafening chorus of boos. Neither man could resist a platform, an interview, or a debate. Both enjoyed sparring with words and manipulating other men's fears with sensational language. They were both fighters."[1] Roberts and Smith provide a reconstructed account of the Ali-X relationship between their first meeting in June 1962 through Malcolm's assassination in February 1965. Via private papers, FBI reports, interview transcripts, personal interviews with witnesses, and media reports, they reassemble a compelling account of "two of the most important black men of the 1960s."[2] The iconicity of both Ali and X heightens our interest in them as individuals, but as friends they occupy a much larger space in public memory. While *Blood Brothers* demonstrates the rhetorical and political collaboration between the two men, it fails to provide a critical account of the ways in which the closeness between them was a transformative intervention into discourses of race and gender. Likewise, where rhetorical

scholarship has focused on either Malcolm X or Muhammad Ali as rhetorical figures, none to date has examined their friendship as a nexus of rhetorical invention.[3]

Ali and X had much to say about their much-lauded friendship. Ali remembers Malcolm fulfilling multiple roles in his life, explaining that it "didn't take
long for us to become friends. In time, Malcolm became my spiritual advisor. He
started calling me his younger brother."[4] Photographs in Ali's memoir, *The Soul
of a Butterfly: Reflections on Life's Journey*, present the boxer bent in study with
Malcolm, showcasing the physical closeness of the two as Malcolm helped Ali
connect with the teachings of Muhammad after Ali announced his conversion to
Islam. However, as Malcolm split with Elijah Muhammad following revelations
of his affairs with young Nation of Islam (NOI) women, Ali broke with Malcolm.
Ali writes, "Malcolm and I were so close and had been through so much, but
there were many things for me to consider."[5] Foremost was his own career and
the kind of political cover that the NOI provided for him, especially in the boxing
underworld. In his memoir, Ali writes, "Turning my back on Malcolm was one
of the mistakes that I regret most in my life. I wish I'd be able to tell Malcolm
I was sorry, that he was right about so many things. But he was killed before I
got the chance. He was a visionary ahead of us all."[6] Ali's lamentation about the
way that he abandoned Malcolm is restated in his memoir even as he recalls the
minister's charisma, intelligence, humor, vision, and pride, describing Malcolm as
a man "who could hold you spellbound for hours."[7] And in their trip together to
New York before Malcolm's excommunication from the Nation, Ali played with
reporters, telling them "Malcolm X got more requests for autographs than I did!
He's the greatest."[8]

For his part, Malcolm's recollections of Ali are minimal because he was
killed so soon after they parted ways (and fifty years before Ali's own death) but
his rememberings in his autobiography are tender, almost that of a lover; they
showcase the eroticism of their connection. He says, "Cassius Clay and I are not
together today. But always I must be grateful to him that at just this time, when he
was in Miami training to fight Sonny Liston, Cassius invited me, Betty, and the
children to come there as his guests—as a sixth wedding anniversary present to
Betty and me."[9] Ali's physician remarked, "Malcolm X and Ali were like very close
brothers. It was almost as if they were in love with each other."[10] This romantic
frame permeates stories about Ali and X and suggests a remarkable familiarity
between the two men.

Of course, Ali was alive and likely to read Malcolm's autobiography so the
minister's tenderness is understandable. And biographer Bruce Perry writes that
Malcolm "felt like a man who was married psychologically but divorced physically"
suggesting that Malcolm's marriage was functionally over and Ali was possibly a
bridge to a new future, particularly since his departure from the NOI was immi-
nent.[11] But in Malcolm's *Autobiography*, Alex Haley recalls finding a notecard on

Ali's feelings about Malcolm X from a 1964 interview Haley did with Ali that appeared in *Playboy*. Haley produced the card and showed it to Malcolm, recalling that it was "one of the few times I ever heard [Malcolm's] voice betray his hurt was when he said, 'I felt like a blood big-brother to him…I'm not against him now. He's a fine young man. Smart. He's just let himself be used, led astray.'"[12] In Haley's recollection here, Malcolm is expressing a deep pain about the break with Ali, suggesting the connection between these two men, while brief, was intense enough to lament. Additionally, this passage is interesting because Haley (an icon in his own right) is using rhetorical intimacy to establish his closeness with Malcolm (as well as Ali) while simultaneously cementing Malcolm's own closeness to Ali. The emotional repertoire, as Haley tells it, is the vector that all three icons share in this textual encounter, highlighting how layered emotional intimacy is among icons. But this moment also reminds us that sharing and re-sharing private moments is a way of creating and reinforcing perceptions of intimacy in networks that amplify social capital.

As Haley's anecdote demonstrates, Malcolm's recollections of Ali are detailed and physical space plays a much more important role in orienting the reader to their relationship. Malcolm's reportage of his closeness to Ali was short-lived because after the two men toured Harlem following Ali's defeat of Liston in Miami in 1964, Elijah Muhammad extended Malcolm's censure and precipitated Malcolm's departure from the Nation, leaving him without Ali as a friend or collaborator. Nonetheless, Malcolm recalls that after the Liston fight, "There probably has never been as quiet a new-champion party. The boyish king of the ring came over to my motel. He ate ice cream, drank milk, talked with football star Jimmy Brown and other friends and some reporters. Sleepy, Cassius took a quick nap on my bed, then he went back home."[13] Malcolm adds that the two men had breakfast together the next morning. Snacking, brunching, sleeping, and meeting with friends all indicate a high level of trust and closeness for two men building their friendship and Malcolm's memories demonstrate how proximity in private spaces helps define the kind of closeness that icons often develop with one another.

In this chapter, I introduce the term "rhetorical intimacy" to understand how the unlikely friendship between Muhammad Ali and Malcolm X produced tremendous opportunity in connecting religion and sport as spaces for intimate black masculinity. Where rhetorical scholarship acknowledges the importance of race-talk in the explicitly political realm of American life, less attention has been paid to the co-constitutive relationship between sport and politics, especially for black men. In public statements, speeches, memoirs, and particularly in photographs, Ali and Malcolm articulate a persistent closeness that connects them as kindred intellectuals in a landscape characterized by white supremacy, demonstrating how sport and religion provide unique and overlapping spheres for rhetorical and political invention. Photographs of the Ali-X friendship suggest to me that the *rhetorical* dimensions of their friendship charted new *public* pathways for black men to occupy affective space that had a tremendous impact on the representational politics of social activism. In particular, public touching became a primary way of expressing the filiation between the two men. And while the break between Ali and Malcolm certainly impacted their intimacy, Ali's own recollections as well as recent scholarship have resituated the friendship as both transformative and enduring, making it an important place to understand how black masculine closeness functions within white civic spaces where citizenship is being interrogated. I conclude this essay with an assessment of the impact of positive depictions of black male rhetorical intimacy, especially in displacing the heterosocial modes of caring that dominate the American media landscape, suggesting that a homosocial mode of brotherhood has significant political consequences that marry both defiance and play.

Particularly because sport provides the most visible site of black male intimacy in American popular culture, the intentional production and circulation of images and narratives of closeness between Ali and Malcolm offer scholars a compelling example that underscores the role of intimacy in visual and non-visual racial discourses. This is due, in large part, to the fact that Ali and Malcolm intentionally augmented their social agency as black men through modes of technological engagement that allowed them to become peers through avenues that are often foreclosed for men, generally, and for black men, especially.

DEFINING RHETORICAL INTIMACY AND BLACK MASCULINITY

While Roberts and Smith catalogue the Ali-X relationship, they don't use the word intimacy once in their book. They characterize only one relationship as "intimate": Ali's relationship with Elijah Muhammad. And even this description only occurs in the penultimate paragraph of the book. Nonetheless, I want to suggest that Ali and X publicly showcased rhetorical intimacy, which created space for positive images of radical black masculinity that underscored how closeness might build new models of political engagement. By rhetorical intimacy, I mean the kind of political and social closeness that builds the architecture of iconicity. As one of the most recognizable figures in sport in the entire twentieth century (inside *and* outside of the United States), Ali is singular in his visibility, bridging multiple spheres of public life. Likewise, Malcolm was also hyper-visible, identifiable to global audiences as a result of his televisual ubiquity and his global travels. Together, the men illustrate how black superstars networked together to build the architecture of black iconicity within a culture that denied them full citizenship and humanity.

Because rhetorical intimacy is built through the scaffolding of social networks and through the collision of icons in different social spheres, it makes sense that sport would be a unique space for the solidification of icons and a platform for rhetorical and political collaboration since spectatorship is a precondition for engaging sport. In this way, rhetorical intimacy is produced and documented through photography, recollection, and memorialization where icons discuss their relationship to one another through their shared understanding of fame and its monstrosity. In commiserating about and augmenting fame, black icons use their connection to one another as a way of navigating the social and political violence that targets them. Building close social support for one another helps inoculate them from the hostility of white public culture. For Ali, that came from those boxing fans and insiders who objected to both the possibility and the reality of a black heavyweight champion. Although he had been widely praised as Cassius Clay, as Ali became more political and more closely aligned with black separatism, the hostility against him increased. For Malcolm, the resentment of black moderates and fearful whites created an environment that was far more navigable with a young, handsome, charismatic sports figure. Their televisual relationship disrupted political negativity, creating a spectatorship anchored in admiration and enjoyment.

Rhetorical intimacy is most closely aligned with Michael Herzfeld's notion of "cultural intimacy," which he describes as "a recognition of that deep sense of a shared fatality, something to be treasured precisely because it is at once impermanent and private, that seems common to all intimacy."[14] Herzfeld sees cultural intimacy as a complex matrix of symbols, signs, and feelings that emerge when "the intimate seeps into public spheres that have themselves been magnified by the technologies of mass mediation."[15] At the personal and the communal level, cultural intimacy demands a high degree of self-recognition and, as Hertzfeld notes, a political cynicism that encourages alternative expressions of nationalism that challenge "the way things are." Cultural intimacy relies upon the persuasiveness of rhetorical artifacts to help create affinity between and among iconic figures in popular culture and memory. Photographs, letters, interviews, and ephemera carve out the space for relationality and provide accounts of closeness that emphasize affinity and/or distance. Given the preoccupation that the American culture has with the singularity of individual greatness and with the "Great Man Theory" of social advancement, rhetorical intimacy is remarkable as rhetorical practice because it resists such narratives, particularly for black men. Instead, the relationality among black men *especially in different social spheres* (like sport or religion), creates a complex tapestry of closeness that emphasizes mutuality. In relationships where the icons are from seemingly incompatible spheres, the closeness becomes even more remarkable, compelling publics to follow the unlikely friends, particularly during the civil rights generation when desegregation propelled social anxiety. However, even in sport, black icons don't generally augment their power through their relationality to black men outside of sport in culturally close ways, especially as we think about the G.O.A.T.s (the Greatest Of All Time). O. J. Simpson, for example, made his career out of his closeness to white icons. Michael Jordan rarely demonstrated any intimacy, let alone outside of basketball (and this is true of most basketball icons). For example, Magic Johnson collaborated with Michael Jackson, and LeBron James and Jay-Z are close, but public intimacy does not define their relationality. Even with high profile friendships like those between Deion Sanders and MC Hammer, Michael Jordan and Will Smith, Jim Brown and Richard Pryor, Floyd Mayweather and 50 Cent, Tiger Woods and Darius Rucker, the mediated rhetorical intimacy is not an *essential* feature of their public connection.

Something about the singularity of Ali being a boxer made the collaboration with Malcolm even more impressive: Ali was a pugilist and was not involved in a team sport. And Malcolm, for all of his involvement with the NOI, was a singular figure even within the organization, and his rhetorical career far surpassed any of his predecessors or contemporaries. But even with some current examples of odd friendships between high profile athletes and icons from outside of sport, the major difference is in the intentionality of Ali and Malcolm in documenting their friendship as a *strategic* and *reciprocal* intervention. As preoccupied with photography and image as both men were, their closeness together was a *fundamental* aspect of their lives and public personas. Because of their intentional mediation, their friendship provides a unique space to interrogate rhetorical intimacy and its relationship to culture.

While cultural intimacy is close to rhetorical intimacy, they do not overlap one to one. Rather, rhetorical intimacy describes the ways in which public figures invent and utilize rhetorical strategies designed to make people feel close to them (or their ideas). This feeling of closeness connects icons to their publics in ways that fuse memories to create microcohorts or to define generations because the intensity of the private closeness is publicly palpable. Where icons may socialize publicly or privately due to their shared experiences in the public eye, it is the magnification of their closeness through mediation and through memory that helps cement icons in relation to one another. Ali and Malcolm mark the 60s in ways that other high-profile friendships do not and the reason that they do is because their positionality *as icons* is defined at least in part by *their rhetorical closeness*. In this way, proximity is an essential part of rhetorical intimacy and it is managed, produced, and circulated through expressions and documentation of relational care between iconic intimates and for particular publics. Documentation of rhetorical intimacy is crucial in establishing closeness, as it cements certain facets of an icon's relationality (their charisma, their mobility, their political sensibility) to other icons, as well as to publics.

In the case of Ali and X, I am particularly interested in how their friendship provided a template for rhetorical intimacy in the public sphere. Against images of abjection that circulated in this historical moment documenting black protest, anti-black terrorism, and black suffering, the rhetorical intimacy of Ali and X was rooted in embodied black male pride. Their hypermediated intimacy was captured through photographs that documented their friendship, the way that they moved in the world together, and the kind of proximity to them that curious onlookers desired. In a hyper-segregated country where vision reigned supreme as the primary means of excluding black men from social participation, the elevation of touch as an avenue of identification seems especially salient in these photographs. This is particularly true since Ali and X were both Muslims and crossed between two separate spheres of sociality: sport and religion. Boxing, in particular, is a sphere that lends itself to a particular kind of sociality because boxers have to become discrete celebrities with personalities that create publics. Ministering is similar, especially for a charismatic preacher like Malcolm, who carved out his own space within the NOI and brought droves of adherents to his mosque as a result of his personality and his hypervisibility in the black press. But as the two most high-profile Black Muslims in America, Ali and X also existed in a religious and political space that is not transferrable to high-profile friendships like those listed above and so collaboration across social location helped to augment their social power and blunt (at least temporarily) the blowback from their opponents.

In addition, visages of Ali and X were ubiquitous in print and on television, making photos of the two men together a kind of aggregation of black masculinity that critiqued white nationalism. Their close proximity functioned as a force multiplier of their rhetorical and political power and demonstrated how well both men improvised, especially in front of a camera. Thus their rhetorical intimacy had a public dimension, as they used their friendship to augment their political power and celebrity *as black men*.

RHETORICAL INTIMACY, PHOTOGRAPHY, AND TOUCH

Photography has long been a method of creating and documenting black intimacy, particularly in relationship to the black freedom movement. In this way, photographs function, in Cara Finnegan's words, not just as a product but "as a mode of inquiry."[16] "For marginalized groups, especially, bearing on their shoulders the burden of representation, photography can simultaneously establish intimacy with its subject and articulate distance."[17] Photography played an important role in cementing the intimacy between Ali and X. Jonny Weeks notes that "Ali's iconic status…is inextricably married to the photographs that exist of him. While his poetic tongue and rapid wit charmed us, and his poise and ruthlessness in the ring thrilled us, the imagery of him toned our appreciation of his personality, craft and beauty. Photographs are now among the defining symbols by which we remember him."[18] Mark Anthony Neal writes similarly that Ali "was one of the most photographed Black men of a generation. In the aftermath of Ali's death, much has circulated with regards to his all-too-brief though powerful relationship with Malcolm X (with Sam Cooke and Jim Brown as fellow travelers). Politically linked as Ali's 'Blood Brother,' Malcolm X shared a passion for photography—and Ali was often his willing subject."[19] Neal's assessment of the closeness between the two men is interesting because he characterizes it in terms of *power* within a nexus that also included singer Sam Cooke and football player Jim Brown, providing us with another template of public closeness. But Neal is also clear about the role of technology in drawing the men together for a larger public because of their shared love of photography. It is in the intentional mediation and documentation of their publicness that Ali and Malcolm become the ultimate power couple (especially since, as two men, their closeness displaces the feminine or the woman) where their social power together is greater than the sum of their parts.

Graeme Abernathy recently charted Malcolm's obsession with photography as an auteur and documented the Nation of Islam orator's photographic savvy as he used images to build his reputation across the world. Abernethy notes that Malcolm staged photographs of himself to craft an image around "the raised fist, the microphone, the riddle, the grin, and the glasses."[20] Malcolm dedicated himself to a defiant masculine image "that could transform and radicalize African American self-images while drawing on a recognizable tradition of resistance in black culture. In so doing, he framed himself as folk hero, prophet and revolutionary."[21] Here, Malcolm embodied black masculinity at the locus of "desire, emulation, and domination."[22] Many pictures of Malcolm showcase him with his own camera, demonstrating the importance of black men (particularly black male icons) documenting and visually narrating their success. Ali and X demonstrate a public closeness that showcases how intimacy "comes with an unforeseen recognition of the self in the world and with an unbounded interaction of the self with the world."[23] While some scholars might be interested in the authenticity of this kind of intimacy, I am much more interested in how it is used to position the subjects.

Probably the most famous series of pictures of Ali and X together was shot by Bob Gomel of *Life* magazine, a white photographer. The series features Malcolm snapping pictures of Ali at a Miami lunch counter in 1964 while Malcolm was in town for the Liston fight.[24] I am interested in how *photographs* of Ali and X connect the men through visualizations of their paralanguage including: proxemics (proximity/space), haptics (touching), and kinesics (body movement). The photographs of Ali and X before their break demonstrate the importance of black biopolitics as both men grappled with fame and publicity. Grinning at one another, clowning at the counter, the two icons capture the moment while dozens of men look on. These iconic photos showcase the ways that Malcolm and Ali played together in public, suggesting the kind of closeness that is a hallmark of rhetorical intimacy. Their bodies are a kind of centrifugal force, pulling the viewer into visual spaces that s/he will never occupy.

Gomel's photos of Ali and X evidence their rhetorical closeness primarily through haptics, or touch. Touch became an important vector in the Ali-X images as well as in news stories, especially about Ali. This is perhaps not surprising, since all judgments about Ali concerned how his gloves touched the bodies of other men. Even so, attention to Ali's and X's closeness demonstrates how touch is a sensory description that emphasizes physical *as well as* emotional contact.[25] As Roberts and Smith remark, Ali's touch was special: "Boxing's savior he was. He had the Golden Touch, the Gorgeous George magic that put people in the seats."[26] The emphasis on touch and touching here reminds us that flesh is the way in which race is understood as a political assemblage. As Darieck Scott reminds us, "the body is both material and discursive," because bodies make stories and are made by them.[27] Helpful, too, is Hortense Spillers' definition of flesh "as that zero degree of social conceptualization that does not escape concealment under the brush of discourse or the reflexes of iconography."[28] But the commentary on Ali's use of his own flesh to interact with others also highlights the exceptionalism of Ali's flesh as well as his touch as defining features of his iconicity.

In contrast, Harold Conrad remembers that Malcolm wouldn't even touch white people when they met in Miami. He refused to shake hands. As they negotiated Malcolm's presence at Ali's fight against Liston, Conrad recalls telling Malcolm that he had to leave town in order for the fight to proceed because there was so much negative attention on him and his relationship with Ali. He says, "I stuck out my hand, but he wouldn't shake. He wasn't into shaking hands with white people then. All he did was reach out and touch my wrist with his finger. But thank God, the fight was on again."[29] Interestingly, Ali himself talked about his involvement with the NOI in terms of touch. In describing his first contact with the Miami mosque in 1961, he said, "that he could reach out and touch what Brother John was saying. It wasn't like a church teaching, where I had to have faith that the preacher was right .... So I liked what I heard, and I wanted to learn more."[30] In these remembrances, touch is the vehicle for expanding consciousness, so it is not surprising that Ali describes touching as essential in describing his conversion to Islam. In these passages, Ali is both *toucher* and *touched*, suggesting that his intimacy was hypermobile.

In Gomel's photos, Malcolm's toothy grin matches Ali's goofy, dimpled smile as both men are featured together. In the early photographs of the series, Ali is seated and Malcolm is leaning over the boxer's left shoulder. These shots, with Malcolm pressed to Ali's shoulder and back, emphasize rhetorical intimacy as the shot's composition points to proximity as a marker of closeness between the two icons. In another shot, Malcolm leans over Ali's shoulder, touching him, as the boxer eats some pie. Here, the firebrand is close enough to whisper in Ali's ear.

Where the other black men are all jockeying and laughing behind Ali and X, these two are very clearly creating the play at the counter, bantering and laughing. Because they are playing, there is a sense of vivacity about both men that renders them legible to viewers. The lived engagement of Ali and X communicates a series of rhetorical transfers within their play that amplify the star power of both icons. Their physical touch functions as a kind of anointment where Ali is transformed into the political figure and Malcolm into the pop figure despite the incongruity of their friendship. Boxing is particularly salient as a space for this kind of rhetorical transfer and amplification because it relies entirely on touching as an interpretive schema. And religious ceremony provides a second lens for the transfer of power between and among men.

Ali and X are aware of Gomel's camera and the play helps accentuate their closeness for the viewer, creating lines of sight and texture in the photograph that heighten our understanding of their familiarity. These pictures capture a visual connection between the two men that cements them as intimates, comrades, and confidantes. They are shown having a kind of relationship that the viewer can only imagine since both camera and gaze objectify their closeness and they are also demonstrating personality, which both invites objectification through the camera and also resists it. bell hooks would call this the "oppositional gaze," where black viewers resist white spectatorship with intense gazes that disrupt white power and make visible the power relations inherent in "looking." In reflecting on the slave experience as one where looking could transgress social boundaries and incur serious punishment, hooks suggests that "all attempts to repress our/black people's right to gaze had produced in us an overwhelming longing to look, a rebellious desire, an oppositional gaze."[31] In resisting this kind of visual dominance by the spectator, Ali and Malcolm demonstrate a powerful rhetorical closeness that allows us to read them as peers.

Because they are in motion in these shots, both men resist the kind of rhetorical capture that would stunt their visual and political mobility by both touching and looking. Thus, a kinesic reading of the photos offers a view of both Ali and Malcolm that reduces their distance from the viewer and invites a more intimate encounter with them as individuals and as friends. This humanizing intimacy undermines what Spillars has called "pornotroping," where the gaze reduces and immobilizes black people to flesh, divested of personhood and available for sexual terrorism.[32] This problem of pornotroping is particularly egregious in sports where white consumption of black masculinity is central. As Thomas Oates explains, sport functions "as a cultural site where the admiration of male bodies by men can circulate with remarkable openness. This openness not only satisfies desires that are in most other arenas strictly policed by taboos, but serves to affirm inter-male dominance based on a hierarchy of race by referencing a gender hierarchy."[33] But the photographs of Ali and Malcolm are different because dominance is not the lens for their encounter. In fact, one of the shots after the Liston fight is Gomel's most lucrative photograph of all time.[34] That shot features a playful Malcolm behind the counter photographing Ali, documenting the minister's use of technology to mediate blackness, masculinity, and success. Malcolm is the auteur, composing his own shots as Gomel demonstrates in these pictures. But even so, Malcolm is the one both causing and recording the moment for posterity, creating a permanent record of the closeness between the men.

RHETORICAL INTIMACY AND BLACK MASCULINITY

While I consider how composition in these photographs documents rhetorical intimacy between the men, these images also document the risk of black masculinity. As Michael Cooke notes, intimacy is "a process, an experiment in human modality, and it is laden with risk. Implicitly it takes away the protections, learned and instinctive, with which the personality routinely operates, and in return it holds out as much a prospect of exhaustion and rebuff and ridicule as it does an enhancement of the spirit and terms of life."[35] Both Ali and X understood physical risk (Ali as a boxer, whose life and body were always on the line, and X as a militant black nationalist whose life was marked by the FBI early on in his career) but the photographs of their friendship seem to identify them as transgressing risk (NOI reprobation, boxing sanctions, etc.) to build closeness. I'm interested in the ethos of these two public figures and the way in which their closeness creates a sense of belonging for black men in the nation, in the press, for black intellectuals, and for black men doing race work in totally different public arenas.

Gomel's photographs of Ali and Malcolm captivate viewers because they showcase tender, playful admiration emerging from men both demonized and lionized for their blackness and their masculinity. Working in opposition to controlling images of black men as rapists or savages, photographs of Ali and X create a more complicated rhetorical tapestry for these two media-savvy icons. The contrast in their professional careers only heightens the visual and rhetorical interest in their intimate encounters. Ultimately, photography of Ali and X helps to underscore the impact of positive depictions of black male rhetorical intimacy, which have the potential to displace the heterosocial modes of caring that dominate the American media landscape. A homosocial mode of brotherhood has significant political implications for prolonging radical social activism, as when Ali famously criticized the Vietnam War. Because Ali and Malcolm were able to document their friendship through photographs that centralize their rhetorical intimacy, the fascination with both men as mobile and multifaceted icons only grew in public memory, demonstrating how their closeness augmented their rhetorical and social power in life as well as death.

The photos also showcase what Bruce Perry terms "the politics of manhood."[36] Ali's doctor and friend, Ferdie Pacheco, once said: "If God sat down to create the perfect body for a fighter, anatomically and physiologically, he'd have created Ali."[37] Ali's father used to tease him that he was "pretty," and would call him "beauty" when he was younger.[38] Ali regularly called himself the prettiest as an adult, as well.[39] Writing about Ali following his death in 2016 from Parkinson's disease, George Willis explained, "Ali was a symbol of hope, particularly for black Americans in the 1960s when racial injustice was rampant. By proclaiming himself 'pretty,' he was saying 'black is beautiful,' at a time when black Americans needed to hear and feel that way."[40] His articulation of self as "pretty" demonstrated a hyperawareness of his own body, his own image. But he was also playing with gendered language and embodied gender performances, juxtaposing beauty and strength.

After the Liston fight and the NOI's excommunication of Malcolm, the relationship between Ali and X transformed. Perry writes "since Ali, not Malcolm, was the hero of the hour, the relationship between the two celebrities had subtly changed. The Nation of Islam quickly capitalized upon the fact and publicly embraced the champ, who had suddenly replaced Malcolm as the leading symbol of black masculinity."[41] Perry's assessment highlights how the end of their friendship also marked the end of frameworks that acknowledged or praised their intimacy, favoring competition as the framework instead. In some ways, this is unsurprising, since sports writing intrinsically relies on competition as a framework of analysis; however, for Ali and Malcolm, the competition is imposed from the outside, demonstrating how this view contrasts with the kind of rhetorical intimacy that permeated their public and private encounters.

RECIPROCAL INTIMACY

Ali was a body but his proximity to Malcolm made him a brain. Malcolm was a brain but with Ali he became a body. Ali made Malcolm cool and helped him move from the mosques to the sports arena, where black athletes occasionally made political statements about their mistreatment in the U.S. And Malcolm legitimized Ali's participation in a broader political sphere where he denounced the Vietnam War and toured college campuses as a rhetorical activist. Malcolm provided Ali with spiritual training and Ali offered Malcolm some short-lived political cover as the NOI debated whether to permanently censure him. Ali softened Malcolm's stern visage and Malcolm gave Ali a political edge. The rhetorical intimacy between these two men served both well, elevating them into new popular arenas where they capitalized on their social cache. We might say that their rhetorical intimacy was reciprocal and that its reciprocity helped scaffold their political power both as rhetorical collaborators and as individuals.

While they were clearly distinct icons across the diaspora, Malcolm reports being mistaken for Ali when he was in Mecca. Notably, he blames the confusion on the technology of photography. In describing the curiosity and excitement, he remembers: "I was mistaken time and again for Cassius Clay. A local newspaper had printed a photograph of Cassius and me together at the United Nations." Malcolm explained that kids loved Ali and said admiringly that he had "captured the imagination and support of the entire dark world."[42] This comment about being mistaken for Ali is interesting because it indicates a dissolvability of the men into each other, making their connection and association permanent, particularly as the slippage between the two men propelled them as icons around the diaspora. This is especially important for Malcolm, whose political capital dropped precipitously after his friendship with Ali ended. Paul Gilroy remarks on this kind of relationality in *Against Race:*

> Blackness as abjection gives way steadily to blackness as vitality, eternal youth, and impartial dynamism. The ideal body of the black male athlete or model now supplies a ubiquitous key signature for this strange theme. An exemplary black physicality, mute and heroic, has been conscripted into service to build a militarized and nationalized version of planetary popular culture in which the world of sports counts for more than the supple, subtle public relationships improvised around the gestalt of song and dance.[43]

Gilroy's comments here are particularly salient since Ali and X were hyper-aware of managing their images and careers in an increasingly global culture. But more importantly, Gilroy demonstrates how blackness itself was an intrinsic part of the rhetorical intimacy between X and Ali, how it augmented their youth and their masculine virility as *bodies* and as *brains, touching* and *being touched*. But because they were also speaking, rather than mute, they broke out of the mold that Gilroy describes so cogently. For Ali and Malcolm to become icons, they had to do the unthinkable and move beyond the spatial locations and static masculinities of their early careers and into new arenas where they would circulate in tandem and apart as models of a different form of homosocial praxis. Indeed, the rhetorical intimacy of Ali and X is remarkable precisely because it transgressed contemporary visual and textual articulations of black iconicity, suggesting that scholars would be wise to excavate the dense networks of intimacy that characterize modern icons.

NOTES

1. Randy Roberts and Johnny Smith, *Blood Brothers: The Fatal Friendship Between Muhammad Ali and Malcolm X* (New York: Basic Books, 2016), xiii.
2. Roberts and Smith, *Blood Brothers*, xvi.
3. For recent studies of Malcolm X, see for example, Lisa M. Corrigan, "50 Years Later: Commemorating the Life and Death of Malcolm X," *Howard Journal of Communications* 28, no. 2 (2017):

144–59; Robert Terrill, *Malcolm X: Inventing Racial Judgment* (Lansing: Michigan University Press, 2007); Keith D. Miller, "Plymouth Rock Landed on Us: Malcolm X's Whiteness Theory as a Basis for Alternative Literacy," *College Composition and Communication* 56, no. 2 (2004): 199–222; Robert Terrill, "Colonizing the Borderlands: Shifting Circumference in the Rhetoric of Malcolm X, " *Quarterly Journal of Speech* 86, no. 1 (2000): 67–85; Robin D. G. Kelley, "House Negroes on the Loose: Malcolm X and the Black Bourgeoisie," *Callaloo* 21, no. 2 (1998): 419–35.

For recent studies of Ali, see Ellen W. Gorsevski and Michael L. Butterworth, "Muhammad Ali's Fighting Words: The Paradox of Violence in Nonviolent Rhetoric," *Quarterly Journal of Speech* 97, no. 1 (2011): 50–73; Daniel Grano, "Muhammad Ali Versus the "Modern Athlete": On Voice in Mediated Sports Culture," *Critical Studies in Media Communication* 26, no. 3 (2009): 191–211; Mike Marqusee, "Sport and Stereotype: From Role Model to Muhammad Ali," *Race & Class* 36, no. 4 (1995): 1–29.

4. Muhammad Ali with Hana Yasmeen Ali, *The Soul of a Butterfly: Reflections on Life's Journey* (New York: Simon and Schuster, 2013), 76.
5. Ali and Ali, *The Soul of a Butterfly*, 84.
6. Ali and Ali, *The Soul*, 85.
7. Ali and Ali, *The Soul*, 76.
8. Taylor Branch, *Pillar of Fire: America in the King Years 1963–65* (New York: Simon & Schuster, 1999), 254.
9. Malcolm X with Alex Haley, *The Autobiography of Malcolm X* (New York: Ballantine, 1964/1999), 349.
10. Roberts and Smith, *Blood Brothers*, ix.
11. Perry, *Malcolm*, 246. See also Manning Marable, *Malcolm X: A Life of Reinvention* (New York: Penguin, 2011).
12. Malcolm X, *The Autobiography*, 472.
13. Malcolm X, *The Autobiography*, 355.
14. Michael Herzfeld, *Cultural Intimacy: Social Poetics in the Nation-State* (New York: Routledge, 1997), 43.
15. Herzfeld, *Cultural Intimacy*, 44.
16. Cara A. Finnegan, "Doing Rhetorical History of the Visual," in *Defining Visual Rhetoric*, eds. Charles A. Hill and Marguerite Helmers (London: Lawrence Erlbaum, 2004), 198.
17. Leigh Raiford, *Imprisoned in a Luminous Glare: Photography and the African American Freedom Movement* (Chapel Hill: University of North Carolina Press, 2011), 15.
18. Jonny Weeks, "Muhammad Ali—Through the Eyes of the Photographers Who Know Him Best," *The Guardian*, October 30, 2014, https://www.theguardian.com/sport/2014/oct/30/-sp-muhammad-ali-through-the-eyes-of-the-photographers-who-know-him-best.
19. Mark Anthony Neal, "Muhammad Ali and the 'Birth' of Black Digital Archive," *New Black Magazine*, June 9, 2016, http://www.thenewblackmagazine.com/view.aspx?index=3566.
20. Graeme Abernethy, *The Iconography of Malcolm X* (Lawrence: University of Kansas, 2013), 5.
21. Abernethy, *The Iconography*, 16.
22. Abernethy, *The Iconography*, 153.
23. Michael G. Cooke, *Afro-American Literature in the Twentieth Century: The Achievement of Intimacy* (New Haven, CT: Yale University Press, 1984), 9.
24. *Ali: A Life in Pictures* (New York: Time Life Books, 2016).

25. See for example, Shannon Walters, *Rhetorical Touch: Disability, Identification, Haptics* (Columbia: University of South Carolina Press, 2014).

26. Roberts and Smith, *Blood Brothers*, 85.

27. Darieck Scott, *Extravagant Abjection: Blackness, Power, and Sexuality in the African American Literary Imagination* (New York: New York University press, 2010), 57.

28. Hortense J. Spillers, "Mama's Baby, Papa's Maybe: An American Grammar Book," in *Black, White, and in Color: Essays on American Literature and Culture* (Chicago: University of Chicago Press, 2003), 206.

29. Thomas Hauser, *Muhammad Ali: His Life and Times* (New York: Simon and Schuster, 1991), 67. Malcolm's touching is also well-documented in post-assassination publications and recollections. Ossie Davis's eulogy, for example, crescendos as he asks if the audience had ever touched Malcolm.

30. Barbara L. Tischler, *Muhammad Ali: A Man of Many Voices* (New York: Routledge, 2016), 69.

31. bell hooks, *Black Looks: Race and Representation* (Boston: South End Press, 1992), 116.

32. See Spillars, "Mama's Baby," 203–29.

33. Thomas P. Oates, "The Erotic Gaze in the NFL Draft," *Communication and Critical/Cultural Studies* 4, no. 1 (2007): 75.

34. Judi Griggs, "Renowned Photographer Bob Gomel Captured 1960s from a Catbird Seat," *Houston Chronicle*, February 19, 2015, http://www.chron.com/homes/senior_living-/article/Renowned-photographer-Bob-Gomel-captured-1960s-6089806.php.

35. Cooke, *Afro-American*, 9.

36. Bruce Perry, *Malcolm* (Barrytown, NY: Station Hill Press, 1991).

37. Weeks, "Muhammad Ali."

38. Perry, *Malcolm*, 245.

39. George Plimpton, "Miami Notebook: Cassius Clay and Malcolm X," *Harper's*, June 1964, 61.

40. George Willis, "What Young People Today Don't Know About Muhammad Ali," *New York Post*, June 4, 2016, http://nypost.com/2016/06/04/what-muhammad-ali-being-the-greatest-meant-to-me/.

41. Perry, *Malcolm*, 249.

42. Malcolm X, *The Autobiography*, 394.

43. Paul Gilroy, *Against Race: Imagining Political Culture beyond the Color Line* (Cambridge: Harvard University Press, 2002), 274.

CHAPTER SIX

Spirits in the Material World

The Rhetoric of the Iroquois Nationals

MIKE MILFORD

The Iroquois Nationals lacrosse team holds the distinction of being the only internationally competitive team in any sport that is constituted solely by indigenous peoples. The team represents the Haudenosaunee Confederacy, which includes the Mohawk, Oneida, Onondaga, Cayuga, and Seneca nations. Their presence in the sport is notable because it is theirs. Lacrosse originated nearly a millennium ago from ball and stick games played by Native Americans all across the nation. This means that when the Nationals compete they not only represent Native Americans but also the sport's mythic origins. International competition is already rife with ideological potential, but the historical, racial, and mythic overtones of the Nationals make their performances even more rhetorically dynamic.

Rhetors in the Native American community discuss the Nationals as representing much more than the Haudenosaunee Confederacy. References to the team are typically accompanied by allusions to Native American identity and national sovereignty. Sometimes the team's achievements are held up as examples of the indomitable Native spirit. Other times the team's appearances on the international stage are a legitimation of the Native American nations. The Nationals' successes against other nations become enthymematic proof of sovereignty of the Haudenosaunee Confederacy as a member of the global community.

In these cases, rhetors rely on symbolic boasting to use the athletes' performances as a means to a particular rhetorical end. Symbolic boasting extends

Kenneth Burke's concept of identification to explore how rhetors use others' accomplishments to create a sense of collaboration with an audience. Through the celebration of the achievements of a particular unit, Burke asserts, a rhetor may associate those successes with the larger corporate body. Previous research has shown that symbolic boasting can quickly become exploitative as rhetors may appropriate others' achievements without their permission, often resulting in an eschewing of complexity in favor of rhetorical effectiveness.[1] However, in the Nationals' case the team and its directors actively engage in symbolic boasting in an effort to promote Native American identity and sovereignty. I argue that the Native American media, the prominent voices in the Native American community, and the Nationals all joined in a chorus celebrating broader themes of Native American nationality and ideology in a new and proactive manner. In recent history Native Americans have tried a number of avenues to argue for sovereignty. Casey Kelly shows how Native American rhetors have coopted larger national movements in an effort to resist assimilation, which they saw as the abdication of their identity.[2] Similarly, as Jason Edward Black has showed in two different analyses, Native American rhetoric that resists colonialism and asserts sovereignty is often muted in favor of the dominant culture or ignored outright.[3]

When it comes to sports, Native Americans are rarely offered the opportunity to take an active role and are instead symbolized in the form of mascots. Jackson Miller and Ellen Staurowsky provide insightful looks at how Native Americans are in a constant struggle for ownership of their likeness and culture, and Black shows how mascots perpetuate neocolonial ideologies at the expense of Native American agency.[4] Danielle Endres considers how those tribes who do work with organizations, such as the University of Utah and its relationship with the Utes, awkwardly straddle a line between resistance and complicity in rhetorical colonialism.[5] The common theme in these important debates is that Native American rhetors are positioned as either passive or reactive. What makes the rhetoric surrounding the Nationals compelling is that it empowers Native American rhetors with a proactive position. Through symbolic boasting the community is able to establish its identity on its own terms, instead of constantly pushing back against others' characterizations.

With that in mind, this chapter contributes to the broader discussion of the ways in which political action is facilitated by sport by looking at how rhetors use others' achievements to make pointed ideological arguments about their communities, specifically considering the ways in which Native American rhetors use symbolic boasting to assert their sovereignty. I begin with an overview of identification and symbolic boasting and then provide a brief history of lacrosse from the Native American perspective. I then examine Native American voices in the Nationals' media coverage to better understand how the team functions for the larger community.

IDENTIFICATION AND SYMBOLIC BOASTING

Symbolic boasting is an extension of Kenneth Burke's concept of identification. Burke asserts that rhetoric revolves around identification because audiences are driven to identify with "manifestations beyond" themselves.[6] As Ronald Carpenter puts it, the "ultimate condition sought by rhetorical endeavor" is corporate identification via communal symbols.[7] Identification functions as a remedy for division because, in Robert Heath's words, "estrangement is a recurring human relation problem."[8] In order to answer this issue, communities coalesce around significant symbols that shape their personal and collective identities. To that end, Carpenter writes, identification is achieved, "by discourse as the persuader's demonstration of 'common' sensations, concepts, images, and attitudes with his audience."[9]

Symbolic boasting takes a deeper look at how these common symbols function for communities. Symbolic boasting is "the development and repetition of symbols that provide consubstantiality to the corporate unit through a sense of collaboration."[10] Such rhetoric revolves around what Burke calls the "doctrine of *consubstantiality*" which is concerned with rhetoric as a means of "*acting-together*" through "common sensations, concepts, images, ideas, attitudes."[11] Rhetors recognize and repeat these corporate symbols, choosing them carefully to frame their community in a particular fashion. Rhetors borrow the successes of others as a means to create identity-based cohesion within a community and advertise their value systems. The boasted symbols are used to characterize the entirety of the community as "symbolic structures that embody the ideal," resulting in powerful icons.[12] Identification in these cases "serves as braggadocio," Burke writes, "By it, the modest men can indulge the most outrageous 'corporate boasting.' He identifies himself with some corporate unit (church, guild, company, lodge, party, team, college, city, nation, etc.)—and by profuse praise of this unit, he praises himself."[13] Through the celebration of these accomplishments the "audience is exalted by the assertion because it has the feel of collaborating with the assertion."[14] The end is a rhetorically vicarious experience that allows audiences to participate in the actions of their chosen representatives.

Previous research has shown how this can be an exploitative act. Because the nature of symbolic boasting extends into the realm of idealism it is easy to reduce communal heroes to only those qualities that reinforce communal ideology. J. F. Walsh shows how this empowers audiences to benefit "without paying the costs entailed by participation in the movement."[15] Mark Wright goes further, arguing that symbolic boasting "can occur even for individuals…that do not share in the unit members' ties to each other."[16] Michael Butterworth provides an excellent example of how the Bush administration appropriated the success of the Iraqi national soccer team in the 2004 Summer Olympics to celebrate the success of the U.S. invasion despite the team's assertions to the contrary.[17] In other research,

I examined how Jesse Owens's performances at the 1936 Olympics in Berlin were coopted as a celebration of American victory over Nazism at the expense of Owens's own struggles with racism in the U.S.[18] In contrast, the Nationals' case demonstrates that rhetors can take ownership of symbolic boasting, using their status in the community as a representation of broader ideological goals. The Nationals have purposefully taken up the role of communal representative, openly using their lacrosse successes as victories for not just the Haudenosaunee Confederacy, but Native Americans and even indigenous peoples worldwide. The rhetoric surrounding the Nationals shows first how rhetors may use their own accomplishments as representations of a larger ideological victory, and second how the scope of the contest may be used to stress communal identity.

IROQUOIS AND LACROSSE

In order to better understand why the Nationals have such rhetorical potency it is helpful to understand the importance of the sport to Native Americans. Skaruianewah Logan notes that of all the Haudenosaunee traditions, lacrosse has "successfully made the transition from pre-contact to modern times."[19] For Native Americans the sport is "rooted in religion, mysticism, devout respect for those who played before, and a sacred link between the earth and heavens."[20] Since its genesis the game has been to honor the Creator.[21] Onondaga Faithkeeper and former Syracuse All-American Oren Lyons claims the game "was played on the other side of the stars when the Earth was still covered with water. That's how old the game is in our perspective."[22] It was the Creator who "gifted the sport to the two-legged" and it serves as a reaffirmation of "each nation's unique relationship with the Creator and embodied Man's [sic] relationship with Nature."[23]

Understanding lacrosse's original form and function is tricky: Jerry Reynolds suggests a close analogy to lacrosse's mythic origins would be to imagine if the rules for tennis were "set forth in the Old English of *Beowulf*."[24] Most estimate the game is between 900–1100 years old and featured between 100 and 1,000 men playing between goals between 500 yards and two miles apart over the course of two or three days from sun up to sun down.[25] Despite its seemingly chaotic form the game served crucial functions. The game centered on Native American concepts of medicine and healing.[26] Former Nationals player Neal Powless said the game brings good medicine "in the form of healing energy. Good thoughts, good emotions, happiness. Medicine is in the ball. Medicine is in the stick. The team has medicine as they work together."[27] "Medicine games" are still played the traditional way: "Two poles are jammed in the ground on each end to serve as goals, an unlimited number of males from ages seven to 70 ranges about, and the first team to score a certain number of goals—sometimes three, sometimes five—wins. Any male can call for a medicine game to deal with personal strife.... The caller doesn't play, but he keeps the ball" because the ball "is the medicine."[28] One player said that a traditional medicine game was organized recently to help two players fight an illness.[29] This coincides with centuries old stories of the game; for example, the Oneida tell the tale of young warriors who put on a match for Hayewat-ha, one of the founders of the Haudenosaunee Confederacy who had recently lost his children.

Along with physical and spiritual healing, the game was also used as a means of social and political resolution. Donald Fisher notes that the games served import-ant political functions, citing matches in 1794 and 1797 played between Seneca and Mohawk tribes to reaffirm political ties in response to threats from American settlers.[30] Though certainly rough, the early lacrosse games that Christian mis-sionaries witnessed were not violent: "They settled disputes that way, played a game of lacrosse instead of fighting."[31] Regarding the purpose of the game, Faith-keeper Lyons concludes, "Put your guns down, pick up a stick...nations would settle a difference with a game."[32]

Once Europeans were introduced to the game they sought to standardize the contest. The first set of organized rules were developed in the late 1860s by William George Beers and early on Native American players were considered the sport's best ambassadors. In the late 1800s Native players traveled around the British Isles leaving new lacrosse clubs in their wake.[33] One reporter from 1885 was both impressed with the "fine field play of the Indians" and disappointed in the "lack of judgment" of the white players, whom they found noticeably inferior.[34] Unfortunately attempts to regulate the game took on a racial tone. One of Beers's rules was, "No Indian must play in a match for a white club unless previously agreed upon," which had a Jim Crow effect.[35] Thomas Vennum pointed out that Beers's frustrations with the Native game simply echoed whites' attempts to civ-ilize perceived savagery, highlighting the impacts of Manifest Destiny and Dar-win's theory of evolution on the exclusion of Native players from the game.[36] Beers "admired the physical prowess evident in the Indian style of play" but felt that the game the Natives played "remained at a primitive level" as in "irrational, unscien-tific, impromptu, or otherwise lacking in organization."[37]

Due to the overt racism in Beers and others' organizational efforts Native Americans struggled to find a place in the rapidly evolving sport. In the 1904 Olympics a team of Mohawks from Canada won the bronze in an exhibition match and at the 1932 Games the Iroquois played similar exhibitions, but that was the last time they competed internationally until the formation of the Nation-als in 1983, who won their first official international victory the next year in a special match with England.[38] Robert Lipsyte notes that these injustices still sting: "Iroquois say that the banning of their lacrosse team [was] all a part of the system-atic policy of stealing lands from the American Indians, of denying their culture and eradicating their nations."[39] Evin Demirel argues that the Iroquois sensitivity was well-founded: "in the 1800s the Iroquois taught others their sacred game only to see their students turn around and bar them from the sport."[40] Between their suspension from play in the 1880s to the introduction of the Nationals in the 1980s there developed two distinct strains of lacrosse: "Indigenous people, for whom lacrosse is inseparable from culture and history, and the non-natives who've played and organized the game for decades."[41] Native rhetors pointed to a contrast between "the perception…of the sport as elitist…weighed against its humble, egalitarian, and distinctly Native American beginnings."[42] Others were direct in their criticism, seeing the modern "yacht-setting, ivory tower elite" who play lacrosse as the scions of those who stole their game from them.[43]

Add to this frustration contemporary stories of racism on the field and one can see why Native players and fans are hungry for recognition. Vennum collected a number of accounts from historical and current players who faced blatant racism in the game.[44] The current stars of the game, brothers Miles and Lyle Thompson, admitted that they commonly heard racist remarks from opponents and fans. Their standout cousin Ty said that players often called him "Pocahontas" or "wagon-burner."[45] For Natives, such frustrations in the sport mirror their ongoing grievances as a people. As one Nationals player commented, most of their opponents thought "we're extinct, that we still live in teepees."[46] In essence, the Nationals program represents a conflict on two fronts; one between its progenitors who seek to return lacrosse to its true nature and those who enjoy the racial and misogynistic privileges that the founders of modern lacrosse built into its structure; and the other defined the efforts of rhetors who use the sport as a celebration and reclamation of Native identity against social, political, and economic marginalization. As one player concluded, "The war's not over…. Not by a long shot."[47]

THE NATIONALS, SOVEREIGNTY, AND SYMBOLIC BOASTING

In response to these frustrations Nationals players and fans engage in symbolic boasting as a means to assert their presence and sovereignty in the global community. Rhetors often refer to the sport and the Nationals as a means of affirming Native presence in the public mind. As one writer put it: "Though the Iroquois population and land has been taken away during the last 300 years, their spirit remains. It's the spirit involving, as you say, identity, belonging, sport, and history that has given the Haudenosaunee resilience that defies belief."[48] The team allowed communities to "create a counter-narrative about Native Americans."[49] The Nationals made it possible "to educate the American public so they can know the real history of this country… Our history."[50]

First the team's appearance on the world stage served as an affirmation of their existence and relevance. Any recognition the team received was turned into an affirmation of Native American identity. This is why despite losing all four of their matches the Nationals called their appearance at the 1990 World Championships a success as it won them respect "as players and as a people."[51] Rhetors celebrated a 2012 statement by the Senate Committee on Indian Affairs asserting the "Nationals program has had a significant impact on Native youth throughout the country as their triumphs have provided an international showcase of indigenous talent and culture."[52] They also pointed to moments like the 2014 World Championships when the New Zealand squad performed a traditional Haka dance to honor the Iroquois as the progenitors of the game.[53] Through these moments, "The Nationals are showing the world that we are on the map... to have a positive there on the world stage is such a big thing for us."[54]

Others used the Nationals as a tool to demonstrate Native American sovereignty. One Native American historian stated the Nationals are "really about asserting our identity, our nationality, and our sovereignty."[55] Repeatedly Native American rhetors used the Nationals' trials and tribulations as examples of Native self-determination, such as the Nationals' recognition from the Kennedy School at Harvard for "promoting Indian Sovereignty and excellence on the playing field."[56] Through such moments the Nationals represented Native American "identity and self-determination."[57] Tonya Gonella Frichner, a member of the Iroquois Nationals Board of Directors, commented, "The mission of making a statement internationally that the Confederacy has a national team that can compete on an international level just like the US, Canada, Australia, Japan, and England, and seeing how long the struggle took just for them to open the door for us to be a competing nation—well, therein lies the expression of Native sovereignty."[58] Even their recent agreement with Nike had overtones of sovereignty: the shoe company was identified as a partner, not a sponsor; a noted departure from the typical language in an apparel and equipment agreement.

The Nationals' passport issues leading up to the 2010 World Championships in the U.K. foregrounded this theme. The Nationals travel on official Haudenosaunee passports, and the U.K. denied the team entry on the premise that they would not be readmitted to the U.S. after the Department of Homeland Security questioned their validity. The team was offered expedited Canadian and U.S. passports which they unanimously declined in the name of national sovereignty. One player argued, "We are representing a nation, and we are not going to travel on the passport of a competitor."[59] Such accommodations were not needed as the Haudenosaunee were "a sovereign nation—our own people, our own government."[60] The language of sovereignty and loyalty is written into the Haudenosaunee passport: "You may lose your Haudenosaunee nationality by being naturalized in, or taking an oath or making a declaration of allegiance to, a foreign state" (Iroquois

Nationals, n.d., para. 7).[61] The incident served as an opportunity for the Nationals to represent Native American sovereignty without scoring a goal.

These functions, the themes of presence and sovereignty, were supported by two common lines of argument. Each line highlighted the ways in which rhetors may use symbolic boasting to rhetorically shape the scope of political discourse through international competition. The first form stressed the disparity between the smaller Nationals and other programs as a means to magnify the team's achievements on the field and vicariously celebrate Native American identity. Many rhetors accentuated the resource gap between the Nationals and their competition as a means of amplifying their achievements. Comments mirrored Demirel's, who noted, "the fact a team drawing on a population base of less than 150,000 people can hang with a nation like Canada of more than 35 million people is one of the feel-good stories of the year."[62] Such refrains were common, particularly after the team's historic first win against Team USA in 2012, the U.S. squad's first loss in 24 years to anyone but Canada. Multiple rhetors spoke of the 150,000 strong U.S. player pool versus the comically small 86 member Nationals pool, which made the victory "astonishing."[63] After recounting the same numbers, Timothy Burke called the win, "a massive upset when the scale of the sport's players is taken into account."[64] Valerie Taliman added the "multimillion-dollar operation that stands behind Team USA," against which the Iroquois "are clearly the underdogs."[65] The premise was that if a small, underfunded program can achieve what the Nationals have achieved, then there must be something uniquely great about the players that empowers them, i.e., their Native identity. Many, like Taliman, concluded that by overcoming such hurdles "history [was] made by an exceptional group of Native athletes and coaches that proved the Iroquois are capable of competing."[66]

The second line of rhetoric went the other direction, enlarging the Nationals' actions as representative of all Native Americans, and occasionally indigenous peoples worldwide. The team's participation on the international lacrosse stage reoriented the issue of national sovereignty. Though the reservations are autonomous states they lack the economic or political clout to be heard in most national conversations. However, international sports empower the Haudenosaunee Confederacy to participate on the global stage by reorienting the scope of the discussion. In this manner, the Nationals became a rhetorical tool that argued for the equality of Native American national identity.

Rhetors frequently spoke of the implications of the Nationals' wins for Native Americans at large. For many, "the Iroquois Nationals have ensured respect for the broader Native American community."[67] Faithkeeper Lyons often integrated national sovereignty with identity, commenting, "We're an international team and we're playing under our flag, but we're representing all Indians."[68] Taliman recounted Head Coach Freeman's pregame talk reminding the team to "play for the Creator…It's our game and we'll do our best to play well for our people back home."[69] In each of these cases the successes of the Nationals were used to represent the resilience of Native Americans. Others associated with the team cast the Nationals as representative of indigenous peoples at large. General Manager Gewas Schindler made much of the Nationals' performance at the 2012 championships, "We feel like we fulfilled a historic goal for our team, for the Haudenosaunee, and for indigenous peoples worldwide."[70] He went on to comment, "We were able to hear the Iroquois national anthem and see our flag flying at this international event with the world acknowledging the legacy of the Iroquois Confederacy's role in lacrosse."[71]

Many rhetors extrapolated from the positivity of the Nationals program a brighter future for Native Americans in general. After recounting troubles on the reservations, Faithkeeper Lyons stated, "We've got to give them hope. A national lacrosse team can do that."[72] Another historian stated, "It's not just a game, it's really about asserting our identity, our nationality, and our sovereignty through lacrosse, and that to me is the legacy we are creating for the future."[73] The Nationals served "as an insulator to protect our communities from the breakdown of individual and community identity during colonization. As our communities continue to heal from colonization our game has become much stronger."[74] Even the win over USA in 2012, though it "spoke to the past" was more about "a different type of future."[75] As Lyons concluded, "The kids are the hope of the people."[76]

Perhaps the most vocal rhetors on the subject were the Nationals' stars. Lacrosse luminary Lyle Thompson stated, "[We are] representing the Iroquois people and by doing that at the world stage, we're representing all Native American people.... I want to be an influence on the next generation and the way I'm doing it is through the game of lacrosse."[77] He went on to say, "Being part of the Iroquois Nationals is more than representing your people...you're joining a fight as a people because we haven't been completely accepted by all the nations. You're... doing what you can do help our people move forward."[78] Miles Thompson commented, "Our motto is 'We win, you win,'.... What that means is...there's a bigger purpose than us playing, we play for the people around us. It's medicine for us ... it's much more than us going out and playing; it's for our people, for ourselves and the younger generation. It's much bigger than us."[79]

CONCLUSION

The Nationals play a prominent role in Native American identity rhetoric. The team's participation and achievements on the world stage are adopted by Native American rhetors as a way to argue for identity and sovereignty. Rhetors symbolically boasted of their activities as a way to challenge racial stereotypes and affirm Native identity and national sovereignty. They added significance to the team's actions by shaping the scope of the contest, either magnifying its disparity into an underdog scenario to celebrate Native American ideology, or stressing a level international playing field to argue for the Haudenosaunee's place in the global community.

The Iroquois Nationals seem to be serving their rhetorical function well. Their self-stated goal is to remind the world, "We're still here," and the world, or at least the lacrosse world, is taking notice.[80] The Tewaaraton Award for the best college lacrosse player was won by Native Americans for the first time: Mohawk brothers Lyle and Miles Thompson, with cousin Ty coming in a close third.[81] The trio scored a Nike partnership for their own line of equipment and camps.[82] The Thompsons made inroads for Native players by attending SUNY at Albany, a break with the Native tradition in attending Syracuse, and since their award-winning performances other state universities have come knocking on the reservations' doors recruiting other players.[83] The team performed well at the last World Championships, establishing a perpetual presence on the medal stand and raising the profile of the Haudenosaunee Confederacy in the process. It would seem that the Nationals program, as envisioned by Faithkeeper Lyons and the others, is performing its intended purpose.

One of the givens in international sports is that they function as ideological contests between nations. In the Nationals' case, scope is highlighted as a significant rhetorical dimension of international sports. Because of sports' structure nations compete under the same rules and regulations, meaning that a nation like the U.S. which abounds in players and resources is contained by the same limitations as a collection of reservations who lack the same. The result is that any victory may be applied to the rhetor's advantage: for a small nation, the ideological nature of the contest may imbue a win with significant rhetorical power, while for a large nation a win may serve as an affirmation of ideological superiority or the mandate of heaven.

Broadly speaking, the rhetoric surrounding the Iroquois Nationals serves as an excellent example of the ways in which sports and politics are rhetorical resources. Sport provides a unique rhetorical opportunity for this phenomenon. Because of their amorphous nature it is difficult to actually compare ideologies or value systems. Rhetors must come at them obliquely and figuratively to assert one's dominance or submission to another. The competitive nature of sports simplifies this task by encasing such debates in definable contests with verifiable outcomes. It is important to remember that sports are not inherently rhetorical statements; they are simply contests between competitors within a defined structure, be it lacrosse, football, or gymnastics. These contests are *made* rhetorical by those that produce and consume them. Whether it is the Thompson brothers playing in the lacrosse world championship or Jesse Owens running in the 1936 Olympics, these events become rhetorical when they are refashioned as arguments about race, politics, and ideology by rhetors who see potential in them. The intersection of sports, rhetoric, and politics is a critical nexus from which much meaning may be gleaned. Focusing on the ways in which sports are used for larger purposes helps to build our understanding of the critical functions these contests serve in our communities.

NOTES

1. Mike Milford, "The Olympics, Jesse Owens, Burke, and the Implications of Media Framing in Symbolic Boasting," *Mass Communication and Society* 15, no. 4 (2012): 485–505.
2. Casey Ryan Kelly, "'We Are Not Free': The Meaning of <Freedom> in American Indian Resistance to President Johnson's War on Poverty," *Communication Quarterly* 62, no. 4 (2014): 455–73.
3. Jason Edward Black, "Native Authenticity, Rhetorical Circulation, and Neocolonial Decay: The Case of Chief Seattle's Controversial Speech," *Rhetoric & Public Affairs* 15, no. 4 (2012): 635–45; Jason Edward Black, "Native Resistive Rhetoric and the Decolonization of American Indian Removal Discourse," *Quarterly Journal of Speech* 95, no. 1 (2009): 66–88.
4. Jackson B. Miller, "'Indians,' 'Braves,' and 'Redskins': A Performative Struggle for Control of an Image," *Quarterly Journal of Speech* 85, no. 2 (1999): 188–202; Ellen Staurowsky, "'You Know, We Are All Indian': Exploring White Power and Privilege in Reactions to the NCAA Native American Mascot Policy," *Journal of Sport & Social Issues* 31, no. 1 (2007): 61–76; Jason Edward Black, "Native American 'Mascotting' Reveals Neocolonial Logics," *Spectra* 50, no. 3 (2014): 14–17.
5. Danielle Endres, "American Indian Permission for Mascots: Resistance or Complicity Within Rhetorical Colonialism?" *Rhetoric & Public Affairs* 18, no. 4 (2015): 649–90.
6. Kenneth Burke, *Attitudes Toward History* 3rd ed. (Berkeley, CA: University of California Press, 1937), 264.
7. Ronald Carpenter, "A Stylistic Basis of Burkeian Identification," *Today's Speech* 20, no. 1 (1972): 19–24.
8. Robert Heath, *Realism and Relativism: A Perspective on Kenneth Burke* (Macon, GA: Mercer University Press, 1986): 208.
9. Carpenter, "A Stylistic Basis," 19.
10. Milford, "The Olympics," 488.
11. Kenneth Burke, *A Rhetoric of Motives* (Berkeley, CA: University of California Press, 1969), 21.
12. Ross Wolin, *The Rhetorical Imagination of Kenneth Burke* (Columbia, SC: University of South Carolina Press, 2001), 94.
13. Burke, *Attitudes*, 267.
14. Burke, *A Rhetoric*, 58.
15. James Walsh, "An Approach to Dyadic Communication in Historical Social Movements: Dyadic Communication in Maoist Insurgent Mobilization," *Communication Monographs* 53, (March 1986): 1–15.
16. Mark Wright, "Burkeian and Freudian Theories of Identification," *Communication Quarterly* 42, no. 3 (1994): 301–10.
17. Michael Butterworth, "The Politics of the Pitch: Claiming and Contesting Democracy Through the Iraqi National Soccer Team," *Communication and Critical/Cultural Studies* 4, no. 2 (2007): 184–203.

18. Milford "The Olympics."
19. Skaruianewah Logan, "Lacrosse: A Sovereign Tradition," *Indian Country Today*, September 18, 2015, https://newsmaven.io/indiancountrytoday/archive/lacrosse-a-sovereign-tradition-ocnKXsqlCECvOtncvRcbQg/.
20. Steve Milton, "Lacrosse, Our Fathers' Game," *Hamilton Spectator*, June 16, 2017, https://www.thespec.com/sports-story/7376710-lacrosse-our-fathers-game/.
21. Katie Barnes, "Meet the Filmmaker Behind Tribeca Documentary on Native American Girls Lacrosse Team," *ESPNW*, May 30, 2016, http://www.espn.com/espnw/culture/article/15272215/keepers-game-movie-director-qa.
22. David Sommerstein, "Iroquois, Inventors of Lacrosse, Bring Its World Cup Home," *North Country Public Radio*, https://www.northcountrypublicradio.org/news/story/29618/20150925/iroquois-inventors-of-lacrosse-bring-its-world-cup-home.
23. Donald Fisher, *Lacrosse: A History of the Game* (Baltimore, MD: Johns Hopkins University Press, 2002), 14-15; Winona Laduke, "The Iroquois Nationals at the World Lacrosse Championships," *In These Times*, August 9, 2014, http://inthesetimes.com/article/17058/the_iroquois_little_war_for_independence.
24. Jerry Reynolds, "Lacrosse Museum Pays Homage to the Sport's Original Masters," *Indian Country Today*, October 31, 2007, https://indiancountrymedianetwork.com/news/lacrosse-museum-pays-homage-to-the-sports-original-masters/.
25. S. L. Price, "Pride of a Nation," *Sports Illustrated*, July 19, 2010, https://www.si.com/vault/2010/07/19/105961100/pride-of-a-nation; Bob Scott, *Lacrosse: Technique and Tradition* (Baltimore, MD: Johns Hopkins University Press, 1976), 7.
26. Katie Barnes, "'Keepers of the Game' Breaks New Ground for Sports Storytelling Around Women," *ESPNW*, April 20, 2016, http://www.espn.com/espnw/culture/article/15273999/tribeca-espn-sports-film-festival-premieres-keepers-game.
27. Logan "Lacrosse."
28. Price "Pride."
29. Price "Pride."
30. Fisher, *Lacrosse: A History*, 20.
31. William Wallace, "Putting Tradition to the Test," *New York Times*, June 12, 1990, http://www.nytimes.com/1990/06/12/sports/putting-tradition-to-the-test.html.
32. Sommerstein "Iroquois."
33. Scott, *Lacrosse*, 9.
34. "The Indians Win Again," *New York Times*, September 25, 1885, https://timesmachine.nytimes.com/timesmachine/1885/09/25/issue.html.
35. J. Censer, "For Iroquois National, Lacrosse is More Than a Game," *Lax Magazine*, January 14, 2014, Retrieved September 27, 2017, http://laxmagazine.prestosports.com/international/men/2012-13/news/011413_for_iroquois_nationals_it-s_more_than_a_game. Article has been removed from the website.
36. Thomas Vennum, *American Indian Lacrosse* (Washington, DC: Smithsonian Institution Press, 1994), 254, 268-69.
37. Vennum, *American*, 269-70.
38. Doug George-Kanentiio, "Now is the Golden Era of Iroquois Lacrosse," *Indian Country News*, August 28 2015, http://www.indiancountrynews.com/index.php/columnists/doug-george-kanentiio/14197-now-is-the-golden-era-of-iroquois-lacrosse; Price , "Pride."

39. Robert Lipsyte, "Another National Team, Another Sort of Dream," *New York Times*, July, 31, 1992, http://www.nytimes.com/1992/07/31/sports/another-national-team-another-sort-of-dream.html.

40. Evin Demirel, "A Millennium After Inventing the Game, the Iroquois Are Lacrosse's New Superpower," *Deadspin*, July 21, 2014, http://www.thedailybeast.com/a-millennium-after-inventing-the-game-the-iroquois-are-lacrosses-new-superpower.

41. Milton "Lacrosse, Our Fathers'."

42. Lucas O'Neill, "Lax Movie Pays Tribute to Game's Origins," *ESPN*, June 1, 2012, http://www.espn.com/blog/high-school/lacrosse/post/_/id/6140/lax-movie-pays-tribute-to-games-origins.

43. Liam Pierce, "The Thompson Brothers Bring Lacrosse Home to the Iroquois," *Vice*, September 27, 2015, https://sports.vice.com/en_us/article/pg5j9g/the-thompson-brothers-bring-lacrosse-home-to-the-iroquois.

44. Vennum, *American*, 279.

45. Demirel "A Millennium."

46. O'Neill "Lax Movie."

47. Price "Pride."

48. Valentina Valentini, "The Whitewashing of Lacrosse," *Good Sport*, May 26, 2017, https://sports.good.is/features/spirit-game-lacrosse.

49. Renée Gadoua, "Lax Doc Emphasizes Haudenosaunee Connection," *Syracuse New Times*, May 31, 2017, https://www.syracusenewtimes.com/lax-doc-emphasizes-haudenosaunee-connection/.

50. Sarah Moses, "Lacrosse Documentary Highlights Iroquois Nationals, Honors History of the Sport," *Syracuse*, June 1, 2017, http://www.syracuse.com/entertainment/index.ssf/2017/06/lacrosse_documentary_highlights_iroquois_nationals_honors_history_of_the_sport.html.

51. "Showing of Pride for the Iroquois," *New York Times*, July 16, 1990, http://www.nytimes.com/1990/07/16/sports/showing-of-pride-for-the-iroquois.html.

52. "U.S. Senate Honors Iroquois Nationals Lacrosse Team," *Indian Country Today*, November 28, 2012, https://indiancountrymedianetwork.com/culture/sports/us-senate-honors-iroquois-nationals-lacrosse-team/.

53. Bill Littlefield, "Lacrosse: A Symbol of Family and Tradition for 4 Iroquois Brothers," *WBUR*, June 2, 2017, http://www.wbur.org/onlyagame/2017/06/02/thompson-brothers-iroquois-lacrosse.

54. Price "Pride."

55. Amy Morris, "Iroquois Nationals Lacrosse Documentary Premieres: *Spirit Game: Pride of a Nation*," *Indian Country Today*, May 26, 2017, https://indiancountrymedianetwork.com/culture/sports/iroquois-nationals-lacrosse-documentary-premieres-spirit-game-pride-nation/.

56. Tom Wanamaker, "Iroquois Nationals Place Fourth in World Lacrosse Tourney," *Indian Country Today*, July 21, 2002, https://indiancountrymedianetwork.com/news/iroquois-nationals-place-fourth-in-world-lacrosse-tourney/.

57. Valerie Taliman, "Beyond the Bronze: The Iroquois Nationals Come Home as Champions in Many Respects," *Indian Country Today*, July 28, 2012, https://indiancountrymedianetwork.com/news/beyond-the-bronze-the-iroquois-nationals-come-home-as-champions-in-many-respects/.

58. Gale Toensing, "Iroquois Nationals Ready for World Lacrosse Championships in Finland," *Indian Country Today*, July 7, 2012, https://indiancountrymedianetwork.com/culture/sports/iroquois-nationals-ready-for-world-lacrosse-championships-in-finland/.

59. Price "Pride."

60. "Lacrosse Is More Than Just a Game to Iroquois Nationals," *North Country Public Radio*, August 6, 2010, https://www.northcountrypublicradio.org/news/story/16092/lacrosse-is-more-than-just-a-game-to-iroquois-nationals.

61. "Iroquois Nationals Lacrosse," *Government Innovators Network: Harvard University*, https://www.innovations.harvard.edu/iroquois-nationals-lacrosse.

62. Demirel , "A Millennium."

63. In 2010 the Iroquois Traditional Council passed strict lineage guidelines which cut a large number of their more talented players (see Price, "Pride"). "Iroquois Nationals Make History, Beat Team USA for First Time in International Competition," *Indian Country Today*, July 17, 2012, https://indiancountrymedianetwork.com/news/iroquois-nationals-make-history-beat-team-usa-for-first-time-in-international-field-competition/.

64. Timothy Burke, "An Iroquois Lacrosse Squad Beat Team USA for the First Time Ever," *Deadspin*, July 17, 2012, https://deadspin.com/5926671/an-iroquois-lacrosse-squad-beat-team-usa-for-the-first-time-ever.

65. Valerie Taliman, "Game On: The Iroquois Nationals Face Team USA in Rematch to Determine who makes the Final," *Indian Country Today*, July 19, 2012, https://indiancountrymedianetwork.com/news/game-on-the-iroquois-nationals-face-team-usa-in-rematch-to-determine-who-makes-the-final/.

66. Taliman, "Beyond."

67. "Iroquois Nationals."

68. Toensing "Iroquois Nationals Ready."

69. Taliman, "Game On."

70. Taliman, "Beyond."

71. Ibid Taliman, "Beyond."

72. Robert Lipsyte, "Lacrosse: All-American Game," *New York Times*, June 15, 1986, http://www.nytimes.com/1986/06/15/magazine/lacrosse-all-american-game.html?pagewanted=1.

73. Morris, "Iroquois Nationals Lacrosse."

74. Logan "Lacrosse."

75. Censer, "For Iroquois National."

76. Lipsyte, "Another."

77. Morris "Iroquois Nationals."

78. Michael LoRé, "What Lacrosse Means to the Iroquois Nation," *The Omnivor*, June 23, 2017, https://medium.com/the-omnivore/what-lacrosse-means-to-the-iroquois-nation-6c41309881e3.

79. LoRé, "What Lacrosse."

80. Price "Pride."

81. Pierce, "The Thompson Brothers."

82. Sommerstein; Elaine Quijano, "Three Lacrosse Players Dominate Sport Their Ancestors Created," *CBS News*, May 8, 2014, https://www.cbsnews.com/news/three-lacrosse-players-dominate-sport-their-ancestors-created/.

83. Zach Schonbrun, "In a Native American Sport, a Family's Giant Leap," *New York Times*, March 9, 2014, https://www.nytimes.com/2014/03/10/sports/college-lacrosse-upended-by-albanys-native-american-stars.html.

CHAPTER SEVEN

(Re)Articulations of Race, Sexuality, and Gender in U.S. Football

Investigating Tyrann Mathieu as Honey Badger

DANIEL C. BROUWER AND KATRINA N. HANNA

In early January 2011, the Honey Badger erupted into the mediascape. Propelled by a video featuring documentary footage of actual honey badgers overlaid with narration by Randall (like Cher or Madonna, he uses only a first name) and his distinct and atypical documentary voice, the Honey Badger quickly took form as a meme, a "cultural unit" or fragment of ideology.[1] Some of the pleasure of the original video and some of the force for its virality derive from the gay-sounding voice of Randall the narrator and the humorous "discrepancy" between the toughness of the animal and the silliness (coupled with respect) of the narration. As a meme, the Honey Badger quickly circulated through myriad popular and officious sites—commercials for pistachio nuts, cocktail lists, lesbian sports team names, news stories about the Colorado Secretary of State, the floor of the U.S. Senate, and elsewhere.

The Huffington Post cheekily named Randall's "The Crazy Nastyass Honey Badger" as "the best nature video of all time" just two months after its upload to YouTube.[2] Marking the atypical endurance of this (or any) meme, a panel conversation at the March 2013 South by Southwest (SXSW) Conference investigated "Why We STILL Love the Honey Badger" more than two years after its initial launch. As part of a marketing scheme for a February 2014 episode about the honey badger (the animal), the *Public Broadcasting Service* (PBS) Nature series enlisted Honey Badger (the meme) by having its originator, Randall, voice-over a promotional trailer. More recently, in the aftermath of White House Chief Strategist Steve Bannon's resignation from the Trump Administration in August 2017, the public was reminded that Bannon had welcomed his "Honey Badger" nickname and had adopted the animal-meme as an "unofficial mascot" for Breitbart News.[3]

We do not attempt here a comprehensive accounting of the meme's travels and meanings. Instead, we feature the articulation of "Honey Badger" to collegiate and professional U.S. football player, Tyrann Mathieu. In our view, the articulation of Honey Badger to Mathieu was the most significant catalyst for the meme's circulation. While Honey Badger has circulated and attached in innumerable ways that exceed Mathieu, it remains enduringly linked to him. In the remaining pages, we focus on Mathieu's rearticulations of Honey Badger, between 2013 and early 2016, as a status to strive for but one that he must earn rather than have assigned. These rearticulations occur in the aftermath of the initial Honey Badger-Mathieu linkage asserted by fans and a coach between Fall 2011 and Fall 2012 and Mathieu's short-lived rejection of the linkage as he transitioned into the National Football League circa 2013. These rearticulations also precede his most recent unconditional residence within and cultivation of a Honey Badger persona from early 2016 on. Specifically, we investigate a collection of newspaper articles, podcasts, and videos as locations where we witness Mathieu and sports writers and commentators collectively laboring to align "Honey Badger" with Mathieu and to accommodate the Honey Badger's circulation into the realm of collegiate and professional sports.

Broadly, we query: What do Mathieu's and others' rearticulations of the Honey Badger disclose about race, sexuality, gender, and sport? Understanding rhetoric as a medium through which ideologies of race are circulated, constituted, and materialized, we argue that articulation theory enables us to track and assess the dynamism of Mathieu-as-Honey-Badger attuned to the force of historical and contemporary racial formations in these articulations. In the 2013–2016 rearticulations, sports writers and commentators collaborate with Mathieu to craft a particular racial redemption narrative through the Honey Badger meme. As there is nothing "necessary" about what Honey Badger sticks to and how it does so, we investigate how Honey Badger travels from the pleasures of Randall's gay-sounding tonalities to narratives of racial redemption.

ARTICULATIONS OF RACE AND SPORT

Broadly, we begin with the assumption that the political nature of ideological elements has no necessary belongingness to how language is used to craft our social world.[4] Conceptualized as articulation theory, this perspective on language permits social critics and scholars to unearth how ideological elements cohere with a given discourse and how specific articulations do or do not become "linked" to create (temporarily) new meanings.[5] For our purposes, articulation theory is the means through which rhetorical scholars can unmask, map, and explicate the discursive practice of speaking forth and linking meaning.[6] This bend towards discourse within articulation theory resonates for rhetorical critics specifically because of how language is used to (re)create the social world.[7] A discursive shift situates identity as a rhetorical construct, through which humans are the products *and* agents of persuasive action. Therefore, this articulated "identity is not a natural assumption, but a rhetorical achievement" through which subjects are interpellated by a number of discourses.[8] For Tyrann Mathieu as the Honey Badger, this rhetorically influenced turn to discourse recognizes him not as a stagnant force, but as a "performance" in flux.

A rhetorical turn to discourse and articulation theory reveals three significant characteristics of articulation important to our analysis. First, while a rhetorical approach to articulation takes discursivity seriously, it simultaneously assumes a dialectical relationship between discourse and materiality, including the materiality of differently raced bodies. Second, articulations can be transformed and altered into different versions based off the original.[9] Consequently, subjects who become the focus of a given articulation have the ability to negotiate the meaning bound within the discursive formations. As our analysis will demonstrate, this permits Mathieu to take a stronger oppositional stance in defining the Honey Badger on his own terms. The third characteristic underscores how the relationship between discourse and social reality is dialectical.[10] In other words, to be recognized as a social subject means that one must become subjected to a worldview and embedded within the limits of its discursive framing. Simply put, subjects have agency within a given articulation, but the "choices" available are dictated within the perimeters of the meaning rooted within discursive and material structures. Mathieu has some rhetorical space to accept, reject, and redefine the articulations, but he is constrained by (at least) the remnants of Randall's video and the structures of professional sport and racial formations.

Critical analyses of sport and race outline the contours of sport as a space for particular cultural and racial formations and specify elements of sport-race articulations that enable and constrain Mathieu's relationship to Honey Badger and the work that Honey Badger can do. In this vein, black athletic bodies are framed and circulated as more aggressive and hypermasculine than white bodies.[11] Further, black professional football players are routinely coded as naturally more athletically talented but also primitive and unstable; thus, instances of "bad behavior" by white and black athletes activate different "evaluative framework[s]" wherein white athletes are permitted redemption through proper realignment of mind and body, while black athletes' bodies are redeemed "through a contingent relationship to external disciplinary structures."[12] Under the influence of neoliberalism professional sports allow certain forms of marking and celebrating racial difference but contain such expressions of racial difference when they threaten league profits.[13] Additionally salient to our project, even where we might expect direct articulations of the intersections of race, sexuality, and gender, sport culture might actively thwart such articulations or route them in particular directions. In his analysis of Michael Sam for example, the first openly gay player to be drafted by an NFL team, Abraham Khan argues that the common media analogy between Sam and Jackie Robinson actually produced a disarticulation of race from sexuality as journalists tried to make sense of Sam's identity and role within sport-based progress; within hegemonic constructions of masculinity and race, Sam's race and sexuality were framed as at odds with each other rather than as integrated.[14]

As we argue later in our analysis, Tyrann Mathieu's rearticulations of his relationship to Honey Badger take particular shape as a racial redemption narrative. Two recent, precedential "breaches" of conduct by NFL players Richard Sherman and Michael Vick alert us to key contours of the racialized redemption narrative in professional sports. During his "interview for the ages" after a 2014 NFL playoff game, Sherman famously affirmed his and his defensive teammates' superior talent and chided a specific opponent for conveying doubt about Sherman and teammates: "Well, I'm the best corner in the game! When you try me with a sorry receiver like [Michael] Crabtree, that's the result you gonna get! Don't you EVER talk about me."[15] Sherman's interview content, style, and intensity generated significant response from sports commentators and fans, coalescing into what Joe Tompkins characterizes as "dialectical poles of representation" of Sherman as either "overtly racist…'thug'" or "self-enterprising talent."[16] Those invested in the "thug" framing assessed Sherman to be unredeemable. Those cultivating or permitting the "entrepreneur" frame did not require him to hide or be silent about race but did expect him, as conditions of his redemption, to manage or overcome the challenges that his openly acknowledged blackness incurred upon him.[17] And yet, in Tompkins' assessment, the effect of that redemptive positionality was to "foreclose alternatives to the privatization and depoliticization of [contemporary] racial discourse."[18]

Michael Vick's breach of supporting a dog fighting operation was quite different from Sherman's. As Vick's prison term neared its conclusion, NFL commissioner Roger Goodell announced that Vick could earn reinstatement by expressing "genuine remorse" for his crimes. Vick worked closely with the NFL and a visible team of supporters that included former NFL coach Tony Dungy—a well-known Christian mentor for "wayward" African American athletes—to perform remorse and earn redemptive return as a salaried player.[19] Diagnosing the racial character of "genuine remorse," Daniel Grano argues that the Vick case demonstrates "the central role sports media play in persistently dramatizing forgiveness through nonwhite male athletes, veritable character-types prone to criminality and interior instability but reformable through deference to socio-cultural norms and thera-peutic structures."[20]

Critical sport scholarship discloses the specific social forces, including avail-able ideological elements and emergent patterns of articulation, that shape under-standings of race, racial identities, and intersections of race, sexuality, and gender in sport contexts. Constrained and enabled by these ideological elements and pat-terns of articulation, Mathieu mobilizes the Honey Badger meme. In our analysis below, we explicate the salience of Mathieu's rearticulations of the Honey Badger to his own career in the NFL and the potentialities for oppositional politics and bodies in professional sports; in doing so, we hope to illustrate how sport-based contexts and discourses manifest unique social formations, identities, and power structures across and beyond the body of Tyrann Mathieu.

RACIALIZED AND GENDERED ARTICULATIONS AND REARTICULATIONS OF THE HONEY BADGER

Whatever else it was, Randall's original viral video was rich with gay signifiers. Characterized by a higher pitch and wider range of modulations than common masculine voicing, as well as by extravagant emotional agility ranging from amaze-ment to disgust, Randall's tonalities replaced the sober, earnest, informed intona-tions characteristic of the documentary genre with vulgarity, exaggeration, and occasional bouts of fact-dropping. These gay-sounding tonalities were wildly out of synch with the nature documentary genre and generated some of the video's pleasure and its viral force. As the video became a meme and proliferated, diverse and unknown permutations were to be expected.

In our view the most significant catalyst for the meme's circulation, the artic-ulation of Mathieu-as-Honey-Badger, also happens to perform an extraordinary disarticulation of the meme from its original gay signifiers. Comparatively small in stature at 5'9" and 175 lbs., yet exceptionally talented playing cornerback for the highly ranked Louisiana State University (LSU) team, Mathieu had previously been given the nicknames "Little Ball of Hate"[21] and "Tyrannosaurus Rex."[22] In the fall of 2011 shortly after the original video, in an online message board for LSU sports fans, an anonymous poster by the name of "Mike Linebacker" advo-cated replacing Mathieu's nickname with "Honey Badger," arguing for the aptness of the convergence of Mathieu's athletic qualities of toughness with the virtues that Randall extols in his video. "Mike Linebacker" posted a link to the video for other sports fans to watch.[23] Naming John Chavis, a defensive coach at LSU, as the first person to introduce him to his new nickname, Mathieu explains: "He showed me this crazy video. ...[Randall] was like, 'this is the most badass animal I've ever seen."[24] The nickname stuck.

In the face of one coach's and many fans' enthusiastic linkage, however, Mathieu initially balked at the nickname. In an interview, Mathieu narrates "I didn't embrace it at first. …I didn't like it. Especially the 'honey' part. But a lot of kids smile because of the Honey Badger. It's grown on me."[25] Importantly, we do not find evidence in this article or any others under our scrutiny of Mathieu directly addressing and repudiating the queer taint of Randall's voice. Instead, he seems, like most of the fans and sports commentators who circulate the nickname, to simply ignore the specter of Randall's tonalities. Along these lines, in the 2016 NFL Films feature "The Tyrann Mathieu Story," Mathieu does not attempt to replicate the sound of Randall's voice when he paraphrases a favorite line from his first encounter with the video.[1] Rather than an affirmative or a phobic position toward Randall and his tonalities, we witness instead a rich silence. To refuse to inoculate yourself against the queer sound of Randall's voice is to suggest that it is not, in fact, something to be feared.

Despite Mathieu's initial reluctance, the articulation of Mathieu-as-Honey Badger intensified, producing particular amplifications that opened the discursive space for Mathieu to negotiate with and to alter and accelerate the circulation of Randall's original meme. After two thrilling, award-winning seasons as a defensive and special teams star at LSU, however, Mathieu experienced a tumultuous beginning to his third year. As he transitioned from his dismissal from LSU to preparing for the NFL draft, for a brief period of a few months Mathieu labored to sever completely the articulation. In August 2012, LSU coach Les Miles announced Mathieu's dismissal from the team for what would later be reported in many outlets as "repeated failures of drug tests," and Mathieu withdrew from LSU and began drug rehabilitation. The next month Mathieu abruptly left rehab and signed up for classes at LSU. Then in October, Mathieu was arrested for marijuana possession with three other teammates in what seemed to be the final event in his severance from the university. In November, he announced his intention to enter the NFL draft in lieu of transferring to another university.

Transitions are thresholds that offer conditions of liminality in which things will be—must be—different after the transition. Confronting a Honey Badger-LSU articulation that had gathered too many odious and weighty meanings, Mathieu's initial solution was to disavow Honey Badger completely—to refuse it over and over. He was collectively denied that solution. As a result, his effort at complete disarticulation was short-lived. Confronting a soured and sticky articulation, Mathieu altered his strategy, retaining a relationship with Honey Badger while disarticulating it from his LSU career. Fans and commentators permitted him considerably more leeway in this trajectory, a series of moves in which Mathieu's own utterances became a prominent force in redefining his discursively constructed positionality as the Honey Badger.

REARTICULATIONS

Across a series of media texts starting around June 2013 and lasting through early 2016, Mathieu refuses to affirmatively name himself as "Honey Badger," but he holds out Honey Badger as an aspirational status achieved only "if I'm able to make the right decisions."[26] The conditional framing is noteworthy: instead of being fatally compromised and requiring rejection, Honey Badger retains its status as an honorific that one has to earn through living up to its standards. Even as he adds new elements of good conduct and role-modeling to the meaning of the meme, Mathieu retains the key virtue of tenacity dramatized in the original viral video and attributed to him; however, he relocates tenacity away from the scene of LSU (a place that must be left behind) and toward both the specific scene of the NFL and the more general scene of his life-journey. Many sports journalists collaborate with Mathieu in these rearticulations, helping him to put into motion a racial redemption narrative not uncommon among professional athletes.

In one interview, Mathieu offers a complex account of his rearticulation. Asked whether he would revive the nickname, he claims "I don't know if he's [the Honey Badger] going to come back this fall. ...I really don't know."[27] After being asked whether there could ever be a positive connotation to the name, Mathieu opens up, saying "I think so, but I think it's going to take some time, just because 'Honey Badger' happened at such a bad time, a time where I wasn't making the best decisions."[28] A new relationship to Honey Badger is possible but not guaranteed. Thus, Mathieu states that "going forward, if I'm able to make the right decisions, able to be that role model for the kids, I think the 'Honey Badger' can be a pretty positive person."[29] Here we see Mathieu seizing the meme and framing it as an identity or persona through which he can revise and renovate his image. Refusing total disconnection, he becomes agentic, disarticulating and rearticulating the meanings of Honey Badger and his relationship with the meme. Mathieu effectively strips himself of the title that others bestowed upon him, but he works to shape for himself the conditions—the "evaluative framework"[30]— in which he might earn back the title. His revised conditions of "mak[ing] the right decisions" and being a role-model for kids are very different from the qualities of fearless, indiscriminate confrontation (with venomous snakes and bee colonies, for example) that Randall valorized in relation to the honey badger animal, and that led others to bestow Mathieu the honorific in the first place.

An ESPN podcast interview with Mathieu propels the force of the racial redemption narrative while simultaneously and awkwardly revisiting the gender dynamics of the transfer of Honey Badger from Randall to Tyrann. In anticipation of their upcoming interview with Mathieu in September 2015, podcast host Dan Le Batard and co-host Jon "Stugotz" Weiner banter about their struggles with the proper forms of addressing Mathieu. Noting a general lack of respect for the 2015–2016 Arizona Cardinals team, Le Batard muses, "I bet you that bothers Ty*rone* Mathieu. …We will have him on, the Honey Badger, next segment…. I thought I was introducing the segment…for the Honey Badger. …And I've been struggling with his name because it's not spelled 'Matthew.' …And it's not Ty*rone*, it's Ty*rann*. [At this moment, someone in the studio interrupts: 'It's actually Ty*rann*.'] The whole thing is difficult. …I've been calling him the Honey Badger, but he doesn't like to be called the Honey Badger."[31] Co-host Stugotz announces his resolution of this struggle: "I'm just going to call him Honey." Le Batard quickly routes us away from "Honey" to other, better renamings: "Okay. That's fine. 'HB'? Something like that?"[32] Anything but "Honey," it seems.

This exchange is awkward but disclosive. First, sport commentators indicate they know they are being asked to shift their understanding of Mathieu's relationship with "Honey Badger" and implicitly agree to keep space open for the rearticulation. Second, although this exchange takes place over two years into Mathieu's rearticulation and four years after his admission about initially balking at "honey," we discern here a tiny earthquake of gay panic, a subtle clue about the lingering feminizing and queering threat of "honey" (and perhaps a faint trace of Randall's voice). In queer culture, men might refer to each other (even strangers) as "honey" as a way of generating or expressing intimacy; in male-female heterosexual relationships, too, "honey" circulates as a common term of intimacy. However, as a medium of exchange among ostensibly heterosexual men, especially those who are strangers to each other, calling another man "honey" threatens to work otherwise, feminizing or queering and thereby diminishing or questioning the masculinity of the man addressed. During the ESPN podcast, we read Le Batard's hasty, clunky rerouting away from "Honey" and toward "HB" as an effort to manage the specter of queerness.

Third, the cohosts' struggle here is not just to understand Mathieu's shifting relationship to the meme but also the struggle to pronounce both his prename and surname correctly, and this banter about the challenges of Tyrann Mathieu's names marks his race. As a point of contrast, it is not "Matthew" and "Ryan" that they are struggling with, for example, to use the conventional white spellings of the common white first and last names of the Atlanta Falcons quarterback at the time of this writing. Prior to this ESPN podcast, Mathieu had self-identified as creole in his Twitter feed (September 13, 2013, and June 21, 2013), a self-identification that in a U.S. context often refers to a multiracial identity of African, European, or Native American ancestries, or someone born in Louisiana who identifies with that state's distinct history and culture. In the texts that we studied as part of the collection of his rearticulations of Honey Badger, however, Mathieu rarely self-identified as a person of color. That is, he did not directly explicate his race as a salient element in his rearticulated relationship to the Honey Badger title. Nevertheless, in the ESPN podcast we read this moment of struggle over Mathieu's creole-sounding name in conjunction with articulation theory's reminder that discourses about race circulate as always already available for interpretation, definition, and interactional norms.

Once Mathieu arrives for the interview, his rearticulation takes center stage. The co-hosts note they have been told Mathieu no longer likes the famous nickname, and they ask him for dis/confirmation. Mathieu explains, "Well, …you know, when I went through my ordeal at LSU, … getting kicked out of school and what not…, the Honey Badger had just taken off and…that's what I was identified as…. When I entered the NFL, obviously I was trying to turn over a…leaf …. I really thought most people when they thought of me they would think of the Honey Badger at LSU, and I didn't want…those two things to get confused, you know what I mean? …When I was the Honey Badger at LSU, …it was a dark place for me…. I was struggling with some issues…. I didn't want people to…remember me as…*that* Honey Badger."[33] Co-host Le Batard checks his understanding of the rearticulation: "Oh, understood. So you just want to erase your mistakes. …You like the nickname; you don't like the time—what the time represents." "Right," Mathieu affirms. These and other sports commentators demonstrate willingness to collaborate in Mathieu's rearticulation of Honey Badger.

To reframe and newly stabilize the meme in ways that he can affirm and inhabit, one of Mathieu's key tactics is to shift the location of its salience. First, as we showed above Mathieu retains the virtue of tenacity linked to the meme but relocates it from the LSU football field to the NFL football field. As the location of "dark times" in his life, LSU must be left behind. The NFL field is the new, now-salient scene of tenacity. Importantly, this spatial reorientation is also a temporal one, focusing our attention on Mathieu's present ("make the right decisions" now) and his future (complete the redemption process and earn back the Honey Badger title). Second, Mathieu collaborates with sports writers who become increasingly interested in Mathieu's difficult past as a context for understanding his recent troubles and current life-journey. Difficulties from his home life in New Orleans include a birth father in prison, a birth mother who abandoned him, and a murdered best friend. In this vein, an NFL Films video features then-Arizona Cardinals teammate Patrick Peterson who narrates how Mathieu "has always made football look easy. But maybe that's because everyday life was the hard part."[34] The tenacity of the Honey Badger is mobilized into a narrative of redemption in which Mathieu appears in progress toward overcoming his difficult past to becoming a "better" man.[35]

Already existing racial redemption discourses about professional athletes of color underwrite Mathieu's particular story to help fans make sense of this gifted but seemingly troubled athlete. As we noted earlier, Grano's analysis demonstrates the force of racialized discourses in sport and alerts us to the pattern of differential treatment of black and white athletes' "bad behavior" and their different pathways toward redemption.[36] With specific regard to the paths of redemption available to NFL athletes Richard Sherman and Michael Vick, the Vick case demonstrates how African American athletes are granted "forgiveness" (or redemption) for violations according to racialized standards for authenticity and remorse; black athletes have to perform these in popular media forums.[37] In the Sherman case, athletes who resist such standards for redeemable blackness might find their anti-racist responses being calibrated to the demands of neoliberal capitalism.[38]

These "breaches" and subsequent analysis of them disclose racialized modes of perception and permissible and preferable ways for black athletes to repair breaches in professional sports that precede and serve as context for Mathieu's racial redemption story. Mathieu's crime did not involve physical violence against person or property, as Vick's did, but instead involved drug possession and failure to pass drug tests at the university level. In the aftermath of his dismissal, Mathieu offered no harsh, unrepentant, or accusatory public statements, so neither the characteristics of his crime nor any sort of agitating public speech placed him at significant risk, as Sherman was, for framing as a "thug." Yet Mathieu, kicked out of a public university with no degree, did not have anything resembling Sherman's 4.2 high school grade point average and scholarship to and degree from Stanford University to facilitate his own redemption narrative.[39] Additionally, compared with Vick, if Mathieu had a team to help orchestrate his redemption, it was not particularly visible.

The multiple forms of hardship that we learn about in relation to Mathieu's upbringing are indisputably challenging, and they create a context for his proximity to crime. Different from Vick's probationary status and the NFL's explicit monitoring of his conduct, we see the NFL collaborating with Mathieu to affirm his challenges growing up in New Orleans and his potential for overcoming those challenges. In a nearly eleven-minute NFL Films video titled "The Tyrann Mathieu Story: Born & Bred In New Orleans," we see scenes of Mathieu's successes on the NFL field and an audio clip of a sports announcer celebrating the skills of "The [Honey] Badger." We also see scenes of Mathieu walking through the gentrified French Quarter (a familiar but flawed synecdoche for New Orleans) and talking on a basketball court with two neighborhood friends near where he was raised in New Orleans East, the three telling stories about some of the dangers they encountered there. Playing basketball against murderers and drug dealers, for example, Mathieu claims to have learned a particular type of "tough[ness]." Released in January 2016, this video bestows the NFL's imprimatur on the plausibility of Mathieu's racial redemption narrative and the possibility for a happy ending.

CONCLUSIONS

By mid-2016 and through the time of our writing, Mathieu had seemingly set-tled into a comfortable inhabitance of the Honey Badger nickname and identity, no longer framing his relationship to it as conditional. In response to a journal-ist's question about his athletic versatility and the proper name for his position, Mathieu enthused "we can just call the position I play the 'Honey Badger.'"[40] Ongoing sport media coverage commonly uses Mathieu's rearticulated, rehabil-itated, and redeemed nickname, a nickname that has largely been disarticulated from its original queer signifiers. For Mathieu personally, the stakes of a success-ful rearticulation and redemption are significant. Temporally, it is crucial to note how compressed the wage-earning, work-life journey is for NFL athletes. A 2017 NCAA report notes that of 73,660 football players at the U.S. collegiate level, 16,369 of those players were eligible for the NFL draft; of those draft eligible athletes, only 251, or 1.5%, were actually drafted to NFL teams.[41] NFL careers are both rare and typically brief. A 2016 *Wall Street Journal* data analysis shows that from 2008 to 2014, the average length of career for all NFL players dropped from 4.99 years to 2.66 years.[42] Coupling rarity and brevity in the NFL with Mathieu's major ligament injuries in 2013 and 2015 dramatizes how precarious his wage-earning power is and how eager he might be to craft a Honey Badger "brand" that might live beyond a brief playing career. These dynamics shape the distinct material conditions of the temporal-spatial work-life journey of the NFL player and illustrate what is at stake for Mathieu as a laborer.

For sport, race, and rhetoric more generally, our analysis of Mathieu's reartic-ulations explicates how sport can create discursive and material arenas for oppo-sitional politics to be fought and potentially won. Mathieu's rearticulations are oppositional in that he insists he is not reducible to racial stereotypes inside or out-side of professional sports, and he resists a kind of economic-determinist reading wherein he is rendered intelligible as someone inalterably forged by his difficult, early-in-life material conditions. Discursively, Mathieu finds himself informed by an 'Africanized Horatio Alger' narrative in which the emphasis on his indi-vidual successes permits the public to ignore "the structural forces of anti-Black racism."[43] Too common in such framings of professional athletes is some form of criminal past (marijuana possession in Mathieu's case) and some effort by the athlete to reframe himself on the field and off the field in interviews. For some professional athletes of color, enfoldment into both fandom and redemption is achieved through the minimization of their race (e.g., Tiger Woods and Michael Vick), while others undergo a process of redemption wherein their blackness is marked and they become a "credit to [their] race" (e.g., Richard Sherman).[44] In this case, Mathieu does not fit clearly into either of these categories. On the one hand, his race is not entirely minimized given his own and interviewers' indirect remarks noted above. On the other hand, our texts do not explicitly promote that he is tokenized for his identity as a man of color. Speaking forth from this in-between space of racial redemption narratives gives Mathieu discursive freedom to be oppositional. Mathieu is unequivocal in his efforts to disarticulate and rearticulate Honey Badger as a means to shed his "criminal" past. Indeed, the meme of Honey Badger functions as a supplemental identity that Mathieu can appropriate for his own redemption narrative — serving as a medium for change and a measure of character that he, by his own account, initially fails and then lives up to. As such, Mathieu is a vernacular practitioner of articulation.

Discourses about race and sport reflect larger political and cultural trends; thus, we must consider how spheres of sport and culture work to reinforce one another. As Tompkins notes, Richard Sherman's post-game comments and the controversy surrounding the killing of Michael Brown occurred at the same time, and the same discourses of race circulated through both cases, illustrating how sport both constitutes and reflects logics dominant in other spheres of public life. In the same vein, the rise, fall, and rebirth of Mathieu as Honey Badger is situated within larger discourses surrounding Black Lives Matter and public criticism about police brutality. Although the discourses of professional football may be informed by larger public conversations, we acknowledge how the game of football is often framed as an inappropriate space to have political conversations about race. In kneeling during the national anthem, Colin Kaepernick performed an act of oppositional politics that extended far beyond efforts at personal branding and spoke directly to racial injustices; as a result, he is not currently employed by an NFL team. So, talking about race is acceptable within professional football primarily when it is separated from the field and guided through the framework of post-racism—upholding the notion of the individualized success of the player of color as defined within the sport itself.

Ultimately, the permeation of ideologies of post-racism sets limits on how discourses about race and identity can be taken up by professional athletes. In this instance, the power of the identity *as* Honey Badger situates Mathieu among the both/and of minimizing race and being a credit to his race. Being the Honey Badger creates an oppositional racial politics largely restricted to Mathieu himself, tethered to the contexts of his own body, his own redemption, and his potential success during and after his NFL career. In effect, Honey Badger as cultural meme *and* identity opens a discursive toolkit for Mathieu, sports commentators, and the public while being constrained by hegemons of post-racism and sport politics. Describing his relationship to football, Mathieu intones, "without sports, I don't…I can't say that I have a true identity…."[45] Even as Mathieu rests comfortably within his current articulation of Honey Badger, its malleability leaves room for him to renegotiate in the future, if need be, his relationship to sport.

NOTES

1. Limor Shifman, "An Anatomy of a YouTube Meme," *New Media & Society* 14, no. 2 (2012): 187–203.
2. Carol Hartsell, "Honey Badger Don't Care: The Best Nature Video of All Time," *The Huffington Post*, March 4, 2011, http://www.huffingtonpost.com/2011/03/04/honey-badger-dont-care_n_831278.html.
3. Tony Lee, "Breitbart, the Honey Badger, and America First: Book Provides Clues into How Bannon Propelled Trump into Oval Office," July 18, 2017, http://www.breitbart.com/big-government/2017/07/18/breitbart-the-honey-badger-and-america-first-book-provides-clues-into-how-bannon-propelled-trump-into-oval-office/. The authors thank Damien S. Pfister for this tip.
4. Ernesto Laclau, *Politics and Ideology in Marxist Theory: Capitalism, Fascism, Populism* (London: Verso, 1979).
5. Ernesto Laclau and Chantal Mouffe, *Hegemony and Socialist Strategy: Towards a Radical Democratic Politics*, 2nd ed. (London: Verso, 1985).
6. Lawrence Grossberg, "On Postmodernism and Articulating: An Interview with Stuart Hall," *Journal of Communication Inquiry* 10, no. 2 (1986): 45–60.
7. Kevin DeLuca, "Articulation Theory: A Discursive Grounding for Rhetorical Practice," *Philosophy & Rhetoric* 32, no. 4 (1999): 334–48.
8. DeLuca, "Articulation Theory," 345.
9. Grossberg, "On Postmodernism," 55.
10. Grossberg, "On Postmodernism," 55.
11. Suzanne Marie Enck-Wanzer, "All's Fair in Love and Sport: Black Masculinity and Domestic Violence in the News," *Communication and Critical/Cultural Studies* 6, no. 1 (2009): 1–18.
12. Daniel A. Grano, "Risky Dispositions: Thick Moral Description and Character-Talk in Sports Culture," *Southern Communication Journal* 75, no. 3 (2010): 263, 256.
13. Abraham Iqbal Khan, "A Rant Good for Business: Communicative Capitalism and the Capture of Anti-Racist Resistance," *Popular Communication* 14, no. 1 (2016): 39–48.
14. Abraham Iqbal Khan, "Michael Sam, Jackie Robinson, and the Politics of Respectability," *Communication & Sport* 5, no. 3 (2017): 331–51.
15. Transcription reported in Ben Eagle, "Richard Sherman Calls Out Michael Crabtree in All-Time Postgame Interview," *Sports Illustrated*, January 19, 2014, https://www.si.com/nfl/audibles/2014/01/19/richard-sherman-michael-crabtree-seattle-seahawks.
16. Joe Tompkins, "A Postgame Interview for the Ages," *Journal of Sport & Social Issues* 40, no. 4 (2016): 291–314.
17. Tompkins, "A Postgame Interview for the Ages," 300–05.
18. Tompkins, "A Postgame Interview,", 291.
19. Daniel A. Grano, "Michael Vick's 'Genuine Remorse' and Problems of Public Forgiveness," *Quarterly Journal of Speech* 100, no. 1 (2014): 86–104.
20. Grano, "Michael Vick's 'Genuine Remorse,'" 82.
21. Brett Michael Dykes, "Anonymous and Humorous, Message Boards Feed Fans' Passion," *New York Times*, November 3, 2012, http://www.nytimes.com/2012/11/03/sports/ncaafootball/college-football-message-boards-feed-fans-passion.html.
22. Dan Patrick Show, *Tyrann Mathieu "Honey Badger" on the Dan Patrick Show (Full Interview)*, YouTube video, 08:00, September 30, 2015, https://www.youtube.com/watch?v=f_hw4tALYwo.

23. Dykes, "Anonymous and Humorous."
24. NFL Films, *The Tyrann Mathieu Story: Born & Bred In New Orleans*, YouTube video, 10:52, January 11, 2016, https://www.youtube.com/watch?v=YVM2TGAIem4.
25. Gary Shelton, "For Tyrann Mathieu, 'Honey Badger' Nickname Is Menacingly Sweet Now," *Tampa Bay Times*, January 6, 2012, http://www.tampabay.com/sports/college/for-tyrann-mathieu-honey-badger-nickname-is-menacingly-sweet-now/1209516.
26. Nate Ulrich, "NFL Rookie Symposium: Cardinals Safety Tyrann Mathieu Says 'Honey Badger' Nickname Could be Revived If He Makes Right Decisions," *Akron Beacon Journal*, June 28, 2013, http://www.ohio.com/sports/browns/nfl-rookie-symposium-notes-cardinals-safety-tyrann-mathieu-says-honey-badger-nickname-could-be-revived-if-he-makes-right-decisions-1.409520.
27. Ulrich, "NFL Rookie Symposium.'"
28. Ulrich, "NFL Rookie."
29. Ulrich, "NFL."
30. Grano, "Risky Dispositions," 263.
31. The Dan Le Batard Show with Stugotz, "Tyrann Mathieu Says 'Honey Badger' Nickname Is Symbolic of Dark Times," *ESPN podcast*, September 29, 2011, https://podfanatic.com/podcast/the-dan-lebatard-show-with-stugotz/episode/lebatard-9-29-15-part-3.
32. Dan Le Batard Show with Stugotz, "Tyrann Mathieu."
33. Le Batard, "Tyrann Mathieu."
34. NFL Films, "The Tyrann Mathieu Story."
35. For example, Pete Prisco, "Honey Badger Don't Care? You Don't Know Anything about Tyrann Mathieu," *CBS Sports*, April 6, 2016, http://www.cbssports.com/general/news/honey-badger-dont-care-you-dont-know-anything-about-tyrann-mathieu/.
36. Grano, "Risky."
37. Grano, "Michael Vick."
38. Khan, "A Rant."
39. Tompkins, "Postgame," 302.
40. Vinnie Iyer, "Tyrann Mathieu Still the 'Honey Badger,' but with a (Honey) Pot of Money," *Sporting News*, August 11, 2016, http://www.sportingnews.com/nfl/news/tyrann-mathieu-arizona-cardinals-honey-badger-contract-training-camp-update-lsu/17k2ngkzedsqv126d2a4kxr0sf.
41. National Collegiate Athletic Association, "Estimated Probability of Competing in Professional Athletics," *NCAA.org*, March 10, 2017, http://www.ncaa.org/about/resources/research/estimated-probability-competing-professional-athletics.
42. Rob Arthur, "The Shrinking Shelf Life of NFL Players," *The Wall Street Journal*, February 29, 2016, https://www.wsj.com/articles/the-shrinking-shelf-life-of-nfl-players-1456694959.
43. Tompkins, "Postgame," 293.
44. Tompkins, "Postgame," 297.
45. NFL Films, "The Tyrann Mathieu Story."

CHAPTER EIGHT

Richard Sherman's Rhetorical Witnessing

ANNA M. YOUNG

Coming off the emotional high of defeating San Francisco for the National Football Conference (NFC) title, Seattle Seahawk Richard Sherman gave a now infamous interview to Erin Andrews in which he announced he was the "best corner in the game," publicly rebuked 49ers wide receiver, Michael Crabtree, for having dissed him earlier, and set Twitter on fire. Richard Sherman was called a "thug" on television 625 times the next day. In response, Sherman stated, "The only reason it bothers me is because it seems like the accepted way to call someone the N-word these days."[1] As Greg Howard writes for Deadspin, "A public personality can be black, talented and arrogant, but he can't be any more than two of these traits at a time."[2] Indeed, black men need to know their place and if they forget for a moment after the joy of victory, the world will soon remind them. Richard Sherman earned a 4.3 GPA in high school, went on to play football at Stanford, and earned a 3.7 GPA, a BA and started an MA in Communication. Richard Sherman is, in his own words, an "All-Pro *mind.*" In this essay, I argue that as a frequent guest writer for publications including Peter King's *MMQB* column on *SI.com*, his contributions to *Huffington Post* and other popular press sites, and his cultivation of his media personality, Sherman has begun to manage a public intellectual space on issues that intersect with sports: masculinity, race, sexuality, money and politics. Most recently, he has called out President Trump for his divisive comments on Colin Kaepernick and others who are protesting racism and police brutality against people of color by taking a knee or abstaining from participating in the spectacle of the national anthem at games. Sherman's public intellectualism is a salient and significant form of witnessing in the black tradition of autobiographic testifying, and counter-narrative to the contemporary iterations of white terror that threaten black agency and legitimacy. More, Sherman-as-testifying-witness provides a productive rhetorical model for the ways athletes of color can enact their own politics in a broader sense.

Instances of white terror are pedestrian these days. Pedestrian is an understatement. Instances of white terror are ubiquitous and escalating. In fact, as I wrote this chapter, Donald Trump used a campaign rally for Republican Senate candidate Luther Strange in Alabama to announce, "We're proud of our country and we're proud of our flag." Continuing, Trump addressed Colin Kaepernick and other players who have kneeled during the anthem at National Football League (NFL) games, recommending that NFL owners should "get that son of a bitch off the field right now."[3] Recently, white supremacists and KKK members marched with lighted torches through the University of Virginia's campus, chanting "blood and soil" and "Jews will not replace us."[4] Similar to mass shootings like Sandy Hook or Emanuel African Methodist Episcopal Church, perpetrators of white terrorist acts are treated as lone operators, singular racists, or people who made an unfortunate mistake (though the victim probably deserved it). In the case of Trump's pronouncement that those who kneel disrespect America, NFL Commissioner Roger Goodell stated, "Divisive comments like these demonstrate an unfortunate lack of respect for the NFL, our great game and all of our players, and a failure to understand the overwhelming force for good our clubs and players represent in our communities."[5] Several NFL owners pushed back against the characterization of players who choose to kneel as unpatriotic, despite the fact that at least 8 of these owners gave $1M or more in support of Trump's inauguration. And yet, even acts of white terrorism committed by a president are bracketed in a category we might call "Trump being Trump" rather than situating Trump as the logical outcome of white supremacist histories, structures, and policies. As Ta-Nehisi Coates so masterfully argues,

> With one immediate exception, Trump's predecessors made their way to high office through the passive power of whiteness—that bloody heirloom which cannot ensure mastery of all events but can conjure a tailwind for most of them…Their individual triumphs made this exclusive party seem above America's founding sins, and it was forgotten that the former was in fact bound to the latter, that all their victories had transpired on cleared grounds. No such elegant detachment can be attributed to Donald Trump—a president who, more than any other, has made the awful inheritance explicit.[6]

Trump does not have a problem with Tim Tebow's kneeling "genuflection," but goes out of his way to vilify black players who dare use their platform to challenge white supremacy.

With the exception of insightful popular and independent media writers like Charles Blow of the *New York Times* and Ta-Nehisi Coates of *The Atlantic* and broadcast media personalities like Joy Reid and Soledad O'Brien, white terror is seen as a discrete loose thread rather than part of the fabric of our national character. And yet, somehow, we continue to be surprised that a black man who dares to be talented and brash and articulate and loud is called a "thug" 625 times in a single day for what seemed to this Seattle fan an appropriately amped post-game interview, dashed with a sprinkling of trash talk and righteous indignation. When people tweeted comments like, "Richard Sherman is a classless hoodrat piece of shit" (@BradEstevanott), "Richard Sherman is definitely in the coon hall of fame" (@Am_AJ), and "Someone put Richard Sherman in an animal hospital because he is a fucking gorilla #noracismintended" (@mmortellito),[7] many people label those one-offs and head to their fainting couches rather than recognizing these tweets as a commonplace articulation of white supremacy.

Of course, Sherman receives racist and racially-tinged criticism all of the time. After posting a new episode of his "Out of Context" video series for the Players' Tribune in which he spoke about the Seahawks' decision to stay in the locker room as a team during the anthem, he received tweets like, "If cops wanted blacks dead, all they'd have do is stop patrolling black neighborhoods and wait,"[8] and "It must suck being black. Nobody trusts black people. They lie! You nags [sic] have no clue about what's going on in the world today! #seachickens."[9]

I opened with the response to Sherman's interview with Erin Andrews because it was what launched him into national fame. What distinguishes the "Sherman incident" from other incidents of white terror is not the speed of the backlash or the nasty character of the racist vitriol flooding broadcast and social media, but rather that racists picked the wrong guy this time. By any traditional metric, Richard Sherman is a very bright man, but more significantly, Sherman is a publicly and civically engaged bright man in an occupation and arena of our culture where we expect an inverse relationship between smarts and size. In other words, I would suggest the severity of the backlash against Sherman in 2014 and today is rooted in his potential for persuasion and change in professional sports, a space where black bodies are owned and traded by white ones and where, if you are a white person, it is perfectly appropriate to wear your jersey, paint your face, and be entertained by black men slamming into one another without giving a second thought to the hegemonic and fundamentally raced character of the NFL and other professional leagues. Billy Hawkins reminds, "the slave plantation demonstrated a relationship of the power white slave owners had over black slaves' labor. This relationship quintessentially represented the complete ownership of the black body and the labor it produced. [The word plantation], though provocative, seeks to capture the relationship where Black males are dispossessed of their athletic labor."[10] And as rhetorical scholar Abraham Khan articulates, professional sports, the NFL included, are part of a larger understanding of the neoliberal market as "the model for structuring all social relations" and a "zone of universal liberty."[11] That is, "the market" is seen not as the means, but as the end—"the market" dictates what is "good" or "bad," "right" or "wrong," "fair" or "unfair." The market, then, becomes disconnected from the people who wield it—in this case, white owners. Richard Sherman makes the masses nervous because they cannot feel superior. As Tim Baffoe writes, "The blob has long enjoyed having that one advantage over athletes—its average intelligence that allows it to work a decent job and provide for a family but otherwise contribute nothing special to the world, to never really think outside the box...The blob has also long hated the group of intelligent people. Smart people hold power, so they must be ridiculed labeled 'nerds' and 'weirdos' to save the ego of the blob."[12] But sport has *always* been a site of political struggle, despite cries for it to be somehow pure or apolitical. The difference with Richard Sherman is in the way he does politics, not that he is political in the first place. Sherman's public intellectualism is a form of witnessing to a set of perspectives that resonates. Sherman scares people because what he does *works*.

In his MMQB column following the Andrews interview, for example, Sherman defended his passion in a thoughtful column writing, "It was loud, it was in the moment, and it was just a small part of the person I am. I cornerback in football, it's with a caveat: There isn't a great defensive backfield in the NFL that doesn't have a great front seven."[13] He hosts a weekly trivia tournament on his website. He created a video series called "Out of Context" that he releases once a week on Twitter. He gives interviews that are polished and thoughtful on a diverse set of topics, and he uses his platform as a Super Bowl champion to engage fans and readers on political and social issues that intersect with sports like homophobia, racism, classism, and other issues of community concern. For instance, in an interview with ESPN radio, Sherman was asked what he would do if elected president. He began by explaining his intention to pay down the deficit, and then launched into a critique of taxpayer-funded stadiums saying, "I'd stop spending billions of taxpayer dollars on stadiums and probably get us out of debt and maybe make the billionaires who actually benefit from the stadiums pay for them. That kind of seems like a system that would work for me."[14] And yet, in his astute critique of Richard Sherman, Abraham Khan argues that Sherman's blackness is rendered invisible because of his public fealty to respectability politics. Khan's point is fair, and we might also note that Sherman's left political flank is taken up by Michael Bennett, making Sherman appear more moderate in a variety of ways. However, I think it is also true that Sherman is acutely market-savvy—he understands what sells and what is a bridge too far—so his activism may not be as radical as Bennett's, but it is more palatable and more marketable to a wider audience, giving him tremendous reach.

There is a Gramscian flavor to Sherman's public intellectualism. Gramsci argued that while all people are philosophers in that they all have "common sense," the collections of beliefs and practices the masses hold as to how the world ought to work in fact subjugate the masses to the ruling class. Organic intellectuals have "good sense," direct "the ideas and aspirations of the class to which they organically belong," perform "an essential mediating function in the struggle of class forces" and provide "theory and ideology (and often leadership) for a mass base of non-intellectuals, i.e., workers."[15] An organic, or public, intellectual is the "thinking and organizing element of a particular fundamental social profession" with a "a conscious line of moral conduct" who "contributes to sustain a conception of the world or to modify it, that is, to bring into being new modes of thought."[16] Although Gramsci's organic intellectual, what today we would call a public intellectual, is understood entirely as a class-based agent, Sherman's public intellectualism is more intersectional, a lived articulation of the overlap of privileges and powers. That is, Sherman helps move audiences from hegemonic common sense to counter-hegemonic good sense because he is able to meet people where they live. His own story of struggle, growing up poor and black in a neighborhood that saw extraordinary violence, his ability to use social and broadcast media because of his scholarly expertise in communication, and his outpouring of energy and time in causes that matter to him are all part of his public intellectual work. Grant Farred emphasizes the power and possibility of a kind of "vernacular" intellectual writing: "(n)ever overlook the vernacular as a means of producing a subaltern or anti-colonial voice that resists, disrupts, subverts, reconfigures or impacts the dominant discourse."[17] Farred articulates the centrality of vernacular to black public intellectuals in particular, that, "In order for a black or marginalized intellectual (more so than for other figures) to be politically efficacious, the historical injunction is overdetermined: vernacularity is an absolute prerequisite."[18] Sherman's ability to vernacularize makes him an adroit public intellectual.

He is also a translator of sorts. Shanara Rose Reid-Brinkley explains that "In interactions with white America, African Americans have often had to speak out of 'two mouths.'"[19] They developed rhetorical practices designed to communicate with white people according to accepted norms of social interaction. The NFL's audience is still more male and more white, and of all professional sports leagues, the NFL enjoys the largest audience share.[20] Particularly germane to this chapter, though, the NFL's viewership skews older than other sports in large part because younger people do not sit down to watch complete games start to finish.[21] So Sherman must reckon with an audience that is statistically more likely to be politically conservative and, for instance, to be against kneeling and other forms of activism seen as "overly political." As a Stanford-educated success, Sherman is able to translate a marginalized experience for a more general audience.

THE TESTIFYING WITNESS

Sherman's public intellectualism is important not only because it stands out in his profession, but also because it is an important form of rhetorical witnessing in the black tradition of testifying. Rhetorical theorist Bradford Vivian argues that witnessing is not limited to singular subjects or even to those who have suffered through history's atrocities. Rather, witnessing is commonplace, "a vital and pervasive mode of influence born in the crucible of modern public culture and intensified in its late modern, or contemporary permutations."[22] In Vivian's conception of witnessing as a commonly deployed rhetorical form, political agents bear witness to "questions of historical representation, delayed justice, and multicultural identity...to address unjust or tragic histories."[23] These attempts to call attention to often egregious wrongs are not the sole provenance of those who experienced the wrongdoing, but can belong to willing representative witnesses who may use a variety of platforms, including mediated ones, to disseminate their narratives. Henry Louis Gates, Jr.'s edited volume, *Bearing Witness: Selections from African American Autobiography in the Twentieth Century*, details the role of witnessing as a meaningfully distinctive practice for black writers and speakers in America. Though his collection highlights autobiographical writings, those writings bear a kind of particular witness to the humanity of the black lived experience. As Gates notes, "If the individual black self could not exist before the law, it could, and would, be forged in language, as a testimony at once to the supposed integrity of the black self and against the social and political evils that delimited individual and group equality for all African-Americans."[24] Autobiography-as-witnessing, then, articulates a "connection among language, memory, and the self" and has been "of signal importance to African-Americans, intent as they have had to be upon demonstrating both common humanity with whites and upon demonstrating that their 'selves' were, somehow, as whole, integral, educable, and as noble as were those of any other American ethnic group."[25] Grant Farred argues that black public intellectual athletes' testifying is integral to their politics. In writing on Muhammad Ali, for instance, Farred asserts Ali's 1967 fight against Ernie "The Octopus" Terrell was not merely a boxing match, but a fight for Ali as a postcolonial political agent as exemplified by his adoption of his Muslim name. Farred notes Ali's renaming "signifies simultaneously the act of negation (of the old) and self-construction (of the new)" and that Ali demanded "not only the right to name himself, but also to be recognized by that name."[26] That is, Ali's testifying bears witness to his vernacular experience as a symbol of black agency and humanity.

Vivian connects witnessing to concerns of public and collective memory, and that sort of witnessing tends to be bound to a specific exigency. That is, a tragedy occurs, and those in its wake provide witness. Gates also identifies the mutuality of witnessing and memory, but argues that black writers and speakers, in this case through autobiography, have adopted witnessing as a rhetoric that establishes an "I am." In this conception, witnessing is a kind of testifying, or what Rosetta E. Ross calls an "uplift practice."[27] Testifying has a long history in the black church, and is generally used in praise, a narration of the ways in which God is at work in a person's life. But as Ross explains, the more contemporary form of testifying mimics slave testimonies. She describes testifying as bifurcated into two parts in which the first involves stating a problem, challenge, or deficit, and the second explores the way God is acting to solve the problem or eliminate the challenge or close the deficit.[28] Said another way, testifying is both witnessing an injustice and offering a response to that injustice. Witnessing is not merely an observation, but is an enactment of political will. Testifying, then, is a rhetoric of agency, not of bystanding.

Working with these frameworks, we might think about witnessing as a public modality, a process "through which individuals and groups engage each other, institutions, and their environment in creating, reformulating, and understanding social worlds."[29] Witnessing entails a responsible subject position, a practice of engagement, and a mode of rhetorical action. Although witnessing requires some democratic postures, it is also a unique public modality through which individuals can act in ways that have the "potential to bolster public life in terms of inclusiveness, diversity, economic justice, and other criteria."[30] Witnessing is a rhetorical act. That is, the witness, having witnessed, gives witness. Giving witness requires that one report what was witnessed and argue for intervention. Unlike the notion of a journalist as witness who merely reports what was observed, the citizen-witness, in this case Richard Sherman, understands himself as responsible for the health of his community and the fairness of the democratic process. Sherman has, therefore, a requirement to do more than merely report; he must also engage in rhetorical exchanges with others. And far from restricting such rhetorical exchanges to engagements with official institutions like the NFL or sports media, the discursive arena in which Sherman gives witness widens to include the many manifestations of vernacular rhetoric, from a story shared between friends over dinner to a Facebook post or blog entry to an op-ed in a prestigious newspaper. In one of his "In this Corner" columns for *Sports Illustrated* titled "Welcome to My League," Sherman articulates what he would do as Commissioner of the NFL. He notes, "It's a difficult job, I'm sure, working for the owners while looking out for the welfare of the players. It always seems like a happy balance is being struck in late April" when draftees are named, "But for the rest of the year it's clear that the interests of the 1700 players pale in importance to those of the 32 owners."[31] He goes on to speak to the system of fining players for violence, the poor handling of retiree benefits in the league, salary, transparency, concussion and head trauma, and ends by saying, "I'd recognize that most of [my players] don't spend more than three years in the NFL, and when they're done, many of them are broken in mind and body, and I'd do everything I could to genuinely help them in their transition from athlete to retiree."[32] Sherman's witnessing as a public modality, then, recognizes the dynamic flux of "the public" as a construct and a material instantiation.[33] In each instance, the important aspect of giving witness is to recount with respect that which was witnessed because one has a responsibility to do so for the good of the democratic community.

In the rhetorical tradition, witnessing is often connected to biblical prophets and the Hebrew traditions of prophesying. Its more contemporary form is the American Jeremiad, for example in Bishop Henry McNeal Turner's "I Claim the Rights of a Man."[34] In prophetic witnessing, a person is chosen by God to serve as a mouthpiece, to condemn those in his community of sin, to demand repentance, and to provide a path to redemption or salvation should the community earnestly absolve itself of sin.[35] As you can imagine, this is not a popular gig. The prophet's entire role is to wait for God to contact him and to let him know who he should berate this time. No one wants to see the prophet coming. So, the role of the prophetic witness is one of burden—the prophet does not choose this path; the path is chosen for him. While witnessing is not in any way limited to religious or biblical instantiations,[36] and while I doubt even Richard Sherman would describe himself as divinely called to testify, the emotional and psychological weight of witnessing is germane. That is, we can understand why so many people who have the same kind of notoriety as Sherman and a similar, or even greater, platform for influence as Sherman, choose not to witness to even enormous injustices. The response to Sherman and witnesses like him is generally immediate and vicious. And in the case of black athlete witnesses, it is frequently violently racist. We do not have to work terribly hard to list athletes who chose to testify or to witness who received vile backlash—Jesse Owens, Jackie Robinson, Muhammad Ali, Tommie Smith & John Carlos, Kareem Abdul Jabbar, Colin Kaepernick. Even if a witness is received without this kind of retaliation, he or she is often met with what I would call a sort of paternalism that would deter testifying or witnessing. If we take athletes kneeling or staying in the locker room during the anthem for instance, protesting athletes hear messages couched as allyship and advice that usually sound something like, "I appreciate what you're trying to do, but I don't agree that kneeling during the anthem is the way to go about it." Certainly there are well-intentioned people out there who may disagree with both means and ends, but the majority of reactions a witness like Richard Sherman draws make the risks of witnessing fraught at best and personally dangerous at worst.

THE WITNESSING BODY

An element of Sherman's particular brand of testifying is that it is embodied. There is a long history in this country of situating the black male body as "buck," as sexually superior, as athletically dominant to white masculinity. This legacy colors black athletes' witnessing in significant ways.[37] In his analysis of Binjamin Wilkormirski's *Fragments: Memories of a Wartime Childhood*, a book that purported to tell the stories of Jewish children during the Holocaust but that turned out to be a fictional telling, Brad Vivian clarifies the role of the body in witnessing. Vivian writes, "Wilkomirski's book unwittingly reveals the primacy of the body as a commonplace of witnessing in modern public culture in the same way that it reveals the primacy of fragmented memory as a commonplace trope of witnessing in public discourse concerning historical and personal trauma."[38] In the sense Wilkormirski centers on, the body is a literal site of trauma, and those who witness the extraordinary bodily trauma inflicted on millions, including millions of Jewish, Roma, and differently abled children during the Holocaust must bear witness to narratives of unimaginable pain. The body functions rhetorically as a topos—a usually metaphorical and in this case literal *place* of memory.

There is a different sense of embodiment in Richard Sherman's witnessing. Witnessing in the commonplace sense means even those who have not experienced trauma or injustice firsthand may serve as witnesses. Sherman speaks on topics with which he has embodied experience like concussions and player safety or having been the victim of police brutality. In these situations, his body serves as a site of memory from which he bears witness to injustice. He places himself, his body, in the way in order to disrupt the status quo and the broader political conscience. He makes himself visible, his body visible as a topos, in a variety of mediated spaces. This embodiment has symbolic resonance for black men in America whose bodies were and are the sites of terrible trauma. Sherman's use of his body as a witness is then more than a rhetorical or persuasive tactic, it is a reclamation of the body as a site of *his own agency*. In the same way that African American autobiography articulates and lays claim to an "I am," Sherman's use of his body as a site of testimony argues that his body is his. He chooses to witness. *He is.*

SUMMARY

Richard Sherman is an All-Pro mind, an athlete at the top of his game who has chosen the very difficult path of outspoken political and social advocate, as witness. While most athletes, even ones with the physical and intellectual talents of Richard Sherman, fulfill their professional duties in silence, isolating themselves from larger political and social concerns, Sherman has taken up the mantle of other black public intellectual athlete witnesses like Muhammad Ali and Kareem Abdul Jabbar. He has become almost as famous for his political activism and savvy as he has for his physical agility and dominance. Certainly, I would argue that the Sherman-as-thug backlash is metonym for the ubiquity of white terror so common in our contemporary moment. But I have also argued that Sherman, though most definitely a victim of racism and white terror throughout his life and professional career, has been admirably successful in his work as public intellectual witness. For Sherman, testifying and witnessing are both nouns and verbs. Sherman is a rhetorical, political, and cultural agent. We may look to Richard Sherman as a productive counter to acts and rhetorics of white terror. Though most people will never enjoy or endure his fame, Sherman's work to meet people where they live, to translate marginalized experiences, to shine a public light on injustice and inequality, to speak in a public vernacular, and to give witness provides something of a blueprint for scholars and activists invested in intervening in and ending the all-too-frequent terrorism of whiteness, and marks a significant topos for articulating the power of Sherman-as-witness and athlete-as-witness.

NOTES

1. Chris Greenberg, "Richard Sherman: Thug Is Now the 'Accepted Way of Calling Someone the N-Word," *Huffington Post*, January 24, 2014, http://www.huffingtonpost.com/2014/01/22/richard-sherman-thug-n-word-press-conference_n_4646871.html.
2. Greg Howard, "Richard Sherman and the Plight of the Conquering Negro," *Deadspin*, January 20, 2014, https://deadspin.com/richard-sherman-and-the-plight-of-the-conquering-negro-1505060117.
3. Fox News, "'Tell That Son of a Bitch He's Fired': Trump Blasts NFL Anthem Kneelers," *Fox News*, September 22, 2017, http://insider.foxnews.com/2017/09/22/donald-trump-blasts-nfl-flag-kneeling-get-sob-field.
4. Meg Wagner, "'Blood and Soil': Protesters Chant Nazi Slogan in Charlottesville," *CNN*, August 12, 2017, http://www.cnn.com/2017/08/12/us/charlottesville-unite-the-right-rally/index.html.
5. Kathianne Boniello, "Roger Goodell Calls Trump's NFL Comments 'Divisive'," *New York Post*, September 23, 2017, http://nypost.com/2017/09/23/roger-goodell-calls-trumps-nfl-comments-divisive/.
6. Ta-Nehisi Coates, "The First White President," October, 2017, *The Atlantic*, https://www.theatlantic.com/magazine/archive/2017/10/the-first-white-president-ta-nehisi-coates/537909/.
7. Samer Kalaf, "Dumb People Say Stupid, Racist Shit about Richard Sherman," *Deadspin*, January 19, 2014, https://deadspin.com/dumb-people-say-stupid-racist-shit-about-richard-sherm-1504843629.
8. Farmer Vincent. Twitter Post. September 30, 2017. 9:06am. https://twitter.com/Capacitor79/status/914159600148021248.
9. Laughing@media2017. Twitter post. September 30, 2017. 9:05am. https://twitter.com/MediaLaughter16/status/914159173725691904.
10. Billy Hawkins, *The New Plantation: Black Athletes, College Sports, and Predominantly White NCAA Institutions* (New York: Palgrave Macmillan, 2010), xi.
11. Abraham Iqbal Khan, "A Rant for Good Business: Communicative Capitalism and the Capture of Anti-Racist Resistance," *Popular Communication* 14, no. 1 (2014): 39–48.
12. Tim Baffoe, "The Scary Smart of Richard Sherman," *CBS Chicago*, January 20, 2014, http://chicago.cbslocal.com/2014/01/21/the-scary-smart-of-richard-sherman/.

13. Richard Sherman, "To Those Who Would Call Me a Thug or Worse," *Sports Illustrated*, January 20, 2014, https://www.si.com/2014/01/20/richard-sherman-interview-michael-crabtree.

14. Eric Edholm, "Richard Sherman to NFL Owners: Keep Taxpayer Money Out of Stadiums," *Yahoo! Sports*, June 10, 2016, https://sports.yahoo.com/blogs/nfl-shutdown-corner/richard-sherman-to-nfl-owners--keep-taxpayer-money-out-of-stadiums-150058211.html.

15. Antonio Gramsci, *Selections from the Prison Notebooks* (New York: International Publishers Co., 1971), p. 3.

16. Gramsci, *Selections*, 9-10.

17. Grant Farred, *What's My Name: Black Vernacular Intellectuals* (Minneapolis: University of Minnesota Press, 2003), 1.

18. Farred, *What's My Name*, 2.

19. Shanara Rose Reid-Brinkley, "Mammies and Matriarchs," in *Standing in the Intersection: Feminist Voices, Feminist Practices in Communication Studies*, eds. Karma Chavez & Cindy Griffin (Albany: State University of New York Press, 2012), 39.

20. Demographic Partitions, "Demographics of Sports Fans in U.S., *DemographicPartitions.org*, July 10, 2017, http://demographicpartitions.org/demographics-of-sports-fans-u-s/.

21. Adam Hartung, "The NFL Has a Bigger Problem Than Kneeling Employees—Demographics and Trends," *Forbes*, September 29, 2017, https://www.forbes.com/sites/adamhartung/2017/09/29/the-nfl-has-a-bigger-problem-than-kneeling-employees-demographics-and-trends/#74f4b41f4efc.

22. Bradford Vivian, *Commonplace Witnessing* (Oxford: Oxford University Press, 2017), 2.

23. Vivian, *Commonplace Witnessing*, 6.

24. Henry Louis Gates, Jr., "Introduction," in *Bearing Witness: Selections from African-American Autobiography in the Twentieth Century*, ed. Henry Louis Gates, Jr. (New York: Pantheon Books, 1991), 4.

25. Gates, "Introduction," 7.

26. Farred, *What's*, 28-29.

27. Rosetta E. Ross, *Witnessing and Testifying: Black Women, Religion, and Civil Rights* (Minneapolis: Fortress Press, 2003), 4.

28. Ross, *Witnessing and Testifying*, 14.

29. Daniel Brouwer & Robert Asen, "Introduction: Public Modalities or the Metaphors We Theorize By," in *Public Modalities: Rhetoric, Culture, Media and the Shape of Public Life*, ed. Daniel C. Brouwer & Robert Asen (Tuscaloosa: University of Alabama Press, 2010), 1-32.

30. Brouwer and Asen, "Introduction," 21.

31. Richard Sherman, "Welcome to My League," *Sports Illustrated*, November 6, 2013, https://www.si.com/2013/11/06/richard-sherman-if-i-was-commissioner.

32. Sherman, "Welcome to My League."

33. Brouwer and Asen, "Introduction," 3.

34. Richard W. Leeman, "Speaking as Jeremiah: Henry McNeal Turner's 'I Claim the Rights of a Man,'" *Howard Journal of Communications*, 17, no. 3 (2006): 223-43.

35. James Darsey, *The Prophetic Tradition and Radical Rhetoric in America* (New York: New York University Press, 1999).

36. Vivian, *Commonplace*, 7.

37. Abby Ferber, "The Construction of Black Masculinity: White Supremacy Now and Then," *Journal of Sport & Social Issues*, 37 no. 1 (2007): 11-24.

38. Vivian, *Commonplace*, 71.

Section III: Confronting Stigmas

CHAPTER NINE

Ableism and Paralympic Politics

Media Stereotypes and the Rhetoric of Disability Sport

JAMES L. CHERNEY AND KURT LINDEMANN

The Olympics play an important role in bringing diverse groups of people together in the spirit of competition. Since their earliest beginnings, the Olympics have been venerated as a time to put aside differences or perhaps settle those differences on the field, court, and track. The Paralympics has a similar history, albeit with initially more emphasis on healing deep societal riffs. Since the introduction of the Stoke-Mandeville Games for the Paralyzed, founded by Ludwig Guttmann as an event concurrently held with the Olympics, the Paralympics has functioned as a way to increase the visibility of disabled athletes[1] and to encourage audiences to view disability sports as elite athletic competitions.[2] Both of these functions rely upon the media attention the Paralympics receives. But while some may adhere to old adage "any publicity is good publicity," the ways in which the Paralympics are covered by the media can have profound, not always positive, implications for the ways disability comes to be understood by audiences. This chapter argues that while mainstream coverage of the Paralympics has increased substantially,[3] its promotion of disability rights and its potential to undermine ableism are undercut by media portrayals that often employ ableist stereotypes that reify negative views of disability.

This conflict between ableist stereotypes and the emancipatory possibilities of the Paralympics amounts to a political struggle over the meaning and value of disability sport and, by extension, over the meaning and value of living with a disability. Widespread ableist assumptions equate having a disability with weakness, incapacity, a poor self-image, and hopelessness. The ableist view perceives life with a disability as less of a life, and sometimes even a life not worth living. Because Western culture traditionally views sports as activities that embody characteristics seemingly opposed to disability, like strength, skill, self-esteem, and optimism, disability sports can operate as arenas that can lead audiences and fans to rethink what they believe about disability. The overwhelming attention given to elite sport makes viewing the Paralympics and similar competitions as elite events particularly significant. Elevation to the elite ranks indicates supreme physical prowess; elite athletes have superior bodies. We view this struggle to change the status of disability sport as articulation, which is the rhetorical practice of shifting the social and cultural meaning of things by changing the contexts and connotations attached to them. Ernesto Laclau and Chantal Mouffe popularized the idea of challenging and disrupting hegemonic views through this discursive practice, which scholars like Kevin DeLuca maintain can reconfigure social reality.[4] In this sense, the conflict that we examine revolves around changing the reality of disability through articulating disability sports as elite athletics.

This political struggle over the articulation of disability sport does not bring into question their value for those involved in competitions. Our sole concern is how the games are perceived, viewed, and understood by able-bodied audiences. We emphatically do *not* argue against the existence of the Paralympics, do not disparage the elite athletes who compete in them, and do not question the value of rewarding the victors. Indeed, the games have numerous benefits, although these benefits are often perceived by audiences in ways that emphasize differences between able-bodied and disabled athletes. For example, in our work with Marie Hardin, we describe a dialectic of Inclusion-Competition that crafts an oppositional relationship based on qualities that undergird disability sport.[5] Substantial evidence shows that disability sport can increase participants' social networks,[6] provide an empowered sense of self,[7] and generally encourage a sense of inclusion.[8] However, competitiveness can disrupt inclusion, as not all participants can be ready and able to play at elite levels, and competitors can dislike their opponents. When able-bodied audiences assume that disabled athletes primarily seek to improve their social networks, the dialectic essentially requires them to assume disability sport features a weakened level of competition.

But, as Paralympic media coverage might reveal to mainstream audiences, disability sport is often played at a highly competitive level. The Paralympics are an elite athletic activity, and athletes who have reached this level participate to compete and win—not simply to feel included in a community or repair a damaged sense of self.[9] Yet stereotypes reifying ableist notions of athletic skill and performance might reconcile such evidence of excellence with negative assumptions about disabled athletes and what motivates them. We see a similar process at work in the gender stereotypes that privilege males and masculinity in coverage of the Olympics. As Susan Eastman and Andrew Billings show in their analysis of the 1994, 1996, and 1998 games, despite increasing parity in the proportion of air time dedicated to men's and women's events, coverage remained biased.[10] In particular, "women athletes were about three times as likely as men (75% to 25%) to be tagged with descriptors about the attractiveness of their faces or manners" (e.g. "beautiful," "elegant," and "charming").[11] These qualities reinforce stereotypical views of women and thus frame women's Olympic performances in ways that contain the threat they pose to sexist beliefs about gender superiority.

We suggest that stereotypes also shape coverage of the Paralympics, thereby diminishing the challenge they pose to ableist assumptions. The text of sport participation—in this case disability sport and the Paralympics—is broader than what is displayed on the court or track, or in the pool.[12] By examining interviews with and "interest pieces" about Paralympian athletes alongside the images used to promote interest in and media coverage of the games, we seek to show how stereotypes limit media coverage's potential to disrupt ableist thinking. Like the coverage of the events themselves, these narratives present disabled athletes in ways that emphasize their heroic struggles to overcome limitations instead of celebrating their athletic accomplishments, which we argue articulates disability sport with ableist perspectives.

TRANSFORMING A CULTURE OF ABLEISM

In shaping the ways that people come to understand and value disability, events like the Paralympics may perform a social function that has received substantially less attention than the potential benefits of the games for the athletes themselves. In general, the games show disabled people as athletic, competitive, victorious, and rewarded. These depictions challenge the conventional ableist view that disabled people are weak and incapable by showing disabled people performing with strength and skill. They show that having disabilities does not necessarily make people feel unworthy, helpless, and pitiable; they show disabled people living full, exciting lives—and valuing them. These images have the potential to undermine ableist perspectives, especially those that assume life with a disability is not worth living. The International Paralympic Committee has identified this "transformational legacy" as a key motive behind the games, which they call the "world's number one sporting event for transforming society's attitudes towards impairment."[13] As such, the Paralympics and similar events could have important social consequences. As Jennifer Hargreaves notes, at their core the Paralympics pose a "challenge to 'ableist' ideology, a reinvention of the (dis)abled body and a redefinition of the possible."[14] In other words, the Paralympics offer an opportunity to rearticulate disability sport by abandoning stereotypes and identifying disabled athletes as elite competitors.

Simply put, ableism, and its widespread influence throughout American culture, remains a serious problem despite years of legislation designed to address the issue.[15] Disability rights activists continue to work toward rectifying misperceptions of disability and their pervasive discriminatory influence on such areas as housing policy and employment, but ableism remains the primary context in which most able-bodied people perceive and understand disability. If sporting events like the Paralympics can challenge misinformed views and biased assumptions about disability, then they might reduce ableism's enduring influence. On the other hand, if watching the games reinforces damaging myths and legitimates discriminatory stereotypes, the games may perpetuate and sustain ableist culture. Such tensions characterize elite-level wheelchair sports, like wheelchair rugby,[16] and this ongoing struggle provides a crucial entry point into media coverage of this and similar disability sports.

Since the overwhelming majority of audiences view, hear, or read about the games through mediated channels instead of attending them in person, whether the Paralympics can undermine ableism on a societal level is largely a function of how the games are depicted and displayed. Otto Schantz and Keith Gilbert argue that "the media coverage of the Paralympics is an indicator of public representations of, and attitudes toward, sport for persons with disabilities." As "the public's knowledge about and attitudes toward individuals with disabilities are mostly constructed indirectly, often by the mass media," such depictions "might serve to change public opinion."[17] But the complex relationship of the games to ableism means that the Paralympics and their media coverage do not necessarily transform the culture, and they may even reinforce an ableist perspective.

The media's key role in the Paralympics' capacity to challenge ableism thus directs our attention to how these games function as what the literature generally refers to as sports "mega events." Researchers contend that such events can have substantial influence over how different groups of people are perceived. For example, Billings and Eastman examined the representation of gender, ethnicity, and nationality in television coverage of the 2000 Summer Olympics.[18] They argue that such stereotypes play an important role for those who watch such "megasporting" events—particularly children and teens who form an especially impressionable segment of the viewing audience—as they can frame such things as viewers' first exposure to people of other nationalities. Billings and Eastman conclude that "the identity stereotypes embedded within the television coverage can readily become this young audience's perception of reality, setting expectations about gender, ethnicity, and national similarities and differences."[19] For many, television coverage of the Paralympics performs a similar function, as viewing the games provides them an initial glimpse of different types of disabilities, prostheses, and adaptive techniques.

THE SUPERCRIP STEREOTYPE

Substantial scholarship has focused on the visual display of disability, including studies that focus on specific disabilities and those that develop comprehensive analyses grappling with the broad issue of how disability in general has been portrayed. Paul Longmore established the conventional approach to the latter by developing a typology of stock disability images, which included the "criminal" and "monster," and by identifying common narratives employing disabled characters, such as the disabled person who seeks suicide as a release from a tragic life and the "portrayal of adjustment."[20] Jack Nelson extended Longmore's thesis and added to the typology by grouping Longmore's "monster" and "criminal" into the category of "threat" and adding four other common stereotypical images: "victim," "hero," "burden," and "one who shouldn't have survived."[21] Other researchers have included stereotypes tied to the theme of pity, such as Johnson Cheu's list of stereotypes that features the "pitiable freak, the charitable, helpless cripple, and the inspirational poster child."[22] As these authors' work shows, such stereotypes inform most of the images of disability found in mainstream media.

Among these, the "supercrip" is one of the most widely encountered stereotypes of disabled people, especially in media coverage of sport.[23] This stereotype extends the "inspirational" quality of the poster child and attaches it to the hero. The stereotype essentially celebrates disabled people—such as athletes—who have "overcome" their disability through exceptional achievement. Cherney, Lindemann, and Hardin describe the supercrip as "an individual who—through courage, dedication, and hard work—accomplishes what is generally seen as the 'impossible' in light of the individual's bodily limitations."[24] In the logic of the stereotype, disabled persons' accomplishments effectively remove the negative association between their disability and their bodies. They remain disabled, but their disability does not matter because they have compensated for it in some way—often exceeding what one might expect from an able-bodied person—and have been validated by that success.

The increasing amount of coverage highlighting disabled peoples' accomplishments does help rectify the discriminatory dominance of able-bodied images and narratives in the mainstream media. Historically, most media outlets have represented disabled characters infrequently, and this absence amounts to a form of social erasure that obscures the importance and prevalence of disability. Many scholars and activists have decried this tendency to ignore disability, which Robert Murphy argues is among the most basic social lessons that many learn in their youth. He notes that "Children are quite understandably curious about disabled people and often stare at them, only to have their parents yank their arms and say, 'Don't look.'" To the child, this command communicates the dangerous idea that "the condition is so terrible that one cannot speak about it or even look at it."[25] Engaging, telling, and displaying the life of a disabled person challenges this inherently discriminatory response.

But *how* one looks at or encounters disability matters at least as much as the act itself, particularly in the context of disrupting ableism. Superficially a positive display, the supercrip ultimately presents disability in a negative light. The supercrip stereotype communicates the idea that the disabled must confront and reject their condition—through rare and superhuman acts of courage or strength—and battle with their bodies.[26] This means the stereotype leaves intact the negative perception of disability itself. Disability still diminishes, devalues, and stigmatizes, but the supercrip has managed to compensate for it—and those who do not do so remain invalid(s). The supercrip is heroic *despite* being disabled, so it does little to encourage people to question ableist perspectives and assumptions.

The supercrip stereotype also isolates the majority of people with disabilities who can never accomplish similar feats, because the distinctiveness and rarity of their acts would be lost to banality if everyone could perform them. Only an elite few people can reach a superlative level, whether they are able-bodied or disabled. The able-bodied audience knows this implicitly when reading about or viewing elite able-bodied athletes, because they encounter able-bodied people every day who are dedicated, talented, and accomplished—yet not super. But the typical able-bodied person does not have such a context for perceiving disabled people, so a focus on the supercrip misleads audiences about what the disabled can do. As Ronald Berger points out, the danger is "that these stories of success will foster unrealistic expectations about what people with disabilities can achieve, what they *should* be able to achieve, if only they tried hard enough."[27]

Berger contends that this "supercrip mystique" encourages public adoption of an ideology centered on the "self-made" person.[28] This frames the disabled body as worthy of attention only when it accomplishes herculean feats of prowess and testifies to the power of the human will. It suggests that disabled people who have not reached such amazing heights have somehow failed. This may make the disabled body more palatable to an ableist audience because it promotes the fantasy that disability can be overcome if only the "afflicted" person would try hard enough. This simultaneously justifies demeaning disabled people who do not accomplish such feats—as the limitations posed by their disabilities become their own fault—and sustains the comforting belief of the able-bodied that they could conquer a physical condition through determination and willpower if they were ever to become disabled themselves. Essentially, these stories reaffirm the ableist bias that "disability is not my problem."

For these reasons, media coverage promoting the supercrip stereotype rearticulates an ableist context for the perception of disabled athletes, which constrains sport's capacity to interrogate ableism. As Carla Silva and P. David Howe explain, it is crucial that we identify and challenge "the pervasive, unreflective beliefs and distortions surrounding disability and its representations in the world of sports," including the supercrip, for the world of sport to transform society.[29] Among disability rights activists and scholars, the supercrip has become one of the most infamous stereotypes. Berger does not overstate the case when he argues that it "is almost universally derided as a figure who is antithetical to the interests of people with disabilities."[30]

We reiterate that we do not critique the Paralympians and other elite disabled athletes who accomplish great things or chase a daunting goal. We critique the stereotype and the way it presents disability in the media. We maintain that the problem with the stereotype is not that it focuses on exceptional accomplishments; rather, our concern is that these accomplishments are viewed as exceptional only within the context of overcoming disability, and not as signs of elite athleticism. Thus the supercrip stereotype actually discourages recognizing that Paralympians are elite athletes who have trained extensively, are extremely talented, and are among a select few who reach these levels of competition. Even when the audience recognizes this, the stereotype suggests that it is not qualities of dedication and talent that make the competitors super. What makes one a supercrip is having these qualities "despite" being disabled. The stereotype articulates elite disabled athletes in a way that fails to disrupt the logic of ableism because it depicts them as heroically overcoming their disabilities, while allowing the perspective that "disability means weakness" to remain intact. Instead of decoupling disability from weakness, the supercrip decouples the athlete from disability.

Thomas Kuhn's famous analysis of the "scientific revolution" provides a useful model for engaging how disability stereotypes work.[31] Kuhn used the term "paradigm" to describe a scientific discipline's coherent set of ideas, theories, and methods at any one time. A scientific revolution is a paradigm shift from one view of the world to another, such as when Western science abandoned the "geocentric" view of the solar system and adopted the "heliocentric" model. The pressure for a shift to a new paradigm arises when discoveries or ideas present confounding puzzles—called "anomalies"—which the old paradigm cannot explain or reconcile. Kuhn notes that when initially encountering pieces of evidence that do not fit with the old paradigm, people usually consider them "novelties" instead of anomalies. Rather than demanding a new perspective, these "strange but true" novelties merely present curiosities that do not expose the existing paradigm's flaws. Thus, a critical point at the start of a scientific revolution is the rhetorical transformation that occurs when scientists begin to view such "novelties" as "anomalies" that require a new way of thinking.

Adopting this terminology, we identify ableism as the current paradigm that dictates how disability should be viewed. For that paradigm to be abandoned, and for a new paradigm to rise, evidence that challenges the ableist perspective must be viewed as an anomaly that reveals the flaws of the ableist perspective. When

disabled athletes' competitions rearticulate athleticism and elite sport performance, they make associating disability with weakness and incapacity untenable.
But viewing these athletes as supercrips undermines their impact on ableist culture, because it isolates them as novelties instead of seeing them as anomalies. The
anomaly of elite disabled athletes presents the ableist paradigm with a paradox that
supercrips do not. Supercrips are novelties because they perform feats presumed
to be "unbelievable" according to ableist assumptions about disability and physical
capacity. Supercrips succeed, then, by overcoming their negative and inherently
disqualifying disabilities; they do not delegitimize the idea that disability ought
to be viewed through an ableist lens focused on physical deficits. The stereotype
deflects the political struggle to rearticulate elite sport to include disability sport,
by rendering the athletes as amazing and heroic exceptions who prove the rule that
disability usually makes people into less capable human beings.

Fortunately, not all depictions, images, and stories about disabled athletes
depend on the supercrip stereotype for their appeal. Images of successful athletes
are distinguished from images of supercrips by the spectacle of "the impossible"
that attracts an ableist eye. Depictions of disabled athletes can receive attention
because they show skilled athletes competing in tests of strength, determination,
training, and talent. Simply put, they appeal to audiences by displaying athleticism. In contrast, depictions of supercrips generate interest because they show
someone exhibiting—according to an ableist worldview—freakish physicality.[32]
A video presents athletes competing in the backstroke as supercrips when it specifically directs attention to the swimmers' lack of arms. No one expects the typical
person to compete like an elite athlete and lacking such ability does not inherently
make someone less worthy. In contrast, supercrip images create unrealistic expectations and devalue disabled people who cannot accomplish similar feats. Not
all swimmers without arms can win Paralympic competitions, but the supercrip
image proves to the ableist what any armless person could accomplish if she or he
would simply work harder at overcoming their condition.

THE SUPERCRIP AND THE 2016 RIO PARALYMPICS

"Human interest" stories in Paralympic media coverage function in complex and
ironic ways, simultaneously undercutting the importance of disability and elevating its status to seemingly insurmountable obstacles in the lives of Paralympic
athletes. The NBC human interest stories of Olympic athletes are a hallmark of
its coverage, as well as that of its affiliates, like CNBC, USA, and Bravo. These
stories are oft-critiqued as superfluous and simplistic, but the network has said
that such stories appeal to female viewers who are more interested in the "journey"
of the athletes.[33] These stories rely on a stock narrative. In this narrative, Olympic

athletes overcome challenges and obstacles to their Olympic dreams that do not always (or even often) have to do with athletic accomplishments. NBC is not the only sports media outlet to promote these stories, but its broadcast rights over the Paralympics ensure the pervasiveness of such narratives on the network and its affiliates. As such, NBC is primarily responsible for broadcasting coverage of the Olympics in the United States, and arguably influences the way other outlets cover the games as well.

The human interest stories of Paralympic athletes follow a similar format and tone. The story of Michelle Konkoly, a US swimmer and former member of the Georgetown University swim team, explains that she fell out of her dorm window and was paralyzed. NBC frames her story as one of overcoming adversity.[34] The clip begins by showing her swimming, her voice-over telling viewers that she "loves the feeling of being in the water" and speaking to swimming's deep meaning for her. She then says "it never crossed my mind that this injury would cause me to give that up." A slow motion video of her swimming then plays in reverse. The video cuts to her face, backgrounded by a pool, explaining how she stood on her desk and opened her dorm room window (as she had many times before) to cool off her room. She slipped and fell five stories. She describes waking up in the trauma center, in severe pain, and feeling shock when the doctors told her she was paralyzed from the waist down. The reporter then describes how Konkoly underwent a series of surgeries to repair her shattered spine and months of rehabilitation to regain the ability to walk. When she rejoined the Georgetown swim team, however, she was unable to be as competitive as she was before the injury. Back at the pool, Konkoly describes this feeling "as a tough pill to swallow" and how coming in last time and time again began to "wear" on her. "But there was hope," the reporter's voice intones, when Konkoly discovered Para swimming. Now hopeful, Konkoly redoubled her efforts and commitment to prepare for "Paralympic glory."

NBC Nightly News profiled the victory of the first US runner to win Paralympic Gold in the 1500 meters, Michael Brannigan, who is Autistic.[35] After shots of Brannigan winning on the track, his old high school classmates cheering him on at home, and his parents telling an interviewer how proud they are of him, a reporter is shown sitting with "Mikey" in the bleachers asking him if Autism makes him a better runner. "A better person," he replies. The reporter repeats these words, more slowly and thoughtfully, as if to make sure viewers understand the profundity of his statement. The story then moves to a history of Brannigan, narrated over photos and videos of him as a child, and describes his early diagnosis with Autism. His mother tells a reporter off-camera that they were told to look into group homes for him. The voice over explains that when he was 7 years old, his parents found a way to channel his energy that had previously caused him to run into walls: a running club for special needs children. Brannigan's father appears on camera, tearing up as he explains that "every time I brought him to a race or practice, he was just a regular kid, and all the other stuff that goes on, everything goes away when he's out on the track." The mother marvels that her Autistic son has taken her all over the world for his competitions. The report voice over says Brannigan will train for the 2020 Olympics in Tokyo and dreams of crossing over to the Olympics. Brannigan says he'll "keep on practicing and improving." "He's already a winner," the reporter concludes.

On the surface, these two narratives seem similar to the traditional NBC human interest stories that permeate their Olympic coverage. But the stories of these disabled athletes present what Longmore called "portrayals of adjustment." In this stock narrative the disabled characters must go through a process of "psychological self-acceptance," spurred in part by non-disabled characters "getting tough" with them, which prompts the disabled characters to become well-adjusted.[36] Longmore's portrayal of adjustment narrative surfaces in the way that both Konkoly and Brannigan are portrayed as using athletics, and Paralympic participation, to adjust to their disability and come to terms with it. Their disabilities are framed as an obstacle they overcome on the way to achieving Paralympic success.

As an obstacle, disability retains its negative status and becomes decoupled from the athletes' success. Instead of serving as integral parts of athletes' identities, their conditions become the very things they must compete against. As a result, these narratives use athletic achievement to undercut the very visibility that coverage of disabled athletes ought to promise. As disabled athletes and disability rights advocates struggle for recognition, and seek to challenge the ableist's impulsive reprimand "don't look," this narrative framing seems to ensure that Paralympic coverage will continue to tell the tiresome story that disability is better when ignored or overcome.

THE LIFE, AND POSSIBLE DEATH, OF A STEREOTYPE

The significance of the stereotype of the supercrip and this stock narrative of the portrayal of adjustment extend beyond undermining the Paralympic potential for promoting social change. Unless they have a specific relationship with a disabled person, uncritical able-bodied media consumers have no reason to reject the ableist implications of what they see on the screen. When audiences repeatedly encounter supercrip stereotypes and portrayals of the adjustment narrative, they can learn to use such frames elsewhere and these become part of how the disabled are viewed and understood in other contexts. Billings and Eastman, in their study of the 2000 Olympics made a similar point: "With repetition over time, differential treatment creates a differential reality ... such perceptions unconsciously get transferred from sports to other arenas, such as business, education, and politics."[37]

One way these frames operate is to make most disabled people and their needs relatively unimportant. As explained above, the supercrip encourages an ableist perspective that discredits disabled people who do not reach superlative heights. The logic of celebrating the supercrip dismisses the everyday disabled body and lets it slip into obscurity, or places it in the context of other damaging stereotypes. Similarly, the portrayal of adjustment suggests that those who do not appear to adjust very well are ultimately responsible for both their conditions and the limitations placed on them by a society primarily built by and for able-bodied people. This positions accessibility and accommodations as things mostly needed by those who have not done their part through heroic adaptations.

Another way these frames work is to constrain the potential of non-stereotypical coverage, images, and stories about disabled people. Even when they do not directly employ common stereotypes or stock narratives, such texts can be interpreted through learned ableist frames. "Yes I Can," the extended-length commercial promoting the 2016 Rio Paralympics, unabashedly and repeatedly displays the supercrip stereotype throughout its 3 minute length.[38] Featuring Australian singer Tony Dee, whose Sinatra-like voice perfectly fits the Sammy Davis Jr. song sung throughout the piece, the video displays images of Paralympic competition spliced with shots of disabled musicians playing the song and clips of disabled people performing everyday tasks. The richly symbolic text deserves a good deal more attention than we can give it here, but its closing caption—"WE'RE THE SUPERHUMANS"—exemplifies the perspectives we engage in this chapter.

In the commercial, the supercrip images craft a frame for viewing the images of non-athletes—disabled musicians, for example, who need not be seen as supercrips—which reduces the potential for anomalous images of everyday people to undermine ableism. Most of the shots of non-athletes feature relatively conventional activities; in one sequence early in the piece a woman works in an office, a girl eats a bowl of cereal, and a mother picks up her child. What makes their acts unusual is that each of them do not have arms and use their bare feet as able-bodied people would use their hands. The woman writes with a pen in her foot, the girl lifts the bowl to her mouth by clutching it in her toes, and the mother raises her infant to a standing position by holding it between her ankles. Similarly, the musicians play their instruments with their feet, prostheses, or partially amputated arms. As the repeated and near constant focus in the commercial suggests, it is these "unbelievable" ways of accomplishing everyday things that deserves attention. If viewed in a different context these subjects' adaptations might be seen as merely interesting or thought-provoking—they might even lead an audience to question its ableist assumptions—but these acts are transformed by the surrounding supercrip images. The images of supercrips emphasize athletes who compete in events that to an ableist seem inherently out of their reach—such as the swimmer who does an armless backstroke, the high jumper who removes his prosthesis and clears the bar leaping with one leg, or the gymnast who turns a one-handed forward handspring. In the context of the commercial's explicit theme of superhumanity, the everyday acts of the office worker, child, and mother become the acts of supercrips who have heroically adjusted to their conditions.

Disabled athletes and the Paralympics need not be presented using the supercrip stereotype and stock adjustment narrative. An example alternative is the Olympic Broadcasting Services' (OBS) video coverage, which presented the Rio Paralympics as elite athletic events. For example, commentary during the hour and a half coverage of the 80 kilogram class Men's Powerlifting competition emphasized the athletes' techniques, training, history of accomplishments, and the rules of the event.[39] The drama in the coverage came from the exertion of lifters' bodies as they pushed personal limits, sought to break the World Record, or had a slight infraction disqualify what otherwise looked like a sanctioned lift. The loudest cheers from the spectators responded to a successful lift that gave the lead to the competitor; failing yet valiant efforts received polite applause and no one was lauded for competing despite being disabled. The lifters were praised for displaying athleticism ("That looks like a very solid opening attempt," "You can see how much effort that took," and "That is a textbook lift—no issues whatsoever"), and not because they seemed incredible. No one made comments like "and what's amazing is that this man was completely paralyzed a year ago," "I can't understand how he can do that," or "what these men do to overcome their disabilities is simply unimaginable." Almost no commentary dwelt on the reason that these athletes were disabled, and the few exceptions were presented as explanations for the amount of time that the athlete had participated in international competition. None of these athletes overcame anything other than the weight they raised on the bar, and the absence of the supercrip stereotype was conspicuous.

The OBS coverage may not have the wide distribution and primetime exposure of NBC stories, but it demonstrates the possibility that disabled athletes can be represented without reiterating a discriminatory framework. Were that to become the standard portrayal, Paralympic media coverage would make an important contribution to the transformation of ableist culture.

(IN)VISIBILITY AND THE PARADOX OF PARITY

The quantity of Paralympic media coverage matters; without it, audiences may not be exposed to images of disabled athletes at all. Yet it is the quality of media coverage that will make the difference in challenging ableist assumptions of disability and disabled athletes.[40] Importantly, critics must consider the formats of such portrayals as well. As we illustrate above, parity and the possibility of resistance seem most evident in the "play-by-play" coverage during the events themselves. These moments offer commentators opportunities to directly focus on athletic prowess and accomplishments as they happen.

Our conclusion extends Eastman and Billings' analysis of gender parity in Olympic coverage. While substantial disparities persisted in the coverage of women and men, and female athletes' looks received more attention than males', they were surprised to find "how similarly women and men athletes were treated in the host and reporter discourse."[41] Paralympic coverage may offer a similar promise with sustained critical attention from media producers. Until then, "human interest" stories may seem like a move toward parity because they feature disabled athletes as they might able-bodied athletes, but these stories may inadvertently reify ableist narratives of disability as an obstacle to overcome, rather than something that is part of an athlete's holistic identity. Overall, this seemingly paradoxical nature of visibility and parity ensures that the Paralympics will remain a contested site of struggle for the communication of a disabled sporting identity.

NOTES

1. We follow many disability scholars and activists and choose to use terms like "disabled athlete" instead of following the conventions of "person-first" language. See James L. Cherney, Kurt Lindemann, and Marie Hardin, "Research in Communication, Disability, and Sport," *Communication and Sport* 3, no. 1 (2015): 18–21.

2. Cheri Blauwet and Stuart E. Willick, "The Paralympic Movement: Using Sports to Promote Health, Disability Rights, and Social Integration for Athletes with Disabilities," *PM&R* 4, no. 11 (2012): 851–6.

3. "NBC Olympics Announces Unprecedented Coverage of Paralympics," *Comcast.com*, September 24, 2013, http://corporate.comcast.com/news-information/news-feed/nbc-nbcsn-to-deliver-unprecedented-live-coverage-of-paralympics; "Rio 2016 Paralympics Smash All TV Viewing Records," *Around the Rings*, March 16, 2017, http://aroundtherings.com/site/A__59449/Title__Rio-2016-Paralympics-smash-all-TV-viewing-records/292/Articles.

4. Ernesto Laclau and Chantal Mouffe, *Hegemony and Socialist Strategy: Toward a Radical Democratic Politics* (London: Verso, 1985); Kevin DeLuca, "Articulation Theory: A Discursive Grounding for Rhetorical Practice," *Philosophy and Rhetoric* 32, no. 4 (1999): 334–48.

5. Cherney, Lindemann, and Hardin, "Research in Communication," 8–26.

6. Kurt Lindemann and James L. Cherney, "Communicating In and Through 'Murderball': Masculinity and Disability in Wheelchair Rugby," *Western Journal of Communication* 72, no. 2 (2008): 107-25.

7. Jeffrey J. Martin, "Predictors of Social Physique Anxiety in Adolescent Swimmers with Physical Disabilities," *Adapted Physical Activity Quarterly* 16, no. 1 (1999): 75–85; Jeffrey Martin, "The Psychosocial Aspects of Youth Disability Sport," *Sport Science Review* 19, no. 5-6 (2010): 49–69.

8. Jeffrey J. Martin and Kerry Smith, "Friendship Quality in Youth Disability Sport: Perceptions of a Best Friend," *Adapted Physical Activity Quarterly* 19, no. 4 (2002): 472–83.

9. See Scott Hogsett's statement in James L. Cherney and Kurt Lindemann, "Sporting Images of Disability: *Murderball* and the Rehabilitation of Masculine Identity," in *Examining Identity in*

Sport Media, eds. Heather Hundley and Andrew C. Billings (Thousand Oaks, California: Sage, 2009), 212.

10. Susan Tyler Eastman and Andrew C. Billings, "Gender Parity in the Olympics: Hyping Women Athletes, Favoring Men Athletes," *Journal of Sport and Social Issues* 23, no. 2 (1999): 140–70.

11. Eastman and Billings, "Gender Parity," 160.

12. Cherney, Lindemann, and Hardin, "Research in Communication," 13.

13. "IPC Strategic Plan: 2015-2018," *Paralympic.org* (2015), 14, https://www.paralympic.org/sites/default/files/document/150619133600866_2015_06+IPC+Strategic+Plan+2015-2018_Digital.pdf.

14. Jennifer Hargreaves, *Heroines of Sport: The Politics of Difference and Identity* (New York: Routledge, 2000), 199; also see Carla Filomena Silva and P. David Howe, "The (In)validity of *Supercrip* Representation of Paralympian Athletes," *Journal of Sport and Social Issues* 36, no. 2 (2012): 180.

15. Tobin Siebers, *Disability Theory* (Ann Arbor: University of Michigan Press, 2008); Fiona Kumari Campbell, *Contours of Ableism: The Production of Disability and Abledness* (New York: Palgrave Macmillan, 2009); James L. Cherney, "The Rhetoric of Ableism," *Disability Studies Quarterly* 31, no. 3 (2011), http://www.dsq-sds.org/article/view/1665; Jay Timothy Dolmage, *Disability Rhetoric* (Syracuse, NY: Syracuse University Press, 2014).

16. Lindemann and Cherney, "Communicating In and Through 'Murderball,'" 120.

17. Otto J. Schantz and Keith Gilbert, "An Ideal Misconstrued: Newspaper Coverage of the Atlanta Paralympic Games in France and Germany," *Sociology of Sport Journal* 18, no. 1 (2001): 69-94.

18. Andrew C. Billings and Susan Tyler Eastman, "Selective Representation of Gender, Ethnicity, and Nationality in American Television Coverage of the 2000 Summer Olympics," *International Review for the Sociology of Sport* 37, no. 3-4 (2002): 351-70.

19. Billings and Eastman, "Selective Representation," 368.

20. Paul K. Longmore, "Screening Stereotypes: Images of Disabled People in Television and Motion Pictures," *Social Policy* 16 (Summer 1985): 31-7.

21. Jack A. Nelson, "The Invisible Cultural Group," in *Images that Injure: Pictorial Stereotypes in the Media*, ed. Paul Martin Lester (Westport, CT: Praeger, 1996), 119-25.

22. Johnson Cheu, "Performing Disability, Problematizing Cure," in *Bodies in Commotion: Disability and Performance*, eds. Carrie Sandahl and Phillip Auslander (Ann Arbor: University of Michigan Press, 2005), 135.

23. Ronald J. Berger, "Disability and the Dedicated Wheelchair Athlete: Beyond the 'Supercrip' Critique," *Journal of Contemporary Ethnography* 37, no. 6 (2008): 647-78; Silva and Howe, (In)validity of *Supercrip*"; P. David Howe, "Cyborg and Supercrip: The Paralympics Technology and the (Dis)empowerment of Disabled Athletes," *Sociology* 45, no. 5 (2011): 868-82.

24. Cherney, Lindemann, and Hardin, "Research in Communication," 14.

25. Robert F. Murphy, *The Body Silent* (New York: Norton, 1990), 130.

26. Silva and Howe, "(In)validity of *Supercrip*,"178.

27. Berger, "Dedicated Wheelchair Athlete," 648.

28. Berger, "Dedicated," 648.

29. Silva and Howe, "(In)validity of *Supercrip*," 176.

30. Berger, "Dedicated Wheelchair Athlete," 648.

31. Thomas S. Kuhn, *The Structure of Scientific Revolutions* (Chicago: University of Chicago Press, 1970).

32. Silva and Howe, "(In)validity of *Supercrip*," 178-91.

33. James Warren, "Is NBC's Olympics Coverage Sexist?" *Vanity Fair Hive*, August 8, 2016, https://www.vanityfair.com/news/2016/08/is-nbcs-olympics-coverage-sexist.

34. "Konkoly's One Paralympic Chance," *NBC Sports.com*, video, 2016, http://www.nbcsports.com/video/michelle-konkoly-sees-rio-2016-her-one-paralympic-chance.

35. "Mikey Brannigan Becomes First American Runner with Autism to Win Paralympic 1500 Meter Gold," *NBC Nightly News with Lester Holt*, video, September 18, 2016, https://www.nbcnews.com/nightly-news/video/mikey-brannigan-becomes-first-american-runner-with-autism-to-win-paralympic-1500-meter-gold-764343363631.

36. Longmore, "Screening Stereotypes," 34.

37. Billings and Eastman, "Selective Representation," 368.

38. Self Confidence Motivation, "Yes I Can—Paralympics Rio 2016—We're the Superhumans!," You Tube video, 5:30, July 18, 2016, https://www.youtube.com/watch?v=vzjuQoNM534.

39. Paralympic Games, "Men's 80kg Powerlifting: Rio 2016 Paralympic Games," You Tube video, 1:29:33, September 12, 2016, https://www.youtube.com/watch?v=MzOh7S4sOZE.

40. Ian Brittain, "Perceptions of Disability and Their Impact Upon Involvement in Sport for People with Disabilities at All Levels," *Journal of Sport and Social Issues* 28, no. 4 (2004): 429–52.

41. Eastman and Billings, "Gender Parity," 164.

CHAPTER TEN

Athletes and Assemblage

Political Struggle at the ESPYs

MEREDITH M. BAGLEY

This chapter examines The ESPYs, ESPN's annual award show, as a contested site of political struggle.[1] While certainly a commercialized space, in recent years the ESPYs has served as a major public, collective, real-time forum for elite athletes to engage issues of social justice. I focus in particular on how the Arthur Ashe Award for Courage opens a space within the ESPYs where elite athletes can express their voices as activists. The 2016 telecast offered the most overt example; in that year, major National Basketball Association (NBA) stars opened the show with a direct message to the audience about gun violence within black communities,[2] and the Ashe Award extended this rhetorical intervention by honoring a black teenage football player killed in a drive-by shooting.[3] The ESPY telecast also occurred days after the shootings of black men by white police officers in Baton Rouge, LA and Tulsa, OK.[4] To some, this marked ESPN's capitulation to "political correctness" or unnecessarily linked sport to "politics."[5] For scholars of sport, politics, and political struggle, these remarkable moments are immediately recognizable as "rhetoric"—but what of prior ESPY telecasts where perhaps more subtle, embodied, conflicted, and contingent political engagements occurred? What happens when we only look for one type of "rhetoric" or "politics" within sport spaces?

The goal of this chapter is to consider the limits and opportunities presented by spaces like the ESPYs telecast. This is not to duck the commercial basis of the event; indeed, I argue that the ESPYs offers us a chance to trace how modes of production, commercial interests, and the rhetorical agency of elite athletes can collide. Specifically, I consider the 2014 and 2015 ESPY telecasts through Deleuze and Guattari's concept of assemblage, defined as the "dynamic collection or arrangement of heterogeneous elements that express a character or identity and assert a territory."[6] Questions that guide this analysis include: How do elite athletes' voices and bodies function within this assemblage? How do sport-rhetoric-politics articulations mobilize political struggle? How might sport-political assemblages shape social change? What insights do these assemblages give us into the power, and limits, of sport rhetoric?

POLITICS AND THE ESPYS

Engaging politics has been part of ESPN's identity from the start, even if in limited ways. From the launch of ESPN's signature show, *SportsCenter*, the network altered the tone of sports commentary, which included the ability to engage the nexus of sport and politics. As Grant Farred states, ESPN offered a "counterdiscourse" within sport that "fashioned itself as a kind of displaced public discourse performed in the realm of cool."[7] This positioning facilitated the network's incredible growth: ESPN launched in 1979, and by 2013 reached 100 out of 108 million cable-subscribing United States homes.[8] In a 2009 volume on sport and cultural studies, theorist Michael Berube pondered the "ESPN-ization of North American sport" media.[9] Throughout this growth, ESPN has navigated a complex relationship to political issues. It drew heavy criticism in 2013 for pulling out of an investigative project on concussions in National Football League (NFL) football.[10] At the same time commentators and competitors have critiqued the network as "too political."[11] Some have pointed to ESPN's shifting financial backing as correlating to vacillations on politics, after a series of financial backers in Disney Corporation purchased the network in 1996 to essentially become the sports arm of the ABC television network.[12]

In 1993 ESPN introduced The ESPYs, mimicking familiar award shows with categories like Best Sports Moment of the Year and Best Male or Female Athlete in a certain sport.[13] For its first nine years the ESPYs aired in early March but in 2001 the ceremony was shifted to early July to occupy a relatively slow spot in the otherwise frenetic American sport media schedule. These calendar considerations are significant; as Whannell reminds us, consumers make choices within the economic structures surrounding them.[14] The ESPY timing is certainly intentional; sport viewers have little else demanding their attention at this time, ostensibly putting a spotlight on the ESPY gala, but the doldrums of summer may also limit the impact of any political statements made during the ceremony.

In addition to the "best of" categories, the network has always presented the Arthur Ashe Courage Award to honor persons of "significant or compelling humanitarian contribution in transcendence of sport."[15] The Ashe award provides one of, if not the highest, points of drama in the telecast, pausing the highlight action reels for a serious focus on "real" issues. Past winners include pioneers and activists such as Billie Jean King, Cathy Freeman, Muhammad Ali, and Tommie Smith and John Carlos. It is here that the most explicit engagement with politics typically occurs during the ESPY telecast.

Despite this, sport rhetoric scholars have paid little attention to The ESPYs. In one of the only scholarly collections to focus on ESPN's communication practices, editor John McGuire goes as far as to suggest that:

> ESPN created an event called "The ESPYs," trying to capitalize on the synergy of bringing celebrities, musicians, and athletes together for a gala awards show that would fill programming slots during the dog days of summer…But there are more important economic, social, cultural, and mass communication impacts of ESPN that must be studied and debated.[16]

To dismiss the ESPYs in this way is to ignore a uniquely productive intersection of popular sport and social justice activism scheduled annually on the most influential source of sport messages in America.

In what follows I engage the 2014 and 2015 ESPY telecasts during which Michael Sam and Caitlyn Jenner were honored, respectively, as the Ashe Award winners. These telecasts attracted millions of viewers and drew a range of critical reaction. While less overtly political than the direct engagement seen in 2016, they merit our attention.

ESPYS AS ASSEMBLAGE

The theoretical framework of assemblage was first offered by Deleuze and Guatarri as part of their larger work on the nature of thought.[17] Developed into a methodological approach, assemblage can capture mass phenomena while still allowing for close reading of texts.[18] Assemblages are comprised of elements such as people, objects, history, or ideas brought into relation to make a concept (or person) comprehensible.[19] As a framework it moves communication research beyond the "monopolistic" triumvirate of transmission, modes, and media that shaped our field.[20] Assemblage allows scholars to identify the relations of meaning that emerge between both structural and symbolic elements in any discursive event.

Assemblage also allows for dialectical materialist critiques of media, in which scholars identify economic trajectories of profit and influence while also allowing for unpredictable messages within pop culture texts.[21] As Wise puts it, "perhaps assemblage is a more complex version of articulation" that includes "qualities, affects, speeds, and densities…flows of agency…and territorialization and expression."[22] Grossberg offers assemblage as cultural studies' version of constructivism and situates it within a commitment to radical contextualization.[23] Without losing attention to processes of production and commercial interest, scholars can drill into the interconnections between textual details and the social forces that surround them. The concept seeks to avoid overgeneralization yet produces systemic insight—what Grossberg calls "anti-anti-essentialism," or the simultaneous denial of a fixed "natural" reality as well as a rejection of "universal contingency" that risks losing sight of embedded systems of privilege.[24] This commitment has value for critical scholars of sport, politics and struggle: there are dominant ideologies and privileged financial positions in nearly every major sport context, but this truth should not lead us to dismiss all of sport as doomed to political captivity, void of potentially productive political struggle.

Engaging frameworks such as assemblage and articulation can help sport scholarship move beyond the "exhaustion of that text-centered social-constructionist paradigm"[25] and into supple yet robust explorations of the opportunities and limitations for political struggle. In assemblage analysis, expectations as to how meanings are interpreted are held at bay, not necessarily precluding critical conclusions but allowing critics to see the full complexity of events and processes.[26] Radical contextualization and a commitment to immanence helps us to move carefully through complex texts like the ESPYs without foreclosing insight into potential social justice engagements despite the obvious commercial trappings of the event.[27] In addition, sport's reliance on bodies—particularly attractive, skilled, physically perfected bodies—can be better documented in assemblage analysis than in traditional communication studies frameworks. This is because assemblage traces how elements intersect "to express meanings of a body, always in a specific time and context".[28] As we work to understand how athletes leverage embodied voice in mediated spaces, analytical frameworks that trace "the state of intermingling bodies, attractions, repulsions, sympathies, penetrations and affects" bear value.[29]

In assessing the 2014 and 2015 ESPYs, I attend to relations of meaning between introduction speakers, video montages, and camera cuts during the telecast and acceptance speeches. After illustrating how these elements connect into meaningful components of an assemblage, I discuss the ways The ESPYs can constitute a complex site of political struggle.

2014: THE ROCK COMES OUT FOR SAM

Michael Sam became a household sports name in February of 2014 when he publicly came out as gay after an award-winning senior season at the University of Missouri.[30] Sam was drafted by the (then) St. Louis Rams in the final round of the draft after a sub-par combine performance (and concerns over anti-gay backlash). The week prior to the draft he was named the Arthur Ashe Award winner. The ESPY telecast occurred at arguably the high point of Sam's media embrace and over two million viewers took in the award show that summer.[31]

Throughout the presentation of Sam's award, we can trace how assemblages both "territoralize" and "de-territorialize" meanings and relations associated with sport, bodies, and sexuality.[32] In many ways, Sam's queer identity is contained within familiar territory, as we might expect at a hyper-mediated, hyper-commercialized event like The ESPYs. The feature video that tells his story encourages viewers to focus on Sam's "fight for survival" amid gang violence and his efforts to "get out of town" and find a better situation via football success. Sam speaks of defying his mom to even play football, showing how desperately he wanted that chance. Sam's sexuality is subtly offered as one reason he needed to flee, though we're told that Sam always knew but did not face "his truth" until college. Meeting his current boyfriend gave him the strength to tell his Missouri teammates he was gay, after which he "couldn't go backwards" and thus plunged into the national media maelstrom. The late draft selection is presented as a disappointment, but the raw emotion when the Rams call is shown as proof of Sam's desire to play in the NFL. The Rams are positioned as welcoming, telling Sam that having openly gay players "will be normal someday"—which ironically underscores the rarity of his situation. Such stories of meritocratic opportunity are common in sport tributes, where hard work and dedication are represented as pathways to acceptance for marginalized people.[33]

Indeed, Sam's speech does not stray from the territory of safe, desexualized "coming out" narratives that align with dominant values. He thanks "father figures" in sport and reiterates the opportunity narrative about college football. In his closing section Sam acknowledges that "my responsibility in this moment in history is to stand up for everyone out there who wants nothing more than to be themselves openly," and expresses pride that his story has already helped prevent queer youth from harming themselves. He closes with a promise to "live up to this honor and become the best football player I can". The relation between football success and gay heroism is synchronized—the same values of hard work and dedication will benefit him in both realms.

However, the presence of Sam's body also "de-territorializes" this normative narrative in several ways. ESPY viewers expect to see, either live or in video, the bodies of awardees during the show, but Sam's image as an openly and actively queer male body has the potential to disrupt the heteronormative space of big-time football. During the video we see original footage of Sam working out, topless in baggy mesh shorts, at a modest football field. The camera angle is low and the focus is soft enough that we can barely even make out his face. The effect is to invoke his nameless past, his humble beginnings. As the story comes into the present day we see action shots from his award-winning season with Missouri, including scenes clearly showing the "C" on his jersey, signifying his status as a team captain and the related support of his teammates. The video closes with Sam in his Rams jersey inside the team's professional facility. The video representation of Sam's body is more complex than the verbal narrative, daring to bring his naked torso to the stage, showing its transformation from undisciplined youth to polished professional. The relation between Sam's developing body and the Ashe award marks out a process of perfecting, honing raw material for elite performance. The attention to, and positive valence of, Sam's body brings a subtle queer reading to the moment, even while it remains anchored to normative markers of sport success.

Other embodied elements add to the potentially productive impact of Sam's award. First, his award is introduced by Dwayne Johnson, a former University of Miami football player who transitioned from WWE professional wrestling—taking the stage name "The Rock"—to become a Hollywood action movie star. Johnson is known for his utterly massive physique and in many ways he embodies hegemonic masculinity. Yet in his on- and off-screen politics The Rock eschews the stigma of male homosexuality, and in his introduction he praises Sam, linking Michael's life to the values of Arthur Ashe before moving easily into a full body embrace of the honoree. The Rock's embrace signifies hyper-masculine acceptance of this openly queer man, performatively challenging both the live and televised audience to do the same.

Sam's race layers into the ESPY assemblage in many ways. Black athletes are consumed, visually and materially, by big-time sports publics in ways that produce economic value for elite white men (e.g. team owners) and that allow cultural dominance in white fan bases. Sexuality and race collide in a variety of ways—at times, and particularly for women, LGBT sexuality is erased or downplayed while for men, particularly men of color, hyper-sexualization can facilitate processes of racial control.[34] Further, The Rock's status as a non-white male (he identifies with Polynesian/Islander heritage), and his affiliation with African-American sport culture, intensify the racial and ethnic meaning-making of the Ashe award. The Rock's literal embrace of Sam challenges the widespread socially constructed view of black men as hyper-masculine and (thus) uniformly homophobic. This association, like all social constructions, has some verity and much exaggeration; scholars of hip-hop culture trace the ways black masculinity and sexuality are in constant negotiation and sport is a prime arena for these ongoing shifts.[35] While the relationship between sport, hip-hop black culture, and non-normative sexualities remains complex, the 2014 ESPY assemblage posed a modest challenge to those communities.

Camera cuts during the telecast of Sam's acceptance speech likewise work in multiple directions to shape the meaning of this ESPY assemblage. At various points of his speech, the camera cuts to white men in the audience, specifically Rams head coach Jeff Fisher and Rams General Manager Les Snead, whose earnest facial expressions imply support for Sam's words about his hopes for a pro career. These white men are given privileged positions within the visual narrative of the telecast, stabilizing Sam's acceptance into upper echelons of sport business and culture. The camera also cuts to openly gay and African American NBA player Jason Collins and openly gay journalist Cyd Zeigler, editor of the longest running queer sports news site, *Outsports*. While these two figures were not identified by Sam in his speech, they provided a broader relation of queer context to Sam's speech that challenged the individuality of his award.[36]

2015: ABBY RE-INTRODUCES "CAIT"

In May of 2015 ESPN named Caitlyn Jenner that year's Arthur Ashe Award winner. This drew criticism from several angles, and with more intensity than the backlash to Sam's award one year prior. Some commentators were opposed to showing support for a transgender person while some disagreed that Jenner had taken "heroic" steps or "transcended" sport in the way that the Ashe Award celebrates. Jenner won a gold medal in the 1976 Olympic decathlon, competing as Bruce, and became a symbol of American triumph. They parlayed that fame into lucrative endorsements, and into popular status as a health guru and reality television star. Critics of Jenner's awardee status focused on her immense wealth, her very new embrace of trans advocacy, and her conservative political leanings. Many surmised that ESPN was interested only in higher ratings by selecting such a controversial person; indeed, 7.7 million viewers tuned in as the telecast was on ABC network airwaves for the first time that year.[37]

The focus of my analysis is not to evaluate Jenner's Ashe bonafides. I am interested in how structural and symbolic elements of The ESPYs can create relations of meaning that challenge cis- and hetero-normative sport spaces. Once again, the bodies on stage played a key role in the overall assemblage created by Jenner's award. In this case, Jenner's introduction was provided by soccer superstar Abby Wambach. Wambach's presence brings three relations of meaning to Jenner. First, Wambach had contemporary star power, having led the U.S. national soccer team to Olympic gold medals in 2004 and 2012 as well as significant World Cup victories. Indeed, weeks after this ESPY moment she would play a senior leadership role on the 2015 World Cup champion team. This linked Jenner to the current U.S. sport landscape, even though three decades had passed since Jenner's own athletic career. Second, Wambach is openly lesbian and has taken overt political stances on topics such as marriage equality. Wambach also played a key part in objecting to the Fédération Internationale de Football Association's (FIFA) decision to allow the 2015 World Cup to be played on turf fields, and she tangled with USA Soccer over compensation rates for women's national team players. Wambach's political stances lent credibility to Jenner's eligibility for the Ashe Award. In her comments, Wambach situated Jenner within the criteria for Ashe Award winners, calling her "courageous" and linking the award to issues facing trans persons such as homelessness, bullying, and suicide. Overall Wambach's introduction bolstered Jenner's ethos by bringing light to sport activism and trans issues.

Finally, extending from the effect of Wambach's sexuality is her gender presentation. Already a tall, strong, fit athlete, Wambach in recent years had foregone the standard soccer player ponytail for a more angular, masculine short hair style.[38] In addition, Wambach's clothing style had favored slim cut slacks, suit jackets, and often narrow neckties or bowties. Indeed, on the ESPY stage she emerged in such an outfit, blending in with the best dressed male stars of the night. In this way Wambach extended the trans challenge of the night, providing audiences with a cisgender but masculine-presenting lesbian. She also, queerly enough, provides a counterbalancing masculinity to Jenner's emphasized femininity; as they stood side by side, Wambach in a suit and Jenner in her sweeping white gown, jewels, and coiffed hair, the pairing evoked heterosexual Hollywood glamour with a 21st century twist. Wambach called Jenner "stunning," signaling her feminine beauty, and close ups during the telecast of Wambach's speech featured primarily strong, hyper-masculine male athletes: Brett Favre, Russell Wilson, Richard Sherman, Derek Jeter, Aaron Rodgers. This backdrop of jock masculinity—whether in male or female form—queered the moment as Jenner swept onto the stage.

Visuals and bodies are at the heart of a second key component of Jenner's Ashe Award assemblage: the feature video. The video works to introduce "Cait" in the same heroic terms that Americans came to know "Bruce"—and Wambach's comments echo this, with promises that "the real story" of achievement is Caitlyln's transformation. The video opens with helicopter footage of Jenner's Hollywood mansion: isolated atop a ridge, its adobe style nearly blending into the singed desert surroundings, a massive wall keeping visitors at bay. With a different climate it could be Superman's fortress of solitude. The voiceover starts with "secrets" and we don't see Jenner's face for minutes. She is shown via mirror reflections, partial shots, as if she is not yet ready for full exposure. The secrecy of Caitlyn is then juxtaposed with a history of Bruce—close ups of him training for the Olympics, his dedication to track and field events, and the tension of elite competition. From the famous laps around the track with an American flag we cut back to the mansion and Caitlyn makes her first appearance—from victorious athlete to transgender icon, from hero to heroine. The film closes with Jenner speaking about her new identity and her "calling" to help others live truthfully in this "social movement." This vow is compromised slightly by shots of Jenner showing off her fully stocked walk-in closet rather than working for trans acceptance. As a whole, however, we are encouraged in the video to see the work ethic of Bruce's Olympic quest to the determination Caitlyn has for her new identity. It is as if ESPN defends its choice by suggesting she *could* become a notable queer advocate—and thus a more fitting Ashe Award winner—due to her Olympic champion past. The standing ovation Jenner receives when walking onstage augments the relations of meaning produced by the video.

Much of Jenner's acceptance speech followed generic standards: she thanked mentors, struck a balance between humility and pride, and pledged to honor Ashe in her actions. Attention to bodies and relations of meaning, however, allow us to see three ways that Jenner's gender transition queers the speech. First, in a floor length white sequined gown Jenner claims solidarity with other "girls" about the pressure of dressing up just right. She then tells the whole women's Olympic soccer team "you clean up well"—a phrase often used as a compliment by sexual admirers. Second, when referencing journalist Diane Sawyer's sophisticated telling of her coming out story, Jenner calls Sawyer "my buddy"—a male colloquialism instead of the earlier "girl" talk. These "little statements"[39] vacillate between female and male subject positions, denying the audience a stable binary gendered subject position through which to understand her appearance. While subtle, these verbal elements introduce the slippery, fluid performance of gender that can destabilize the speech from its initially generic acceptance speech format.

The third place where the speech is rhetorically gender fluid is when Jenner discusses her potential spokesperson role. When she locates this power in her "spotlight" status, acknowledging her celebrity, she emphasizes Cailtyn the Hollywood paparazzi target. However, when she speaks directly to her audience of athlete celebrities, building commonality with them, she reminds us of her male-body sporting past. She says, "As a group, as athletes, how you conduct your lives, what you say, what you do, is absorbed and observed by millions of people." This offers a parallel between the experiences of sport's top athletes, who are primarily cisgender male, and the boundary-pushing experiences of a trans athlete. The second person "you" navigates the transition from "guy like you" to "new woman" today who understands these pressures. Similarly, when Jenner refers to herself as "still learning" to be brave like Ashe, the focus is on Caitlyn the newly-emerged. But when she owns that she is buffered from everyday abuse she pulls from her male-body's sporting past. She says "I owe a lot to sports. It has shown me the world, it has given me an identity. If someone wanted to bully me, well, you know what? I was the MVP of the football team. That wasn't going to be a problem. And the same goes tonight." Jenner's former male athletic prowess will serve her well in her new female manifestation. Jenner makes this clear, stating "If you want to call me names, make jokes, doubt my intentions, go ahead, because the reality is, I can take it." Further, when Jenner transitions to how she will pursue her new spokesperson role she maintains the linkage with sport: hard work, dedication, and training.

Jenner's pledge to fight for trans issues may be unfulfilled, but the rhetorical elements in the speech pull from male and female eras of her life, keeping attention on the remarkable transition from potential jock bully to potential trans protector. Further, the contextual ESPY elements of introduction and feature video add emphasis to issues of non-normative gender identity, expression, and sexuality. The speech closely aligns sport with the strength needed to make courageous stands—a theme that echoes Sam's messages the year prior.

ASSEMBLAGE, SPORT, DISRUPTION

It is clear that The ESPYs can offer rich, complex, layered assemblages of sport rhetoric. Turning to the "overarching structures that express rules and definitions by which elements can become meaningful,"[40] I offer four observations about the tenuous connection between sport and political struggle in spaces like this.

First, throughout all the elements assessed here, neo-liberal ideals territorialize the ESPY stage and restrict the resistive relationships of the awardees. Sam's feature video is strongly rooted in a traditional narrative of individual achievement, overcoming the odds, earning the lucky breaks that can help one person at a time escape systems of poverty, crime, racial privilege, or access to education. Sport is familiarly placed as the route to a better future. Jenner benefitted from normative male success and attempts to convert that social capital to her new trans existence as a type of "role model." These narratives serve ESPN's business model well, presenting "safe" connections to political topics by emphasizing sport's ability to provide for escape or the improvement of one's social standing.

As a countervailing force, however, structures of meaning around the athletic body disrupt and de-territorialize this space and allow more subversive understandings of The ESPYs. Bodies constantly interrupt the smooth narrative of American dreams that Sam's life offers: we see his half naked body in his feature video, in partial focus, from a low angle and at middle distance, creating a sense that he is just out of our view or reach, but nearby. His body is then shown in sharp detail as a football star, a common feature in a sport awards show but also an image that brings an out, gay male body into a taboo space. The camera cuts to audience members who supported Sam, adding to these disruptions. Jenner's body is likewise present but in motion during her feature video, like a surprise guest just around the corner that you can't quite see, building excitement for the full encounter during her on-stage appearance. Her body is presented as successfully passing for a beautiful, attractive woman, and this new identity is sanctioned by the applause of a primarily cisgender heterosexual male athlete audience. They are invited to view her as an object of attraction, and while this structure of viewing and appraisal is familiar, especially to men of privilege, the ESPY stage becomes, for a few moments, a site of queered consumption if not desire. These moments are fleeting, but as Grossberg argues these brief openings can produce a "potentially but never actually chaotic assemblage or articulations of contradictions and contestations."[41] In these spaces of contradiction, change may begin.

Adding to these contradictions is the fact that the awardees' bodies do not function in isolation. Jenner's body is both understood through and destabilized by Wambach's butch lesbian presence near her on stage. Wambach anchors Jenner's femininity through her own masculinity, but as an open lesbian and cisgender female Wambach also queers the moment, perhaps further than Jenner would on her own. Their warm embrace, like the way Dwayne Johnson eagerly embraces Sam, provides an embodied meaning that is at once accepting and destabilizing. In our studies of sport, especially elite celebrity sport, we often isolate the athlete body or voice and expect it to do all the work of de-territorialization alone. The ESPY moments show how interrelations between bodies-in-context must be central to our study of sport and political struggle. We can consider The Rock and Wambach as a "line of flight" moving out and away from the territory of the sport status quo.[42] These lines of de-territorializing are crucial and easy to overlook. Yet, Slack reminds us that "real change in assemblages happens when such lines of flight burst forth, allowing something to escape."[43]

The third observation connects the first two: in both of these Ashe award ceremonies (and in the 2016 ESPY speeches as well) the ideals and practices of sport align with the work of social change. This can occur in "role model" discourse and may thus further contain the threat posed by openly gay, openly trans, or overtly political speech within sport. However, Sam and Jenner also illustrate a link between athletic *praxis* (training, hard work, teamwork, dedication, pursuit of perfection, challenge, transcendence) and the agency necessary for social change. This theme, inasmuch as it can be amplified in a hyper-commercial space such as The ESPYs, may alter the "machine of expression" in which sport operates.[44] It opens up space to think about sport as a cultural realm that can produce activists, world-changers not just world-record-holders.

Finally, I want to suggest that ESPN's carefully cultivated image is also a structure of meaning that needs to be tracked. The Ashe Award constitutes a major avenue for ESPN to navigate this image, and recent ESPY telecasts suggest that ESPN continues to engage political struggle as part of its brand.[45] We know the network's roots of offering "smart" sports commentary and many scholars have argued how its success has led to a watering-down of this effect.[46] Not every Ashe Award winner produces a sweeping critique of American institutions,[47] and we know, of course, that the Ashe Award is highly scripted, planned, staged, and controlled by ESPN's producers. However, the familiar notion of sport as a "platform" on which athletes can bring attention to "worthy" causes cannot be fully contained.

Once a platform exists it can support a variety of topics and structures, and can even be appropriated for expanded reach and change.

CONCLUSIONS

We must take sport rhetoric like The ESPYs seriously. Scholars who have used ESPN's growth and wealth to dismiss its potential to engage with political activism risk throwing the baby out with the bath water. Certainly sport can proffer "false engagement" with politics by elevating idealist narratives of individual achievement through meritocratic processes.[48] But additional effects are also possible, including sustained, systematic, justice-oriented critique. The scripted, flawed ESPY moments of 2014 and 2015 can be viewed through broader frameworks to identify rhetorical resources leveraged at unprecedented levels by athletes in 2016 and beyond.

In the analysis offered here, I do not wish to excuse ESPN from any motivations driven primarily by profit and self-interest. However I also defend The ESPYs as worth exploring. Assemblage shows us how bodies can disrupt status quo meanings, how multiple athlete bodies and voices can combine into messages that contest political issues, and how visual and textual elements combine into complex assemblages. This work answers Whannell's call for sport studies to pay "close attention to the multiple levels in which [sport rhetoric] occurs, to the unevenness, the lack of fit, the discontinuities, the tensions and contradictions…" In these moments, Whannell argues, sport "can never be totally subsumed by commodity, and retains on occasion the ability to offer the sublime and transcendent moment."[49] Sport scholarship provides a valuable reminder of the ways bodies-on-display, while mediated, commodified, objectified and "ESPN-ized," still retain the possibility of rhetorical and political impact.

NOTES

1. The author would like to thank Sydney Brasfield for her help transcribing ESPY telecasts.
2. See *3CK News: NBA Stars address the recent shootings at the ESPY Awards 2016*, YouTube Video, 3:44, July 13, 2016, https://www.youtube.com/watch?v=ZpQ9JWK1djA. Ratings indicate that 5.5 million viewers tuned into the 2016 ESPYs ("TV Ratings Wednesday: ESPYs fall, 'America's Got Talent' leads," TV By The Numbers, July 14, 2016, tvbythenumbers.zap2it.com.)
3. NBA superstar Steph Curry introduced the award, speaking directly about rates of gun violence in black communities. See: *3CK News: Steph Curry Gives an Anti-Gun Violence Speech While Presenting Arthur Ashe Award for Courage*, YouTube Video, 0:49, July 13, 2016, https://www.youtube.com/watch?v=XrOvwbfIJOY&feature=youtu.be. The 2016 Ashe Award was given posthumously to Zaevion Dobson; the tribute video as well as Dobson's mother's acceptance

speech included several overt calls to action regarding gun violence, police violence, and racism in America. The video and her comments can be seen at: *3CK News: Zaevion Dobson honored at 2016 ESPY Awards*, YouTube Video, 12:22, July 13, 2016, https://www.youtube.com/watch?v=zX4qgTGoqOo.

4. Philandro Castille and Alton Sterling were killed in the summer of 2016, bringing to a head protests over police shootings that trace to the killing of Trayvon Martin in 2012, and include the deaths of Michael Brown and Eric Garner in 2015. Six weeks after the 2016 ESPYs, San Francisco 49ers quarterback Colin Kaepernick would begin his season-long protest during national anthems, inspiring dozens of other pro and amateur athletes in similar demonstrations.

5. Parker Lee reviews a range of responses to various decisions ESPN made during 2015–16, including Ashe award winners. See Parker Lee, "How ESPN Went from America's Sports Network to That Guy in the Bar Who Won't Shut Up About Politics," *IJR*, August 31, 2016, https://ijr.com/2016/08/683680-how-espn-went-from-americas-sports-network-to-that-guy-in-the-bar-who-wont-shut-up-about-politics/.

6. Jennifer Daryl Slack, "Beyond Transmission, Modes and Media," in *Communication Matters: Materialist Approaches to Media, Mobility and Networks*, eds. Jeremy Packer and Stephen B. Crofts Wiley (London: Routledge, 2012), 143–58.

7. Grant Farred, "'Cool as the Other Side of the Pillow': How ESPN's *SportsCenter* Has Changed Television Sports Talk," *Journal of Sport and Social Issues* 24, no. 2 (2000): 100.

8. Ray Gamache, "The ESPN Assemblage: The Political and Cultural Economy of Late Sports Capitalism," *Journal of Sports Media* 9, no. 1 (2014): 71–93.

9. Michael Berube, "Afterword," in *Marxism, Cultural Studies and Sport*, eds. Ben Carrington and Ian McDonald (London: Routledge, 2009), 236.

10. In 2013 ESPN was set to collaborate with Frontline for an investigative report on NFL and concussions, but pulled out late in the project. See James Andrew Miller and Ken Belson, "N.F.L. Pressure Said to Lead ESPN to Quit Film Project," *The New York Times*, August 23, 2013, http://www.nytimes.com/2013/08/24/sports/football/nfl-pressure-said-to-prompt-espn-to-quit-film-project.html.

11. ESPN's public editor Jim Brady responded to political tensions within the company at the close of the tumultuous 2016 presidential election; his comments are available at: Jim Brady, "Inside and Out, ESPN Dealing with Changing Political Dynamics," *ESPN*, December 1, 2016, http://www.espn.com/blog/ombudsman/post/_/id/767/inside-and-out-espn-dealing-with-changing-political-dynamics.

12. Getty Oil provided early funding for the novel station. Then a partnership with ABC allowed ESPN to start broadcasting major sports events. Finally, Disney bought both networks. Currently Hearst Media has a 20% interest.

13. The Emmys began awarding sport categories in 1950, and created a standalone Sports Emmy event in 1979. The Oscars have also regularly featured sport-themed films, including Best Picture winners *Million Dollar Baby* (2004), *Chariots of Fire* (1981) and *Rocky* (1976).

14. Gary Whannell, "Between Culture and Economy: Understanding the Politics of Media Sport," in *Marxism, Cultural Studies and Sport*, eds. Carrington and McDonald (London: Routledge, 2009), 72.

15. See www.espn.com/espys. The inaugural Ashe Award winner was cancer-stricken basketball coach James "Jimmy V" Valvano, who gave a passionate speech that has taken its place in sport rhetoric legend. Indeed, in 2007 the ESPYs launched a Jimmy V Perseverance Award, which typically honors a figure battling chronic, serious health conditions.

16. John McGuire, Greg G. Armfield, and Adam Earnheardt, eds., *The ESPN Effect: Exploring the Worldwide Leader in Sports* (New York: Peter Lang, 2015), xiv.

17. Gilles Deleuze and Felix Guatarri, *A Thousand Plateaus: Capitalism and Schizophrenia II*, trans. Brian Massumi (Minneapolis, MN: University of Minnesota Press, 1987).

18. J. Macgregor Wise, "Assemblage," in *Gilles Deleuze: Key Concepts*, ed. Charles J. Stivale (Montreal: McGill/Queen's University Press, 2005), 85.

19. Judy Liao & Pirkko Markula, "'The Only Thing I'm Guilty of Is Taking Too Many Jump Shots': A Deleuzian Media Analysis of Diana Taurasi's Drug Charge in 2010," *Sociology of Sport Journal* 33, no. 2 (2016): 169–71.

20. Slack, "Beyond Transmission," 144–145

21. Gamache, "The ESPN Assemblage."

22. Wise, "Assemblage," 84

23. Lawrence Grossberg, *Cultural Studies in the Future Tense* (Durham, NC: Duke University Press, 2010).

24. Grossberg, *Cultural Studies*, 22.

25. Jeremy Packer and Stephen B. Crofts Wiley, "Introduction: The Materiality of Communication," In *Communication Matters: Materialist Approaches to Media and Networks*, ed. Jeremy Packer and Crofts Wiley (London: Routledge, 2012), 3–16.

26. Liao and Markula, "The Only Thing," 170.

27. For instance, Gamache argues that assemblages contain a "duality" in "offering complex social experience while also profiting off it." See "ESPN Assemblage," 72.

28. Liao and Markula, "The Only Thing," 171.

29. Grossberg, *Cultural Studies*, 37.

30. John Branch, "Michael Sam Proudly Says What Teammates Knew: I'm Gay," *The New York Times*, February 9, 2014, https://www.nytimes.com/2014/02/10/sports/michael-sam-college-football-star-says-he-is-gay-ahead-of-nfl-draft.html.

31. "TV Ratings & Research," ESPN Event Wrap Ups, http://espneventwrapups.com/espys-2014/tv-ratings.

32. Slack, "Beyond Transmission," 153–54.

33. Meritocratic narratives mark much of mainstream sport discourse. Within a queer context, linear narratives of "coming out" are preferred by media and sport communities. See, for example: Joah G. Iannotta and Mary Jo Kane, "Sexual Stories as Resistance Narratives in Women's Sports: Reconceptualizing Identity Performance," *Sociology of Sport Journal* 19, no. 4 (2002): 347–69; Andrew C. Billings, Leigh M. Moscowitz, Coral Rae Marshall, and Natalie Brown-Devlin, "The Art of Coming Out: Traditional and Social Media Frames Surrounding the NBA's Jason Collins," *Journalism & Mass Communication Quarterly* 92, no. 1 (2015): 142–60. Palatable gay and lesbian identities are often understood through spokesperson opportunities. See, for example: Megan Chawansky, and Jessica Margaret Francombe, "Cruising for Olivia: Lesbian Celebrity and the Cultural Politics of Coming Out in Sport," *Sociology of Sport Journal* 28, no. 4 (2011): 461–77. And stable identity categories are preferred over fluid queerness. See Samantha King, "What's Queer About (Queer) Sport Sociology Now? A Review Essay," *Sociology of Sport Journal* 25, no. 4 (2008): 419–42.

34. Intensity of sexuality is a key point of ideological control in discourse of sexuality. LGBTQ persons are often de-sexualized to contain their social threat. See Helene A. Shugart, "Reinventing Privilege: The New (Gay) Man in Contemporary Popular Media," *Critical Studies in Media Communication* 20, no. 1 (2003): 67–91. Conversely, queer bodies, especially nonwhite bodies,

are hypersexualized or fetishized in ways that many scholars see as equally ideological. See, for example, Thomas P. Oates, "The Erotic Gaze in the NFL Draft," *Communication and Critical/Cultural Studies* 4, no. 1 (2007): 74–90.

35. The nexus of race, sexuality, sport and hip hop is vast and complex. Hill (Marc Lamont Hill, "Scared Straight: Hip-Hop, Outing, and the Pedagogy of Queerness," *Review of Education, Pedagogy, and Cultural Studies* 31, no. 1 (2009): 29–54 examines the risk of "outing" that queer men in hip hop face, while Brown (Joshua R. Brown, "No Homo," *Journal of Homosexuality* 58, no. 3 (2011), 299–14) delves into the "linguistic dexterity" required to survive in black hip hop communities. Most recently, Penney (Joel Penney "'We Don't Wear Tight Clothes': Gay Panic and Queer Style in Contemporary Hip Hop," *Popular Music and Society* 35, no. 3 (2012): 321–2) explores disciplinary processes within hip hop as elements of the industry embrace queer style or even openly-LGBT persons or behaviors.

36. His video is also narrated by Jeffrey Wright, the award-winning actor from the television adaptation of the HIV/AIDS-themed "Angels in America." Wright's voice-over is a subtle aural element that adds authenticity to Sam's nascent gay identity.

37. The ratings argument was supported by the 2.2 rating the show earned that year, suggesting 7.7 million people watched Jenner's speech. See "ABC Towers Over Wednesday, with the 2015 ESPYS Dominating the Night," TV By The Numbers, July 16, 2015, tvbythenumbers.zap2it.com.

38. The symbolic and ideological value of the "soccer ponytail" has been well documented. See Helene A. Shugart, "She Shoots, She Scores: Mediated Constructions of Contemporary Female Athletes in Coverage of the 1999 US Women's Soccer Team," *Western Journal of Communication* 67, no. 1 (2003): 1–31, and Jamie Schultz, *Qualifying Times: Points of Change in U.S. Women's Sport* (Urbana, IL: University of Illinois Press, 2014).

39. Slack, "Beyond Transmission," 153.

40. Liao and Markula, "The Only Thing," 171.

41. Grossberg, *Cultural Studies*, 41.

42. Slack, "Beyond," 153.

43. Slack, "Beyond," 153–154.

44. Slack, "Beyond," 155.

45. The ESPYs also have competition: Sport Illustrated launched the Muhammad Ali "Legacy" award in 2014 and now offers its own red-carpet awards show for that and its longer-running Sportsperson of the Year award. SI earned intense media attention in December 2017 when it awarded NFL quarterback Colin Kaepernick its Muhammad Ali "Legacy Award" after two seasons (one unemployed) of spurring anti-racism protests among pro football players. Kaepernick accepted the award wearing all black, his hair combed out into a large afro, and wearing large wooden beads, all visually reminiscent of Black Panther and Black Power icons. See "Colin Kaepernick Wins SI Muhammad Ali Legacy Award," *NBC Sports*, http://www.nbcsports.com/video/colin-kaepernick-receives-si-muhammad-ali-legacy-award-beyonce.

46. Gamache ("The ESPN Assemblage") reports on Farred (2000) moving away from his "cool side of the pillow" comments. Many others have dissected ESPN's ambivalent relationship with politics, such as pulling financial support for the investigative documentary on head trauma in the NFL. The relationship is not simple or necessarily consistent.

47. In July of 2017, former first lady Michelle Obama presented the Arthur Ashe award to Eunice Kennedy Shriver, founder of the Special Olympics. While this cause is typically viewed as far less polarizing than topics of race and LGBTQ persons, the presence of Mrs. Obama brought a risk of politicization to the ESPY stage once again. For video of the award presentation see: Erin

Jensen, "Michelle Obama Stuns in Sleek Cushnie et Ochs Dress for ESPY Awards," *USA Today*, July 13, 2017, https://www.usatoday.com/story/life/entertainthis/2017/07/13/michelle-obama-stuns-sleek-cushnie-et-ochs-dress-espys/474917001/.

48. Gamache, "The ESPN Assemblage," 81.
49. Whannell, "Between Culture and Economy," 84.

CHAPTER ELEVEN

"I'd Just Like to Let Everybody Know"

Pete Harnisch on the Disabled List and the Politics of Mental Health

RAYMOND I. SCHUCK

"Baseball is 90% mental and the other half is physical."[1] So goes a famous Yogi-ism, the name given to memorable quotes from Hall of Fame catcher Yogi Berra, who had a habit of saying things containing elements of wisdom, but the expression of which included grammatical or logical errors. In this case, the statement involves a clear mathematical error, but its kernel of wisdom comes from its recognition that mental aspects constitute a substantial part of playing baseball despite common associations of sports with physicality. Presumably, then, mental health substantially affects the ability to play baseball—something Major League Baseball (hereafter, MLB) has increasingly acknowledged, as evidenced by mental health joining physical health as justification for placing a player on the disabled list (hereafter, DL).[2] As a 2010 *Sports Illustrated* article by Pablo S. Torre suggested, "baseball has led the way in supporting a growing number of players who have been brave enough to seek assistance for such problems and speak out about them."[3]

Yet, while MLB has developed practices and programs to address it, mental health has not always received such support, and progress has depended on players' public admissions of mental health conditions. As Torre quotes psychologist Ray Karensky as saying, "Baseball's older generations like to say, 'Guys these days just aren't as tough.' … But what's different is just that guys have come out and actually admitted their problems."[4] Torre's account highlights such high-profile cases as former Cy Young Award winner Zack Greinke and former Most Valuable Player

Joey Votto, who both publicly acknowledged their mental health conditions in the 2000s. Yet, examination of public admission of mental health conditions can go back to the previous decade when in April 1997 pitcher Pete Harnisch admitted he was on the DL for depression—an admission sportswriter Robert Lipsyte argued "made [Harnisch] something of a mental health role model."[5]

In the following essay, I examine Harnisch's admission as a significant event in the development of sports practices regarding mental health. To do so, I theorize DL placement as a rhetorical event constituting what Mikhail Bakhtin has termed an "utterance," or a basic unit of discourse. I argue that in Harnisch's DL placement in 1997, two utterances occurred: Harnisch's actual DL placement and Harnisch's later explanation that he was on the DL for depression. Focusing on the second utterance, Harnisch's admission, I build from Bakhtin's theorization of utterances as ideological and two sided to examine how Harnisch's admission both advanced discourse on mental health in sport and was constrained in its advancement of that discourse. Specifically, I argue that Harnisch's admission advanced discourse by making discussions of mental health more public and open, allowing further recognition of mental health to occur, while the admission remained constrained by maintaining a focus on individual pathology that did not account for how broader social practices and structures of sport, particularly those based in neoliberal capitalism, affect mental health. Additionally, I situate Harnisch's admission within sport's status as an ideological state apparatus that reifies broader social and political relations. Within that context, I argue that the discursive advancements and constraints of Harnisch's admission contributed to a fuller inclusion of individuals with mental health conditions within the political structures of U.S. society, but those contributions were limited because they maintained focus on individual causes of mental health and did not implicate the effects of neoliberal capitalism's systematic and structural conditions. By illuminating the advancements and constraints in Harnisch's admission, I seek to contribute toward mapping out the terrain of mental health discourses in sport to demonstrate how those discourses have developed and to provide a basis for determining how they might proceed so that sport institutions, including MLB, can foster a culture and enact policies and programs that are more inclusive and supportive of mental health conditions.

MENTAL HEALTH AND SPORTS

While statements such as Yogi Berra's have acknowledged mental aspects of sport, research dating back to at least the early 1990s, particularly in psychology, has solidified the connection. Among that work, Parham finds that numerous factors relating specifically and directly to participation in college sports affected individuals' mental health.[6] More recent work has confirmed similar kinds of findings.[7]

Meanwhile, recent research in fields such as sociology has examined the social and cultural conditions under which sports workers perform. Such research includes demonstration of mental health effects of the "slim to win" ideology central to the culture of swimming, the conditions of touring life for professional golfers, and the loss of "feel for the game" for a stable worker in horse racing.[8] In examining scope and future directions for the study of confluences among mental health and sports work, Roderick, Smith, and Potrac also connect the conditions of sporting work explicitly to broader social structures and the power relations embedded within those structures. As they state,

> Some (sport) psychologists have become revered for their work in tackling so-called "negative" athlete emotions and enhancing performance via various emotional management techniques, yet ironically they are part of a wider system of sport science that has been an essential component in delivering the neoliberal drive for perfection in sport, which underpins in the first instance the generation of anxiety. Little scrutiny has been afforded to the forms of shame, humiliation and fear for those entangled in the process of "measuring up." Examining the structure of feeling in sports work might help expose the hidden injuries of the neo-liberal sports industry and offer a starting point to slow down the dehumanization of high level athletes-as-workers who remain largely silent behind the veil of the dominant cultural ideology of sport: a part of which is that they love what it is that they do and consider themselves privileged.[9]

By connecting athletes' emotional responses and the pressures athletes face to neoliberalism and dehumanization, Roderick, Smith, and Potrac implicate broader political and economic contributors to mental health conditions—a connection also articulated by Wagg, who in analyzing English football, demonstrates how the vocabulary of the free market "finds no place for mental distress, the symptoms of which are instead generally seen as signifying self-indulgence and lack of moral fibre."[10] Research on mental health in sports can thus reveal how structures of neoliberal capitalism, deployed through athletes' emotional experiences including their passion for their work and their motivation to succeed at that work, cultivate environments that produce mental health conditions and attribute production of those conditions to individual pathology.

For baseball specifically, accounts of major leaguers who have experienced mental health conditions have indicated broader elements of sports and particular aspects of baseball that contribute to the players' conditions. Broader sport elements include associations between sports and masculine toughness, pressure of having one's mistakes occur in a highly public forum, and persistent ridicule from fans.[11] Particular to baseball, Torre argues that "baseball … might be the team sport that puts the most mental stress on players" because of the high levels of rate of failure, time to think, and solitude that occur within the professional game.[12] Features such as rate of failure and time between game action may be so foundational to baseball that they cannot be removed (or at least not completely removed); however, baseball organizations can acknowledge these foundational features, develop policies and programs that provide adequate resources for addressing issues foundational features produce, and seek to foster a culture that includes and encourages individuals rather than marginalizing, excluding, and dismissing them. Furthermore, organizations can seek to address how broader pressures of neoliberal capitalism both function through and exacerbate the specific pressures associated with elements of athletes' experiences such as rate of failure, time to think, and solitude.

Rhetorical approaches to the confluence of mental health and sport provide a means of demonstrating how sport discourses and practices create experiences, the processes of acculturation upon which those experiences are constructed, and the pressures that accompany those experiences. Toward that end, communicative and rhetorical research has examined such topics as representations of mental health, forms of mental health discourses, and the rhetorical construction of mental health itself.[13] Limited research in the field, though, has examined the connection between mental health and sport explicitly.[14] My analysis seeks to address that connection and to consider the confluence of mental health and sport as a site of political struggle by examining how even as Pete Harnisch's admission that he was on the DL for depression helped open space for public discourse on mental health, it elided connections to structural influences on his condition and, thus, contained constraints on the discourses it enabled. I specifically argue that even as Harnisch's admission made public the need to recognize the significance of mental health in sports, it framed mental health as a consequence of individual pathology and did not implicate the influences of neoliberal capitalism as manifest through athletes' emotional experiences.

THE POLITICAL SIGNIFICANCE OF MENTAL HEALTH SPORTS DISCOURSES

Rhetorical analysis of sport has demonstrated that sport does both symbolic and material political work as it reinforces, enables, and constructs social and political structures and relations of power.[15] As such, sports can be understood as what Louis Althusser called ideological state apparatuses, which he described as "distinct and specialized institutions" including such aspects of society as education, the family, religion, the arts, and more, as opposed to repressive state apparatuses such as the government, the military, the prison system, the police, and other related institutions that use direct force and violence to maintain structures of power.[16] According to Althusser, ideological state apparatuses "function massively and predominantly *by ideology*, but they also function secondarily by repression, even if ultimately, but only ultimately, this is very attenuated and concealed, even symbolic."[17]

The connection of ideology to symbolic means of articulation corresponds to the work of Mikhail Bakhtin, whose theorization of communication has been connected explicitly to the rhetorical tradition.[18] Bakhtin argued that "any … artistic-symbolic image to which a particular physical object gives rise is already an ideological product."[19] Connecting this argument to communication, he added that "nowhere does this semiotic quality and the continuous, comprehensive role of social communication as conditioning factor appear so clearly and fully as expressed in language."[20] In other words, communicative discourse is inherently ideological. Communication also, according to Bakhtin, occurs in units he termed utterances. An utterance is "a moment in the continuous process of verbal communication," and it can take many forms and sizes.[21] As communication, utterances are ideological, and they reflect and reify the political structures invested within their ideological attachments. Also, according to Bakhtin, an utterance is "a two-sided act. It is determined equally by whose word it is and for whom it is meant. … A word is a bridge thrown between myself and another. If one end of the bridge depends on me, then the other depends on my addressee."[22] As such, utterances can advance interests but are constrained by the need to advance those interests to audiences, with this entire process taking place within the ideological situation in which an utterance has occurred.

Bakhtin's theorization of utterances provides a means through which to understand the political work of the rhetoric of sport, aligning with critical rhetoric, which, as theorized by Raymie McKerrow, has a goal of "demonstrating the silent and often non-deliberative ways in which rhetoric conceals as much as it reveals through its relationship with power/knowledge."[23] In the specific case of discourses on mental health, applying Bakhtin's work can illuminate the advancements and limitations contained within particular utterances, the ideological work regarding mental health performed by those advancements and limitations, and the political ramifications of that ideological work. Such illumination aligns with recognition of the discursive construction of disability and the political implications of such construction. As Wilson and Lewiecki-Wilson suggest,

> How disability is defined and who does the defining have important political and social consequences to stakeholders—in receiving services, seeking protection against discrimination, or suing for compliance under ADA law. … Disability provides one of the best examples of how the language of institutional discourse systems determines material practices in ways that can work to the advantage—and disadvantage—of the disabled person.[24]

Identifying advantages and disadvantages built into disability discourses conveys the kinds of constraints and advancements Bakhtinian analysis can elucidate. Additionally, it can build upon work such as Cherney and Lindemann's analysis of how construction of disability in wheelchair rugby both challenges and reinforces ableist discourses.[25] More specifically in regard to mental health, as Wilson and Lewiecki-Wilson note, reliance in constructions of disability on the mind/body split "reinforces the deep prejudices against disabled people with mental illness and cognitive impairments."[26] As other research on the rhetorical construction of mental illness has shown, such prejudices have led to individuals with mental health conditions facing stigmatization and associated consequences including lack of access to resources and disqualification from holding political office.[27]

THE RHETORICAL ACT OF GOING ON THE DL

Within baseball practice, nothing more explicitly names disability than the act of placing a player on the disabled list. As such, DL placement constitutes a rhetorical act, marking an individual as unable to perform. This act alone creates rhetorical substance by advancing a statement about the individual's ability to perform. Additionally, DL placement typically also includes explanation of why the action is occurring—a reason for going on the DL. This adds to the rhetorical substance of the act by offering an argument to explain the action's need. Indication of the reason for DL placement legitimizes conditions deemed worthy of such placement while delegitimizing conditions not articulated as justifications. When mental health is not available as a means of articulating the reason for going on the DL, the practice delegitimizes concerns about mental performability, reproducing stigmatization of mental disability and reinforcing lack of access to services and resources that might aid in the treatment of mental health conditions. Still, while preceding discourses regarding inability to perform inform an individual utterance of DL placement, the utterance can challenge the preceding structures to advance new and/or alternative discourses.

In practice, the two elements of going on the DL usually work as a single utterance since the reason for DL placement typically accompanies placement itself. Sometimes, though, a DL utterance splits when the reason for DL placement does not come—or does not come in full—alongside actual DL placement. In the case of Pete Harnisch's DL placement in 1997, such a split occurred. The reason he was on the DL was not explicitly stated until three weeks after his team placed him there.

THE CASE OF PETE HARNISCH

Entering the 1997 season, thirty-year-old major league starting pitcher Pete Harnisch had pitched in nine seasons, the last two with the New York Mets.[28] After Harnisch began the season as the Mets' opening day starting pitcher on April 1, just six days later the Mets placed him on the DL.[29] Originally, explanations for the DL placement were vague, with accounts speculating about possible recurrence of Lyme disease as well as loss of confidence and other nebulous reasons.[30] Many accounts linked Harnisch's DL placement to withdrawal he was experiencing after quitting chewing tobacco, with some accounts associating that reason with a larger national social movement against the use of tobacco.[31] Then, during a twenty-minute conference call with reporters on April 25, 1997, Harnisch provided fuller indication of why he was on the DL, saying, "I'd just like to let everybody know I've been diagnosed with depression."[32]

In the following analysis, I examine Harnisch's statements in that conference call. In doing so, I do not have access to a recording of the call. Rather, my analysis must rely on media accounts—specifically, newspaper articles—reporting on the event. While many newspapers around the country mentioned the news, and many carried syndicated accounts of the call, I have culled contents of what Harnisch said from three firsthand reports—one from Rafael Hermoso of the *Bergen County Record*, one from Thomas Hill of the *New York Daily News*, and one from Buster Olney of the *New York Times*. At times I will contextualize my analysis using relevant statements from these reporters; however, my examination focuses on Harnisch's statements during the call and is thus based on what Harnisch himself said. I rely on Harnisch's own words, because as reporters choose what to include and not include in their stories, the possibility remains that Harnisch's utterance did articulate themes I will indicate he elided, and none of the three reporters chose to use statements that included that articulation.

Additionally, I want to make clear that while my analysis will critique Harnisch's utterance and what it failed to address, my analysis is not meant to attack Harnisch himself, nor is it meant to diminish the significance of his utterance and his willingness to make the utterance, both of which I find commendable. Rather, this analysis is designed to articulate the conditions of the utterance, both in terms of how the utterance advanced mental health discourse and how it was constrained in doing so, as would be the case for any utterance. My claims constitute a critique of the ideological milieu within which the utterance occurred—a milieu within which Harnisch's consciousness and the utterances expressing that consciousness appear to have been invested, in line with Bakhtin's point that "the individual consciousness is a social-ideological fact."[33]

In analyzing what Harnisch said, I looked for themes he articulated, which I then examined for elements of advancement and constraint regarding mental health. Three themes arose in the analysis. The first theme is Harnisch's admission that he was experiencing depression, including comments about the timing and/or context of that admission and comments about the symptoms he was experiencing. The second theme includes Harnisch's discussion of his reaction to being diagnosed with depression. The third theme involves Harnisch's statements about his condition, including causes of his depression, details of his diagnosis, and treatments he was undergoing. As my analysis shows, each of these themes contained elements that advanced discourse on mental health while also containing elements that reflected and reinforced constraints on such discourse. Specifically, I identify two major functions of Harnisch's discourse occurring across the three themes: (1) advancement of public discourse through public admission and (2) constraint as Harnisch's utterance did not implicate structures of sport that contribute to mental health conditions.

ADMITTING DEPRESSION

One of the most significant aspects of Harnisch's utterance was his explicit admission he was on the DL for depression. While during the 2000s MLB began to enact policies providing for DL placement explicitly for mental health reasons, in the mid-1990s organizations continued long-time traditions of dismissing mental health and/or seeking to treat mental health conditions as physical ailments. Within the same organizational context and general timeframe as Harnisch, the Mets organization looked only at physical mechanics to treat pitcher Bill Pulsipher, who would later be diagnosed with general anxiety disorder and clinical depression.[34] Harnisch's admission thus advanced discourse on mental health by offering public acknowledgement of his condition and thereby designating the legitimacy of mental health, at least in the form of depression, as a reason for DL placement. Harnisch also stated symptoms he was experiencing, including describing himself as "withdrawn," "having trouble communicating," having "a lot of anxiety," experiencing a "sleeping problem," "not eating," being "down a lot of weight," and feeling "pretty weak."[35] Like admission of depression, Harnisch's statement of these symptoms advanced mental health discourse by making them public.

Yet, Harnisch's admission contained constraints. His description of his symptoms located the condition within himself as an individual without indication of structural conditions of working in sport that may have contributed to them. Meanwhile, Harnisch's admission came eighteen days after he went on the DL. That time gap created a lull during which speculative explanations that might mitigate some of the forcefulness of the admission circulated. Mets general manager Bob McIlvaine had publicly surmised that Harnisch was experiencing a mental health condition.[36] Yet, media discussion of Harnisch had already begun focusing on tobacco, and that focus even framed Harnisch's admission, as he explicitly indicated withdrawal from tobacco had "possibly precipitated" his depression, but was not its sole cause.[37] In addressing the time gap, Harnisch said, "This is the first time I've felt up to talking about it."[38] Here, Harnisch located the reason for the delay within himself rather than implicating baseball and/or sports as contextualizing factors—something he could have done by discussing how the culture of sports stigmatized admitting mental health conditions and/or how the sport of baseball produces solitary isolation that might contribute to anxieties about such admission.

HARNISCH'S REACTIONS

By suggesting this was the first time he was ready to discuss his depression, Harnisch's explanation of the time lag between his DL placement and his depression announcement relayed some of his own reaction to learning of his condition. Harnisch elaborated on his reaction by focusing on his well-being and his desire to return to playing. Among statements addressing this, Harnisch said, "I am feeling better. I've been told to take a certain amount of time for the medication to balance everything out. I feel considerably better than I did two weeks ago. I expect to feel better day by day."[39] Harnisch also said, "I hope to be able to go back on the road soon, get my arm stronger. It's just kind of a day-to-day thing. Over the last six or seven days, I've had some good days and some bad days."[40] Like Harnisch's other statements, these statements advanced mental health discourse by making aspects of Harnisch's experience public, but they also located the condition within himself, focusing on his strength and determination to return, without discussing organizational and cultural barriers such as lack of support resources for dealing with public failure, public humiliation, and periods of inactivity that can cause anxieties to incubate. Perhaps more notable was Harnisch's statement "The way I feel from two weeks ago to now is a drastic improvement. There's nothing seriously physically going on. As soon as I can, I'll be back pitching, there's no doubt about that."[41] This statement forcefully indicated Harnisch would return, and it occurred within the context of Harnisch acknowledging he was receiving treatment; however, by stating "There's nothing seriously physically going on," Harnisch reified the privileged status of the physical over the mental. If mental health occupied an equal position of legitimacy as physical health, mention of the physical would be unnecessary. Harnisch's statement thus emphasized physical performability as mattering more, relegating mental health to a personal obstacle he must overcome, as opposed to physical conditions as obstacles that can stem from the sport itself.

Harnisch also said, "I've never really thought about depression at all. You know what the word means, but I never thought about the actual condition" and "I can't say I ever really consciously thought about it. Sure, I've had some rough nights sleeping in the past. I never really thought I'm a different person than normal. I never considered that."[42] Acknowledgement that he had not thought about depression before could advance mental health discourse by implying people should think about these kinds of conditions and/or be prepared to confront them. Yet, by suggesting his depression made him "a different person than normal," Harnisch's statement stigmatized mental health and attributed his condition to individual abnormality rather than recognizing structural issues of sport such as hegemonic masculinity and neoliberal preoccupations with specialization and productivity that enforce particular conceptualizations of the normal. Harnisch's statement also enacts the kind of self-disciplining suggested by Wilson and Lewiecki-Wilson when they state that the mind/body split "pressures persons with disabilities to compartmentalize the disabled 'part' of themselves as separate from some essential, nondisabled self."[43]

CAUSES, DIAGNOSIS, AND TREATMENTS

As mentioned, Harnisch recognized that accounts of his DL placement had framed it in terms of tobacco withdrawal, and he indicated doctors informed him that while quitting tobacco contributed to his depression, it was not considered the cause. Harnisch identified a "chemical imbalance" as a cause and added, "It's hard to pinpoint exactly why it happened or what caused it. They feel maybe it's been coming for a long time. But there's no way to quantify the time. It's just gotten severe the last several weeks."[44] Harnisch also referenced family history as a contributing factor doctors had identified, elaborating by saying, "I'd rather not go into that, but there is some, yes, and the doctors feel that has something to do with it."[45] These statements publicly acknowledged causes such as chemical imbalance and family history. Additionally, given public movement against tobacco occurring at the time, quitting tobacco provided a convenient excuse for admitting depression. By disassociating his condition from that cause, Harnisch offered legitimacy to mental health itself as a reason for limitation on his performability. However, these statements also located his depression within himself as an individual without indicating how structural aspects of sport such as solitude, inaction, and public failure without organizational support resources may have contributed to his condition. Ironically, because Harnisch's utterance happened at a time when baseball was recognizing more fully how the culture of the game contributed to tobacco usage, the tobacco explanation might have offered a less constrained route for implicating the sport.

Additionally, Harnisch acknowledged the specific treatments for depression he was undergoing, which included a combination of therapy and medicine. As Rafael Hermoso summarized, Harnisch "has been taking two anti-depressant medications for the past 2 1/2 weeks and is undergoing therapy with his own doctors ."[46] Again, explicit acknowledgement of mental health treatment offered legitimacy to mental health discourse. Yet, Harnisch also made a point to indicate his depression was not manic depression.[47] Such indication constrained advancement of mental health discourse by offering only limited legitimacy for mental health conditions. Perhaps Harnisch was differentiating his form of depression from a more serious form of depression, akin to differentiating a physical injury from a more serious physical injury. However, Harnisch's disassociation from manic depression, at least in part, stigmatized manic depression as an assumedly less viable and acceptable mental health condition. Juxtaposed against Harnisch's statement about the "normal," mention of manic depression further distanced manic depression from the ability to be "normal," as if a person who is normal can return from Harnisch's form of depression, while manic depression marks an individual as definitively abnormal.

Meanwhile, as Hermoso's, Hill's, and Olney's reports corroborated, Harnisch indicated he was receiving treatment from his own personal physicians, not Mets team physicians.[48] This statement conveyed the Mets organization's failure to address mental illness effectively, which may be the most salient part of Harnisch's utterance for implicating the structures of sport, as it provided a moment upon which to develop a larger criticism of how the culture of baseball—and of sport in general—has failed to address anxiety, depression, and similar kinds of conditions. Yet, this implication was mitigated by indication that no doctor had a clear sense of how to diagnose and treat Harnisch's condition, represented in Hill's summation that "Harnisch revealed that doctors expressed some uncertainty about how to treat his depression and that he had 'no exact course of treatment.'"[49] That even Harnisch's personal doctors had no clear treatment for him reveals the extent to which, as a society, the United States in 1997 lacked understanding of and support for mental health, a situation correlating with how other institutions such as the military treated mental health at the time.[50] As such, Harnisch's statement called attention to lack of cultural and organizational mental health support, but by offering a sense of a broader societal lack, the statement elided specific lacks endemic to sport in general and baseball in particular.

POLITICAL IMPLICATIONS

More than two decades after Harnisch's conference call, on February 14, 2018, a 19-year-old man killed seventeen people in a school shooting in Parkland, Florida—adding yet another incident to the recent history of U.S. mass shootings. In the discursive cycle that followed, some commentators, often seeking a scapegoat to deflect attention from gun use, suggested the need to address mental health to stop this kind of violence. These commentators included U.S. President Donald Trump, who raised the issue of mental illness in his first public comments on the shooting.[51] Yet, the federal budget proposal Trump had just submitted contained significant reductions in mental health support, including cutting $665 million from the Substance Abuse and Mental Health Administration and decreasing the National Institute of Mental Health's funding by 30 percent.[52]

This juxtaposition typifies a neoliberal position that acknowledges mental health's significance but leaves mental health treatment to individual action and decreases government assistance—and thus societal assistance—for addressing mental health. Aligning with the kinds of advancements and constraints I have discussed, Trump's position publicly recognized mental health as a legitimate concern but relegated that concern to individuals and lessened recognition of societal impacts. It seems inaccurate to characterize Harnisch and MLB as having the same position as Trump. Harnisch's statements did draw slight attention to his team's lack of resources, and he did not advocate removal of resources the way Trump's budget proposal did. Meanwhile, since Harnisch's utterance, MLB has added programs and practices that address mental health. Harnisch's 1997 team, the Mets, are among the many teams that have added mental skills coaches, and heading into the 2018 season, the Mets restructured their medical department, moving away from an old model relying on trainers and seeking a more all-encompassing view of player needs. That said, under the restructure, the department is headed by a "director of high performance."[53] Given its emphasis on "high performance," that position title suggests the move could end up reinforcing pressures of neoliberal capitalism rather than addressing them.

Meanwhile, Trump and many of his supporters have quite willingly invoked sports' roles as ideological state apparatuses when it has suited their interests, most prominently when arguing that athletes must stand for the performance of the national anthem. Such arguments rely on acceptance of sports' symbolic and material contributions to society. Similarly, as baseball and other sports address mental health, their practices and policies contribute to broader attitudes and perspectives on mental health. Insofar as Harnisch's conference call influenced the trajectory of mental health practices in baseball and other sports, it reinforced an emphasis on individual pathology that did not implicate neoliberal capitalist effects on work and life experiences. Accordingly, we would do well to examine the programs and practices MLB and other sports have developed since Harnisch's utterance to determine the extent to which they maintain and/or have moved away from the messages his utterance offered, for sports organizations' messages contribute to the ideological milieu from which Trump and others throughout U.S. society draw as they address mental health in not just sports, but all areas about which they invoke the topic.

NOTES

1. Nate Scott, "The 50 Greatest Yogi Berra Quotes," *USA Today*, September 23, 2015, http://ftw. usatoday.com/2015/09/the-50-greatest-yogi-berra-quotes.

2. Jay Cohen, "Baseball Offering More Mental Health Support to Players," *Yahoo Sports*, April 10, 2015, https://sports.yahoo.com/news/baseball-offering-more-mental-health-support-players-065303072--mlb.html.

3. Pablo S. Torre, "A Light in the Darkness," *Sports Illustrated*, June 21, 2010, https://www.si.com/vault/2010/06/21/105951448/a-light-in-the-darkness.

4. Torre, "A Light."

5. Robert Lipsyte, "Harnisch a Reluctant Role Model," *New York Times*, November 22, 1998.

6. William D. Parham, "The Intercollegiate Athlete: A 1990s Profile," *The Counseling Psychologist* 21, no. 3 (1993): 411–29.

7. For example, Yulia Gavrilova, Bradley Donohue, and Marina Galante, "Mental Health and Sport Performance Programming in Athletes Who Present Without Pathology: A Case Examination Supporting Optimization," *Clinical Case Studies* 16, no. 3 (2017): 234–53.

8. Jenny McMahon, Kerry R. McGannon, and Chris Zehntner, "Slim to Win: An Ethnodrama of Three Elite Swimmers' 'Presentation of Self' in Relation to a Dominant Cultural Ideology" *Sociology of Sport Journal* 34 (2017): 108–23; John Fry and Daniel Bloyce, "'Life in the Travelling Circus': A Study of Loneliness, Work Stress, and Money Issues in Touring Professional Golf," *Sociology of Sport Journal* 34, no. 2 (2017): 148–59; and Deborah Butler, "Regaining a 'Feel for the Game' Through Interspecies Sport," *Sociology of Sport Journal* 34, no. 2 (2017): 124–35.

9. Martin Roderick, Andy Smith, and Paul Potrac, "The Sociology of Sports Work, Emotions and Mental Health: Scoping the Field and Future Directions," *Sociology of Sport Journal* 34, no. 2 (2017): 102.

10. Stephen Wagg, "'With His Money, I Could Afford to be Depressed': Markets, Masculinity and Mental Distress in the English Football Press," in *British Football and Social Exclusion*, ed. Stephen Wagg (London: Routledge, 2004), 108.

11. Shirley Wang, "Professional Baseball Faces Loaded Issue: Mental Health," *Wall Street Journal*, July 1, 2009; and Pablo S. Torre, "Dangerous Minds," *Sports Illustrated*, August 15, 2011, https://www.si.com/vault/2011/08/15/106097861/dangerous-minds.

12. Torre, "A Light in the Darkness."

13. Examples include Catherine Prendergast, "On the Rhetorics of Mental Disability," in *Embodied Rhetorics: Disability in Language and Culture*, ed. James C. Wilson and Cynthia Lewiecki-Wilson (Carbondale, IL: Southern Illinois University Press, 2001), 45–60; Nicole E. Hurt, "Disciplining Through Depression: An Analysis of Contemporary Discourse on Women and Depression," *Women's Studies in Communication* 30, no. 19 (2007): 284–309; Davi Johnson Thornton, "Race, Risk, and Pathology in Psychiatric Culture: Disease Awareness Campaigns as Governmental Rhetoric," *Critical Studies in Media Communication* 27, no. 4 (2010): 311–35; Maureen Donohue-Smith, "Telling the Whole Story: A Conceptual Model for Analysing the Mental Illness Memoir," *Mental Health Review Journal* 16, no. 3 (2011): 138–46; and Cathryn Molloy, "Recuperative Ethos and Agile Epistemologies: Toward a Vernacular Engagement with Mental Illness Ontologies," *Rhetoric Society Quarterly* 45, no. 2 (2015): 138–63.

14. Kristen Harrison and Barbara L. Fredrickson, "Women's Sports Media, Self-Objectification, and Mental Health in Black and White Adolescent Females," *Journal of Communication* 53, no. 2 (2003): 216–32.

15. Examples include Michael L. Butterworth, "The Politics of the Pitch: Claiming and Contesting Democracy Through the Iraqi National Soccer Team," *Communication and Critical/Cultural Studies* 4, no. 2 (2007): 184–203; Michael L. Butterworth, "Purifying the Body Politic: Steroids, Rafael Palmeiro, and the Rhetorical Cleansing of Major League Baseball," *Western Journal of Communication* 72, no. 2 (2008): 145–61; and Barry Brummett, ed., *Sporting Rhetoric: Performance, Games, and Politics* (New York: Peter Lang, 2009).

16. Louis Althusser, "Ideology and Ideological State Apparatuses (Notes Towards an Investigation), " in *Lenin and Philosophy, and Other Essays*, trans. Ben Brewster (London: New Left Books, 1971), 136–7.

17. Althusser, "Ideology," 136-7.

18. John M. Murphy, "Mikhail Bakhtin and the Rhetorical Tradition," *Quarterly Journal of Speech* 87 (2001): 259–77.

19. V. N. Vološinov, Ladislav Matejka, and I. R. Titunik, trans., *Marxism and the Philosophy of Language* (Cambridge, MA: Harvard University Press, 1973), 9.

20. Vološinov, Matejka, and Titunik, *Marxism*, 13.

21. Vološinov et al., 95.

22. Vološinov et al., 86.

23. Raymie E. McKerrow, "Critical Rhetoric: Theory and Praxis," *Communication Monographs* 56, no. 2 (1989): 92.

24. James C. Wilson and Cynthia Lewiecki-Wilson, "Disability, Rhetoric, and the Body," in *Embodied Rhetorics: Disability in Language and Culture*, ed. James C. Wilson and Cynthia Lewiecki-Wilson (Carbondale, IL: Southern Illinois University Press, 2001), 10–11.

25. Kurt Lindemann, "'I Can't Be Standing Up Out There': Communicative Performances of (Dis) Ability in Wheelchair Rugby," *Text and Performance Quarterly* 28, no. 1–2 (2008): 98–115; and James L. Cherney and Kurt Lindemann, "Sporting Images of Disability: *Murderball* and the Rehabilitation of Masculine Identity," in *Examining Identity in Sports Media*, ed. Heather L. Hundley and Andrew C. Billings (Los Angeles: SAGE, 2010), 195–215.

26. Wilson and Lewiecki-Wilson, "Disability, Rhetoric," 10.

27. Examples include Cynthia Lewiecki-Wilson, "Rethinking Rhetoric through Mental Disabilities," *Rhetoric Review* 22, no. 2 (2003): 156–67; and Jenell Johnson, "The Skeleton on the Couch: The Eagleton Affair, Rhetorical Disability, and the Stigma of Mental Illness," *Rhetoric Society Quarterly* 40, no. 5 (2010): 459–78.

28. "Pete Harnisch," *MLB.com*, http://m.mlb.com/player/115487/pete-harnisch.

29. Buster Olney, "Troubled Harnisch Put on Disabled List," *New York Times*, April 8, 1997.

30. Examples include Marty Noble, "Mystery Illness/Harnisch Returns for Diagnosis," *New York Newsday*, April 7, 1997; and Buster Olney, "Harnisch Struggling After Quitting Tobacco," *New York Times*, April 7, 1997.

31. Examples include Buster Olney, "Quitting Smokeless Tobacco Exhausts Harnisch," *New York Times*, April 3, 1997; Judy Battista, "Pete's Perils Not Unusual, Doctors Say," *New York Newsday*, April 8, 1997; and Alan Truex, "Trying to Kick the Habit Costs Harnisch His Confidence," *Houston Chronicle*, April 13, 1997.

32. Buster Olney, "Harnisch Says He Is Being Treated for Depression," *New York Times*, April 26, 1997.

33. Vološinov et al., *Marxism*, 12.

34. Torre, "A Light in the Darkness."

35. Olney, "Harnisch Says"; Rafael Hermoso, "Harnisch Ailing from Depression," *Bergen County Record*, April 26, 1997; Thomas Hill, "Harnisch Reveals Depression," *New York Daily News*, April 26, 1997.

36. Buster Olney, "Harnisch Struggling."

37. Hill, "Harnisch Reveals."

38. Hill, "Harnisch."

39. Hill, "Harnisch."

40. Olney, "Harnisch Says."

41. Hermoso, "Harnisch Ailing."

42. Hermoso, "Harnisch;" Olney, "Harnisch Says."

43. Wilson and Lewiecki-Wilson, "Disability, Rhetoric," 10.

44. Olney, "Harnisch Says"; Hill, "Harnisch Reveals."

45. Olney, "Harnisch Says."

46. Hermoso, "Harnisch Ailing."

47. Olney, "Harnisch Says."

48. Olney, "Harnisch;" Hermoso, "Harnisch Ailing"; Hill "Harnisch Reveals."

49. Hill, "Harnisch Reveals."

50. Charles W. Hoge, Christopher G. Ivany, Edward A. Brusher, Millard D. Brown, John C. Shero, Amy B. Adler, Christopher H. Warner, and David T. Orman, "Transformation of Mental Health Care for U.S. Soldiers and Families During the Iraq and Afghanistan Wars: Where Science and Politics Intersect," *American Journal of Psychiatry* 173, no. 4 (2016): 334–43.

51. Brian Naylor, "Trump Calls for Steps That Make 'A Difference' on School Shootings, Without Specifics," *NPR*, February 15, 2018, https://www.npr.org/2018/02/15/586009781/president-trump-to-address-the-nation-on-florida-school-shooting.

52. Vanessa Romo, "Trump Calls for Mental Health Action After Shooting; His Budget Would Cut Programs," *NPR*, February 15, 2018, https://www.npr.org/sections/thetwo-way/2018/02/15/586095437/trump-calls-for-mental-health-action-after-shooting-his-budget-would-cut-program.

53. James Wagner, "Mets, Playing Catch Up, Hire Specialist to Avert Injuries," *New York Times*, January 12, 2018, https://www.nytimes.com/2018/01/12/sports/mets-fitness-expert.html.

CHAPTER TWELVE

When Sport Facilitates Saying the Unsayable at the Boundaries of Race and Sexuality

Jason Collins and Michael Sam

BARRY BRUMMETT

Sport in American life is a terrain that facilitates thinking about multiple categories and dimensions of athletes and fans. We may know that an athlete is a football player but also a Christian, sometimes ostentatiously so. Another athlete is a tennis player but also LGBTQ. Yet another athlete is known for prowess on the field but also for championing causes for social diversity. Sport is also a site in which social change, and a shifting in our social categories, is more visible than in other terrains. If women are becoming more involved and successful in society, we will see that powerfully represented in sport. Change as represented in sport is more likely to be shown to us in our living room than is change in, for instance, business. Joan next door coming out as queer is smaller public news than is a major athlete doing the same thing. When Michael Sam, the first openly gay football player ever drafted into the National Football League (NFL), kissed his boyfriend on national television (an event I discuss below), one commentator called it "my sports moment of the year, hands down."[1] Note that the kiss itself was not in any kind of sport setting, but sport as an institution framed the change in social mores that it reflected. It will be bigger news when a variety of sexualities, gender identities, and so forth are exposed and perhaps socially accepted in sport than in everyday life. This is because sport is connected to so many dimensions of experience and is seen by so many. As a spectator experience, it facilitates the viewing of social issues that emerge within its frames.

In this chapter, I argue that the intersection of a multiplicity of social categories, especially when those categories are shifting, facilitates the saying of what is otherwise often socially unacceptable. I want to suggest that discourse at the borders of human categories, especially the borders of changing, morphing categories, is a kind of discursive outlaw space for saying what we generally would not say. Just as one could claim that the election of Donald Trump fed oxygen to hateful and oppressive speech, so can the creation of such outlaw spaces on the boundaries empower saying the unsayable. Boundaries can thus undermine civility, decorum, and public discourse. Discourse emerging from boundaries therefore has political consequences. Using the two examples of Jason Collins and Michael Sam, I want to suggest that sport is a site for saying the unsayable at the borders of shifting categories, especially around sexuality and race.

THE DIALECTIC OF SOCIAL RELATIONS AND CHANGING HUMAN CATEGORIES

A key theme in the thinking of rhetorical theorist Kenneth Burke is the idea that discourse and its structures tend to slide into each other. Come up with a scheme to organize categories of people, or even of discourse, and because of the nature of language, thinking in terms of one category within the scheme will inevitably morph into another category. Ambiguity is the essence of language. We can rarely (perhaps never) say just what we mean, Burke argues. "Accordingly, what we want is *not terms that avoid ambiguity*, but *terms that clearly reveal the strategic spots at which ambiguities arise*."[2] Burke made that statement in introducing his famous pentad. What he means is that terms in the keys of act, agent, agency, scene, and purpose are all miscible with each other. Start talking about the nature of an act and soon you will be discussing the nature of the agent performing the act, and so forth. Another example of Burke's idea of moving from one category of language to another is found in his "Four Master Tropes," of which he says, "I refer to metaphor, metonymy, synecdoche, and irony.... . Give a man [sic] but one of them, tell him to exploit its possibilities, and if he is thorough in doing so, he will come upon the other three."[3]

Everybody manipulates categories within different social structures linguistically. When we do this using the terms we have for different human categories, we might call that the dialectic of social relations. We are all of us caught up in this ongoing dialectic in which we categorize ourselves and others according to schemes we find socially useful and important. These categories change and merge into other categories, in ways described by Burke. Of course, those categories themselves get redefined from time to time. In terms of sexual orientation, greater awareness of a wide variety of orientations has, over the last few decades, resulted in increased divisions of that overall category and a proliferation of sub-categories as reflected by the term, LGBTQ. Increased awareness and acceptance of multiracial people follows the same process. Increasing public awareness of the porous and unstable nature of racial categories is weakening the venerable system of racial identification in the United States and other countries. The categories we use in a dialectic of social relations always show some degree of fluidity and instability. Another way to put this is to say that discourse about human categories often tends to shift toward the borders of those categories where change is taking place vis a vis other categories.

When we consider how people are at the intersection of many dialectical categories, interactions among these categories can create great social complexities. Let me propose a thought experiment: Hold in your mind one social category and come up with a list of widely attributed qualities for that category. So, what are widely attributed properties for being white? Now complicate that by juggling two or three such categories together at the same time. What are white, straight, rich people widely supposed to be like? It won't do to refuse stereotyping in this case because that is what we all do so as to navigate our social worlds. Such questions are asked in the media all the time about political constituencies (who did Roy Moore appeal to in Alabama, what is Trump's base, and so forth). I believe in this thought experiment you will begin to sense some instability in those categories, you will have many "well, it depends" moments.

There is another important dimension of this dialectic of social relations, and that is what may be said permissibly in social circumstances. We all know what is civil and acceptable to say out loud, in the presence of others, about different ethnicities, class positions, sexualities, and so forth. Our dialectic of social relations is more comfortable negotiating single categories at a time. At any given social and historical moment, there are things about our categories that may not be talked about with ease and frankness. These are results of the stereotypes and innuendoes that haunt our discourse. All our categories come with politically and socially "incorrect" baggage, but what conditions bring that baggage out onto the loading dock? Burke describes this sense of how things ought to be as "piety," the preservation of which upholds received social arrangements, while impiety is subversive.[4] For Burke, piety is very much a matter of constructing or deconstructing categories, and thus it is a matter of the borders between them.

I think it can be shown, and this study is an attempt to do so in a limited way, that when we begin combining these categories in thought or discourse, the unsayable comes closer to the surface of public utterance. The unsayable may be more easily facilitated in sport because it is a site of multiple, intersecting categories.

You might think of "white" all day and know that one is "not supposed" to say certain things about a category of people. Similarly, we know what to say and not to say when we think of "poor" people. But when we start to think of "poor + white," can't we feel negative stereotypes pushing themselves closer to the tongue? Why might this be true, rhetorically and linguistically? One example may be found in a commentary cartoon showing two working class men drinking at a bar and disparaging Michael Sam's coming out. Clearly, the working class clothing, "gimme" ball caps, and portly physiques instruct us to read the men as poor. It is clear that two of the three are white, which then leads to further implications and associations. One man's pants are sliding down over his bottom, and so the commentator remarks "Because of the perspective, we don't see the butt crack, but we know it's there and it is revealed."[5] And beyond what is revealed is what may then be said: people know what to attribute when multiple categories are invoked.

I think there is a propensity of the discursive location of borders that destabilizes categories, or perhaps shows more clearly a destabilization that is underway, and with the destabilization comes a greater willingness to say the unsayable. When we move from speaking of white people to the border between white and poor, derogatory thoughts of hillbillies, rednecks, trailer park trash, catfish noodling, and the like can, I think, be shown to be facilitated precisely by being on the border. These things may or may not be said aloud, but audiences will say them in their heads enthymematically, and will be attuned to hints and implications.

All of this brings us to sport, which is, and for the last few decades of American life has been, a major site of intersectionality. Sport is where different categories of human identity are put into play with each other and made visible. Bodies, with markers of race and gender at least, are more visible than they are at the office.[6] The physical markers of at least gender and race are more visibly available for remarks in sport. Ever since major league sports began to be racially integrated, ever since issues of female participation in sport began to be socially and legally discussed, ever since athletes from other countries began to arrive on American playing fields, sport has been a place where the public can hardly avoid thinking of athletes—and perhaps of sport itself?—as A + B. The unsayable begins to edge into public discourse when the borders among categories destabilize our understandings of those categories. For example, Jon Entine's book, *Taboo: Why Black Athletes Dominate Sports and Why We Are Afraid to Talk About It*, clearly references the unsayable at the borders of sport.[7]

If athletes have "always" been white, or male, or straight, then the rise of athletes of color, or of athletes who are female, or of different sexualities, will destabilize categories and thus draw forth the unsayable more vigorously, I think, than discourse in most other sites of American life. We have reached the point where a prominent blogger can proclaim, "I try to be mindful about and supportive of efforts to eliminate discrimination and promote equality regarding race and ethnicity, regarding sexual orientation; regarding gender; and regarding socioeconomic class."[8] As the public observes intersectionality in the spectacle of sport, the public can work out its own shifting allegiances and identifications.[9] Sport is a major site for participants and spectators alike to work out their identities. Those identities are often grounded, as Thomas Oates observes, in the categories of "race, gender, class, and sexual identities." And Oates adds that sport, football in particular, strongly facilitates discussions of sexuality.[10] Abraham Khan also notes many examples of how sport facilitates saying the unsayable, the politically incorrect, about gayness. [11] I want to offer two cases studies that illustrate this happening, both related to the outing as gay of African American athletes: Michael Sam and Jason Collins.

In the spring of 2013, National Basketball Association (NBA) player Jason Collins announced he is gay. The act of outing oneself, or another, is an act of manipulating categories. We have categories of sexual identity, and to claim this or that identity is to declare membership in a category. Collins announced a category of sexual orientation in which he now included himself. Hitherto, if anyone thought about it, they might have likewise included him in a different category, that of being straight. But nobody is in only one category; we have many alignments, and whether our various categories align or not is a matter of the dialectic of social relations in which we constantly engage. Because being gay was not a category typically aligned with the category of professional athlete, or even African American, his announcement caused a short-lived stir in the media.

COLLINS'S STATEMENT OUTING HIMSELF

In April of 2013, Jason Collins issued a statement on the *Sports Illustrated* website in which he outed himself.[12] He begins by immediately identifying himself with three categories: "I'm a 34-year-old NBA center. I'm black. And I'm gay." In doing so, he announces the three social categories that would structure his statement. But the rest of his statement explores the boundaries and intersections among those categories, and he does so in two main ways.

First, Collins employs a number of terms and metaphors that referenced the crossing of borders. He refers to his "journey of self-discovery," and of course a journey often involves crossing borders. He talks about his "double life" of crossing between the borders of being gay but appearing straight. He references two of his categories—professional sports and sexual identity—in declaring himself "a free agent, literally and figuratively," and freedom is a state in which one can move and cross boundaries. He refers several times to the spatial metaphor of "coming out," which implies the crossing of a border if only the threshold of a closet. His first mention of coming out occurs in the same paragraph where he makes the first of two mentions of the 2011 NBA "lockout," thus making the move of coming out reverberating with the condition of being locked out. This coming out was a "sweet release," which he compares to being "in the oven, baking," and then being freed. To emerge from an oven or a closet is almost certainly a kind of boundary crossing.

I find it telling that, in his statement, Collins references his twin brother, beginning a story about being born first by joking, "When I came out (for the first time)..." In telling the birth story, he acknowledges that the very common lack of boundaries between brothers dissolved into some distance as his gay identity developed into a contrast to his heterosexual brother. Collins also discusses his family's intentional introduction of his brother and him to different cultures and experiences, an "early exposure to otherness," which bespeaks boundaries between differences.

A second way in which Collins explores the boundaries and intersection among his multiple identity categories in the statement is by talking about more than one category at once. He juggles three main categories in writing, "After I was traded by the Celtics to Washington in January [sports], I took a detour to the Dr. King memorial [race]. I was inspired and humbled. I celebrate being an African-American and the hardships of the past that still resonate today. But I don't let my race define me any more than I want my sexual orientation to [sexuality]. I don't want to be labeled, and I can't let someone else's label define me." Note the tension of his beginning announcement of precisely those labels and yet his discomfort with staying within those boundaries even as he shows his travels across them. This acceptance and refusal of categories is echoed in his aside to Shaquille O'Neal, who once had attributed Collins's "flops," or dramatic collapses during games, to his sexuality. Collins asserts, "My flopping has nothing to do with being gay," and he further insisted that, by being an aggressive player, "I go against the gay stereotype."

In another paragraph of the statement, Collins references sport and sexual identity together in saying, "My one small gesture of solidarity was to wear jersey number 98 with the Celtics and then the Wizards. The number has great significance to the gay community," because of the infamous murder of Matthew Shepard in 1998, a young gay man beaten to death for his identity.

RESPONSES TO COLLINS: SHERMAN ALEXIE

If you google "Jason Collins outing" or a similar string of terms you will get a sense of the explosion of commentary in the media, blogs, and online to his statement. Of course, the comments displayed a whole range of reactions. I want to focus on one remarkable blog by Sherman Alexie, on the blog site *The Stranger*, and to an even more remarkable cartoon illustration for that article by Mark Kaufman.[13] I present this article and cartoon not as the finest example of commentary I could find, but as an illustration of how talk at the borders dances around sensitive issues *and* may be facilitated by borders as well.

Alexie invokes the same intersections among categories as Collins, thus referencing the same borders. His first sentence links sexual identity with sport, two of Collins's three categories, beginning with the words "As a straight-boy jock... ." The same two categories are later introduced at the same time when Collins describes himself as "a heterosexual lifelong basketball player." He defines expectations for his sexual identity by noting that "we straight boys aren't supposed to think of other men as beautiful." All three of Collins's categories are referenced in describing Collins as "the Jackie Robinson [race] of homosexual [sexual identity] basketball big men [athlete]."[14]

Alexie plays along the intersections of these three categories to enable talk that one does not very often observe in mainstream media or discourse, and that talk is to sing the homoerotic praises of athletes. Alexie does this through insisting on his own heterosexuality at the same time that he swoons for male athletes. He is able to express vigorous homoerotic feelings by clinging to the conventionally defined intersection of athletes and sexual identity.

Alexie admits to a fair bit of homoerotic behavior in his own life, while constantly reminding us that he is straight. As a long-time frequenter of gyms, he has "seen a lot more cock and man-ass than many gay men." He claims that "gay men have hit on me." Speaking from the borders, he is enabled to hint that gay men can be sexually aggressive. On the one hand, he denies that "gay men hunger for" straight men. On the other hand, he reports a history of gay men making sexual advances toward him, whispering room numbers at hotels and leaving keys with him, or pushing a "crotch against my blue-jeaned butt." He discusses these experiences explicitly in terms of crossing the borders, observing that "men are boundaryless animals." He was most likely referring to a crossing of boundaries between gay and straight, but his comment illustrates all the more clearly how talk located at any border facilitates saying what cannot otherwise be said, such as discussing being hit upon by other men. Yet we are constantly (even feverishly) reminded that he is straight. In talking about spectators looking at professional athletes' superb bodies, he claims, "It might not be homosexual, but it certainly is homoerotic." And, in expressing his "pride" in Collins's self-outing, he claims, "I was aroused, politically speaking."

Clinging to his claims of his own hegemonic sexual identity, Alexie defines professional sport as a homoerotic experience in which male-to-male gaze and physical fetishism is commonplace: "When we're talking about professional athletes, we are mostly talking about males passionately admiring the physical attributes and abilities of other males." He argues that basketball is especially a sport that invites homoerotic gazes because of the scanty clothing worn by the athletes, compared to other sports. Collins himself is a "highly attractive dude." Indeed, as the article title proclaims, "Jason Collins is the Envy of Straight Men Everywhere." That envy arises because, Alexie claims, even he "wants to be sexually objectified by women. And men. Truly, when it comes down to it, don't we all want to be universally desired?" I don't think we have to make much of a stretch to connect envy to penis envy, and from there we are not far from stereotypes and allegations, otherwise often unsayable, about the sexual prowess of African American males.[15]

There is one more important component of this article that I want to mention because I think it very clearly references a theme that everyone knows of but few, if any, will say in public. That component is the remarkable cartoon by Mark Kaufman that accompanies the article. It shows a shower room scene in which four men stand facing the viewer. Three of the four are African American. One is close enough to the front frame of the image that his body is hidden from the midriff down, and he has his arms crossed. The other two African American men have their hands over their genitals. Oddly enough, nobody seems to be actively showering; the showers pictured in the cartoon have no water running from them. In the background is a lighter skinned man with black hair, perhaps Alexie himself, who is an American Indian. He is wrapped in a towel around his waist. All four men are looking slyly askance at one another, and the Alexie stand-in in the back has a big grin on his face as he watches the other three men from his physically but perhaps also culturally privileged position.

Now, this image occurs just below the article title featuring the word, "Envy," and I think that the unspoken and perhaps unspeakable folk tale that African American men have larger genitalia is powerfully but silently referenced by this conjunction of the word, "Envy" (as in penis envy), and a homoerotic cartoon featuring one non-African American and three African American men. All the men are frankly leering at the other African American men. The Alexie character in the back is not being regarded by any of the other men. Doesn't all this homoerotic leering, in the context of the Collins statement, also invoke the unspeakable stereotype of gay men as sexually aggressive, as unable to shower with strangers without panting? Doesn't it reference the stereotype of hyper-endowed African American men? The article and its accompanying cartoons, being on several borders, become ways to say what cannot be said.

SAM COMES OUT

Michael Sam was an all-Southeastern Conference (SEC) football standout at the University of Missouri. In the fall of 2013, his senior season, he first announced to his teammates that he is gay and then made a major public announcement before the NFL draft in 2014. He was taken much lower in the draft than expected. After he was selected by the St. Louis Rams, a widely circulated televised kiss with his boyfriend, Vito Cammisano, drew much attention and commentary. As one observer said of the kiss, "this was something nobody had ever seen before,"[16] which must surely be a reference to the kiss in a sport context, as one must have led a sheltered life indeed not to have seen a public kiss, even a same-sex one. We might note that while sexual identity is not always as visibly evident as markers of gender and race, queer public kissing makes sexuality visible, even ostentatious.[17] Sam was not able to launch a career in professional football despite tryouts with several NFL and Canadian Football League teams. Whether that was because of anti-gay bias or his relatively small stature and slow speed vis a vis other professional players remains a contentious issue (Cyd Zeigler endorsed a statement by Sam in 2015 that if he had not come out, he would have made it professionally).[18]

An abundance of comments by Sam and others clearly articulated his location at the intersections of multiple categories. In general, Khan notes that Sam's race and his sexuality would be perceived to be at odds and thus to make an unstable intersection. Indeed, Khan summarizes Sam in general as having an "intersectional identity."[19] At least one blogger tried to force the issue by asking, "Is Michael Sam gay? Or is he black?" but of course the attempt to simplify categories was useless.[20] Sam was described by others, and described himself, as a person on the boundaries. One cartoon depicted Sam holding a newspaper announcing his sexual identity while consulting a bust of Jackie Robinson as to what to do, announcing and conjoining two dimensions of his identity.[21] Some descriptions by himself and others echoed those of Collins. For example, he declared, "I'm Michael Sam: I'm a college graduate. I'm African-American, and I'm gay." He was described as facing "the twin problems of being the first openly gay NFL player, and also actually performing once out."[22] Note that "performing" is a term often linked to sexual prowess, perhaps even more often than it would be linked to athletic skill. Clearly, the categories of gay and athlete are referenced, but not the sexual connotations that "performing" might evoke even if the comment was literally about athletics. Another blog quotes Sam as saying, "I am an openly, proud gay man," on the one hand, and, "I want to be a football player in the NFL" on the other hand.[23] However, Sam's problems with being on borders are also reflected in a report that "Sam said he grew up uncertain about what his sexual orientation was." And Sam's location in different categories put him on uneasy borders, as in this border fight between athletics and masculinity: "I could imagine that masculinity just screamed … *Ahhh! You betrayed me, football!*"[24]

One comment called attention to the rhetorical problems created through active assertion of Sam's categories, stating, "Coming out wasn't the problem. Flaunting it was,"[25] which was his way of saying that elevation of the sexual category created rhetorical problems for Sam vis a vis the athletic category. On the other hand, another blogger reported that "Sam said he wanted to be a 'football player,' full stop. Jason Collins and Robbie Rogers could have told him that his wish was naïve at best."[26] Actually, Sam did from time to time request membership in the solely athletic category, as when he said "I just wish you guys would see me as Michael Sam the football player instead of Michael Sam the gay football player."[27] However, his lack of success with that request, and his own multiplicity in declaring who he was, shows that on the borders complication cannot be avoided. Thus, as to the reference just above, announcing himself as gay was bound to seen as "flaunting it."

HINTS AND ALLEGATIONS: SAYING WHAT CANNOT BE SAID

Rather often, Sam's location on multiple boundaries was coupled with hints and allegations of what might be said about him but was not, could not be articulated openly due to "political correctness." These unsayable statements may be summed up as "homophobic locker room chatter" whether by players or the public. The unsaid sort of homophobic comment was in this case echoed by widely known stereotypes about the sexual prowess of African American males, as in one blogger's mention of "the jokes that could be made about a black man being represented by a ram" (a reference to Sam's initial drafting by the St. Louis Rams). As Sam correctly observed, "Everyone can say hurtful things and hateful things"; exactly what those things were remained unspoken, yet the public could consult Sam's border location to figure it out. One commentator on a blog argued that "Michael Sam is right society is too afraid of the gay black man"; what there was to fear remained unarticulated here, yet implications of sexual aggression and prowess seemed clear.[28] It was precisely Sam's membership in more than one category, and his location at the border, that invoked the unsayable, for "the intersections of race and sexual orientation in … professional sports in the U.S. are a virtual minefield."

The "kiss" itself, innocent and sweet as it was, was an open demonstration of affectional if not sexual vigor. A commentator to a blog noted that a cartoon depicting Sam and his white boyfriend kissing identified a range of unsayable comments in regard to the cartoon, from "miscegenation" to references to President Barack Obama's ethnicity to "'redneck' stereotypes." Another appeal through implication and allusion was in a blogger's posting which begins, "How'd you feel when you saw the kiss? You know the one I mean."[29] Another commentator on the same blog agreed that discourse about Sam evoked, even if it did not clearly articulate, "stereotypical ignorance." Because what could be said was stereotypical, allusions in effect said the unsayable. Even commentators who disapproved of Sam, or specifically of the on-air kiss, kept their disapproval at the level of innuendo and implication, as when Miami Dolphins safety Don Jones tweeted, "'horrible' and 'OMG' after the kiss aired." Similarly, Patrick Dollard tweeted, "'any straight person who says '#MichaelSam/bf kiss plc doesn't look disgusting' can't pass a lie detector test saying it. Prove me wrong.'" It is worth noting that some commentators approached concerns about the kiss from a comic perspective. Andy Kerman tweeted, for example, "'How do I explain Michael Sam to my kids? A man with TWOfirst names?'"[30] And, if it was true, as Grantland's Bryan Curtis suggested, that "players and reporters tried to say the right things, to give no offense," then even these efforts to not offend invoked the unspeakable that was being suppressed.[31]

Even though they were rare, explicitly homophobic reactions to the kiss gave voice to what was hinted at but not fully articulated elsewhere. One commenter said, perhaps ironically, for example, that we "can't have these fairies mincing around the field." Yet, for the most part, the unspeakable things that might be said about sexuality or race were repeatedly hinted at in terms so strong they need not be openly articulated, as in the report that "Sam rejects the appalling slanders that sometimes have been hurled at gay men." Sam did articulate one such slander, "that gay people are predators." Note the evasiveness in one blogger's comment, made following Sam's statement, that "other such negative stereotypes seem too absurd for him even to consider,"[32] and yet every reader will have them called forth in his or her mind and be able to recite them *sotto voce.*

A common site for concerns about sexual aggression was the locker room.[33] One commenter said, "Sam said that despite some comments from current players, he doesn't anticipate difficulty gaining acceptance in an NFL locker room." Note that of all the scenes and venues in an NFL career, the one location where men are naked with each other is chosen as a synecdoche; not the playing field or conference room, for instance. Sam himself made use of the figure in anticipating a future NFL job: "Hopefully it will be the same like my locker room. It's a workplace. If you've ever been in a Division I or pro locker room, it's a business place." It was reported that "Players asked [Wade] Davis [a former NFL player who is gay] the inevitable question about showering with a gay teammate." The locker room continued as a focal point for saying the unsayable, as "an anonymous player … wondered if Sam was going into the showers after the rest of the Rams so as not to make his teammates uncomfortable." Actually, in Dallas, where Sam had an unsuccessful second attempt at the NFL after St. Louis, he was criticized for being standoffish in locker room terms: "He would rarely be in the locker room. If he was, he was grabbing stuff out of his locker and walking away."[34]

CONCLUSION

We have several theoretical instruments to help us understand the conjunction of different categories. Kenneth Burke writes of perspective by incongruity, which is surely what you get when you think of one category in terms of another, viewing a constellation of categories from the borders among them. We also have the theoretical concept of queerness. Although it began as a way to think about non-normative sexualities, queer theory also has a use in thinking about discourses that violate expected category constructions or emerge on the borders of categories and respect none of them. I think either theoretical perspective may be useful to apply to the Collins and Sam cases.

It is not conventionally acceptable in a heteronormative context to express homoerotic desires by men toward men. Yet Alexie does this in the Collins case precisely by manipulating the intersections among the main categories introduced by Collins himself. It's ok to be homoerotic if one is really, really, really straight, and ok to be homoerotic if the object of the gaze is a professional athlete in scanty clothing. And the racial leg of this triangle of categories is referenced in the cartoon by Kaufman, which voices the unspoken folk tale that African American men are better endowed genetically than other men, an unspoken assumption that here combines with the folk tale of gay men as sexually aggressive. The unspeakable is spoken, or pictured, or strongly referenced precisely by standing on and manipulating the symbolic resources of crossing categorical boundaries. And, as noted above, we found similar discourse in the Sam case. With the kiss as the central performative focus of Sam's coming out as a professional, much was hinted at and implied rather than explicitly articulated, but nevertheless, blog followers and the public knew what was being said. This study then suggests the possible value of exploring other texts that straddle borders to explore whether my suggestion is true, that border talk enables the unspoken and unspeakable to be expressed.

NOTES

1. Bryan Curtis, "The Kiss," *Grantland*, December 12, 2014, http://grantland.com/features/the-kiss-michael-sam-nfl-what-we-saw-dallas-cowboys-st-louis-rams/.
2. Kenneth Burke, *A Grammar of Motives* (Berkeley, CA: University of California Press, 1962), xviii.
3. Burke, *A Grammar*, 503.
4. Kenneth Burke, *Permanence and Change: An Anatomy of Purpose*, 3rd ed. (Berkeley, CA: University of California Press, 1954), 72–89.
5. Frank Bramlett, "Editorial Cartoons: Is Michael Sam Gay? Or Is He Black?" *The Hooded Utilitarian*, May 22, 2014, http://www.hoodedutilitarian.com/2014/05/editorial-cartoons-is-michael-sam-gay-or-is-he-black/.
6. For more on intersectionality, see Kimberle Crenshaw, "Mapping the Margins: Intersectionality, Identity Politics, and Violence against Women of Color," *Stanford Law Review* 43 (1991): 1241–1299; Karma Chavez and Cindy Griffin, eds., *Standing in the Intersection: Feminist Voices, Feminist Practices in Communication Studies* (Albany, NY: State University of New York Press, 2012); and Michelle Kelsey Kearl, "'Is Gay the New Black?': An Intersectional Perspective on Social Movement Rhetoric in California's Proposition 8 Debate," *Communication and Critical/*

Cultural Studies 12, no. 1 (2015): 63–82. For scholarship on intersectionality and sport, see Philip E. Wagner, "Bulking Up (Identities): A Communication Framework for Male Fitness Identity," *Communication Quarterly* 65, no. 5 (2017): 580–602; Emily Deering Crosby, "Chased by the Double Bind: Intersectionality and the Disciplining of Lolo Jones," *Women's Studies in Communication* 39, no. 2 (2016): 228–48; and Kristin Skare Orgeret, "The Unexpected Body: From Sara Baartman to Caster Semenya," *Journal of African Media Studies* 8, no. 3 (2016): 281–94.

7. Jon Entine, *Taboo: Why Black Athletes Dominate Sports and Why We Are Afraid to Talk About It* (New York: Public Affairs, 2001).

8. Bramlett, "Editorial Cartoons: Is Michael Sam Gay?"

9. Barry Brummett and Andrew Ishak, eds., *Sports and Identity: New Agendas in Communication* (New York: Routledge, 2014).

10. Thomas P. Oates, "The Erotic Gaze in the NFL Draft," *Communication and Critical/Cultural Studies* 4, no. 1 (2007): 74–90.

11. Abraham Iqbal Khan, "Michael Sam, Jackie Robinson, and the Politics of Respectability," *Communication & Sport* 5, no. 3 (2017): 331–51.

12. Jason Collins, "I'm a 34-Year-Old NBA Center. I'm Black. And I'm Gay," *Sports Illustrated*, May 6, 2013, https://www.si.com/vault/2013/05/06/106319492/im-a-34yearold-nba-centerim-black-and-im-gay.

13. Sherman Alexie, "Jason Collins Is the Envy of Straight Men Everywhere," *The Stranger*, May 1, 2013, https://www.thestranger.com/seattle/jason-collins-is-the-envy-of-straight-men-everywhere/Content?oid=16638642.

14. For more on this idea, see Khan, "Michael Sam, Jackie Robinson."

15. For a parallel scholarly treatment of the erotic gaze, sport, and race see Oates, "The Erotic Gaze."

16. Curtis, "The Kiss."

17. See Charles E. Morris, III and John M. Sloop, "'What These Lips Have Kissed': Refiguring the Politics of Queer Public Kissing," *Communication and Critical/Cultural Studies* 3 (2006): 1–26; and Charles E. Morris, III and John M. Sloop, "Other Lips, Whither Kisses?" *Communication and Critical/Cultural Studies* 14, no. 2 (2017): 182–6.

18. Cyd Zeigler, "Michael Sam Says He'd Be in the NFL If He Hadn't Come Out as Gay. He's Right," *Outsports.com*, September 28, 2015, https://www.outsports.com/2015/9/28/9413055/michael-sam-gay-dan-patrick-comments.

19. Khan, "Michael Sam," 341.

20. Bramlett, "Editorial Cartoons: Is Michael Sam Gay?"

21. Bramlett, "Editorial."

22. Chris Connelly, "Mizzou's Michael Sam Says He's Gay," *ESPN.com*, February 10, 2014, http://www.espn.com/espn/otl/story/_/id/10429030/michael-sam-missouri-tigers-says-gay.

23. For Khan, this would be viewed as a bid for "respectability." See Khan, "Michael Sam."

24. Curtis, "The Kiss."

25. Holly Yan and Dave Alsup, "NFL Draft: Reactions Heat Up After Michael Sam Kisses Boyfriend on TV," *CNN.com*, May 13, 2014, https://www.cnn.com/2014/05/12/us/michael-sam-nfl-kiss-reaction/.

26. Curtis, "The Kiss."

27. Zeigler, "Michael Sam."

28. All comments from Connelly, "Mizzou's Michael Sam."

29. Curtis, "The Kiss."

30. Tweets quoted in Yan and Alsup.
31. Curtis, "The Kiss."
32. All comments from Connelly, "Mizzou's Michael Sam."
33. Sport and culture scholars have produced interesting work on the locker room as a signifying site. See Elizabeth Cavalier, "Men at Sport: Gay Men's Experiences in the Sport Workplace," *Journal of Homosexuality* 58, no. 5 (2011): 626–46; Caroline Fusco, "Spatializing the (Im)proper Subject," *Journal of Sport & Social Issues* 30, no. 1 (2006): 5–28; Mary Jo Kane and Lisa J. Disch, "Sexual Violence and the Reproduction of Male Power in the Locker Room: 'The Lisa Olsen Incident,'" *Sociology of Sport Journal* 10 (1993): 331–52; Donn Short, "The Informal Regulation of Gender," *Journal of Gender Studies* 16, no. 2 (2007): 183–6; and Gordon Waitt, "Gay Games: Performing Community Out from the Closet of the Locker Room," *Social and Cultural Geography* 4 (2003): 167–83.
34. All quotations from Connelly, "Mizzou's Michael Sam."

Section IV: Future Provocations

CHAPTER THIRTEEN

"My Whole Life Is about Winning"

The Trump Brand and the Political/ Commercial Uses of Sport

THOMAS P. OATES AND KYLE W. KUSZ

On July 2, 2017, Donald Trump re-tweeted a video depicting him at Wrestlemania a decade earlier, body-slamming World Wrestling Entertainment (WWE) founder Vince McMahon with the CNN logo photoshopped over McMahon's face. The tweet generated widespread outrage for its seeming endorsement of violence against the institutional press. To many, the tweet seemed to be yet another outrageous violation of presidential norms. Much of his political base loved it. The tweet also offered a reminder of a key, if underappreciated component of Trump's personal and political brand—his demonstration of white male dominance through sport.

Trump's political appeal is not based in his ability to articulate traditional Republican values. During the primary campaign establishment Republicans repeatedly attacked the candidate for being a faux conservative who had openly supported Democratic candidates in the past. These broadsides failed to sink Trump's candidacy because it was never rooted in conventional campaign logics. Instead, it was about communicating a carefully manufactured guise. As Alison Hearn has argued, Trump's political entreaty is partially rooted in his background in reality television. Hearn observes that, "The 'reality' rules of self-promotion are simple: craft a notable persona, say whatever will set you apart and garner attention, break the rules of the game wherever possible, choose your message, and repeat it clearly and often."[1] Naomi Klein contends that "the Trump brand" positions the candidate as "power and wealth incarnate."[2] Both Hearn and Klein stress Trump's stint on the reality program "The Apprentice" as the key venue through which Trump refined this appeal.

But Trump's strategies of self-presentation did not begin with his career in reality television. In this chapter, we examine Trump's efforts over forty years to associate his brand with sport. Long before his career as a television personality, Trump carefully built and maintained an identity as a dominant white male figure, consistently fostering associations with the gendered and raced power that sport routinely promotes. In the pages that follow, we examine how this was done and what developments in and beyond sport made this articulation possible. At the end of this essay, we consider how alternative narratives about the political in contemporary sport might offer opportunities for resistance.

Of course, Trump is not the first U.S. president to make political appeals through sport. Since at least the days of Theodore Roosevelt, chief executives have publicized connections with athletics by declaring formative experiences in organized sport, releasing publicity photographs of themselves engaged in sporting competitions, predicting outcomes of major championships, and throwing out ceremonial first pitches at baseball games. However, Trump's deployment of sport differs from these precedents in important ways. In contrast to the more typical appeals to populism or demonstrations of sound health, Trump's alignment with sport deploys three major strategies to communicate his identity as a dominant white man: (1) As a businessman and politician, Trump has fostered a view of himself as athletic. His career as a high school athlete has an important role in his personal biography, and as a real-estate mogul, reality television star, and politician, he has sought metaphors that frame his work in the physical, competitive terms common to sporting narratives. (2) As owner of the USFL's New Jersey Generals and as a partner with mixed martial arts and boxing promotions, Trump sought to align himself with and in control of physically imposing and athletically accomplished men. (3) As a presidential candidate Trump strategically employed endorsements from white sportsmen as embodied symbols of his project to reassert white male prerogatives.[3]

Together, these features of Trump's appeal do more than simply spell out the link between sport, commerce, and politics. They demonstrate the extent to which mainstream sporting discourses lend themselves to reactionary agendas and they illustrate the urgent need to craft new meanings of sport that can effectively challenge these dominant discourses.

"ALWAYS THE BEST PLAYER": TRUMP AND THE "NATURAL QUALITIES" OF LEADERSHIP

To an extraordinary degree, Donald Trump presents his childhood as a window on his future personality. "When I look at myself in the first grade and I look at myself now," he told journalist Michael D'Antonio, "I'm basically the same. The temperament is not that different."[4] Trump believes that innate qualities, rather than learned behavior, are the best predictor of prosperity.[5] Of the requirements for financial success, Trump told *Playboy* in a 1990 interview, "I'm a strong believer in genes…I don't think any of it can be learned. Either you have it or you don't."[6] Fourteen years later, in another interview with *Playboy*, he reiterated: "Some people aren't meant to be rich…It's just something you have, something you're born with."[7] Since, in Trump's view, hierarchies can be explained primarily through inborn differences, those at the top of the social hierarchy should be expected to demonstrate their superiority early on. Accordingly, Trump presents his biography in ways that provide examples of his "natural" talent for leadership, with sporting triumphs frequently presented as evidence.

After many disciplinary problems at the progressive Kew-Forest School, a then 13-year-old Trump was enrolled in New York Military Academy (NYMA) in Cornwall, New York in 1959. He identifies his time at NYMA as a turning point in his life, noting that he thrived in the school's hyper-masculine homosocial environment and he began to ascend the male pecking order through his athletic accomplishments—success that signals his "natural" greatness and future prominence. Interscholastic sport was the primary way Trump distinguished himself as an alpha male. "Always the best player," he remembers of his high school days. "Not only baseball [which Trump claims he could have pursued professionally, declining only because "there was no real money in it."], but every sport."[8] Trump's high school teams were not particularly accomplished, but this is not significant in his story because it is his individual achievement that matters.

As Trump's wealthy status and business career led him toward the elite pastime of golf, it remained important for him to demonstrate masculine credentials via athletic prowess. In a 2013 Twitter exchange with fellow billionaire Mark Cuban, for example, Trump reiterated his oft-repeated claim to have won eighteen amateur championships, adding that Cuban "swings like a little girl with no power or talent."[9] "I've won many club championships," he summarized in a 2015 interview with *Time* magazine. "So my life has been about winning. My life has not been about losing."[10] This dominance among men in athletic competitions is meant to illustrate his fitness for leadership. "I'm not bragging when I say that I'm a winner," Trump explains in his campaign biography. "I have experience in winning. That's what we call leadership."[11]

In addition to highlighting his purported athletic prowess, Trump regularly invokes sport in metaphorical ways that position him as an athlete. During his presidential campaign, Trump repeatedly framed the contest in physical terms and asserted his superiority. He maligned Republican challenger Jeb Bush as "low energy," derided Marco Rubio as diminutive, and questioned (as a Victorian physician might) the "strength and stamina" of his female competitor Hillary Clinton.

Trump even suggested a scourge plaguing athletic competitions was marring the presidential debates when he asserted that performance-enhancing drugs had unfairly aided Clinton's effectiveness. "Athletes, they make them take a drug test. I think we should take a drug test prior to the debate," Trump asserted just weeks before the election.[12]

Though perhaps unprecedented in their brazenness, invocations of physical superiority are not new to presidential politics. Trump's rhetorical moves resemble those feminist film scholar Susan Jeffords identified in Hollywood film during Ronald Reagan's presidency. For Jeffords, action blockbusters of the 1980s and early 1990s positioned symbolic bodies in the service of Reaganite agendas. She advises readers not to see bodies only as ways to imagine power, but also as a representation of the nation's ills. Jeffords writes "it is important to see [these bodies] not simply as images for Reagan's own self-projections or idealizations of an outdated Hollywood heroism but to recognize their successful linkage in Reaganism to the national body as well."[13] Jeffords illustrates several examples of how a disgraced national "soft-bodied" masculinity, represented by state bureaucracies, is contrasted with the hard-bodied outsiders with whom Reagan aligned himself.

Similarly, Trump's stories about his athletic accomplishments are more than boasts. In his campaign biography *Great Again: How to Fix Our Crippled America*, Trump contrasts himself, a proven winner, with an American nation (not coincidentally led by the United States' first black president) he perceives as physically compromised, disgraced, and aggressively taken advantage of by its many competitors. The tome begins with the declaration, "America needs to start winning again. Nobody likes a loser."[14] Trump, who through sport has aligned himself not only with able-bodiedness but with exceptional physical prowess, sees himself as uniquely positioned to restore this impaired, blackened, and emasculated loser of a nation to its rightful status as a virile winner. Trump asserts himself as a "winner" in part because he has triumphed in athletic competitions, but also because these accomplishments bespeak a potent and unassailable claim to ableist, hegemonic white masculinity.

BIG LEAGUE: TRUMP'S SPORTING ENTREPRENEURIALISM

Trump is best known as an entrepreneur. Though his businesses are vast and complex, ranging from Manhattan real estate to brand licensing deals in Asia, he has shown an enduring interest in sport as a site for investment. These projects have rarely produced profit for Trump, but they offer dividends of another kind, creating associations that have enabled him to extend and deepen his public image of racialized and gendered dominance.

In 1983, while still emerging as a public figure, Donald Trump bought a majority share of the New Jersey Generals, a team in the United States Football League (USFL). In owning the Generals, Trump saw an opportunity to promote himself as a purveyor of quality and success. "[Y]ou have to give quality," Trump boasted to the *New York Times* of his plans for the team. "And I've always gone first class."[15] As owner of the Generals, Trump pursued and landed top NFL and college players, including Heisman trophy winner Herschel Walker (whom the *New York Times* described as "the epitome of strength") and Lawrence Taylor (whose extraordinary size and strength were conveyed by his nickname: "Godzilla").[16] In the role of team owner, Trump was able to connect himself with icons of masculinity, generating speculation about how Trump's interventions might alter their futures. Thus, by owning the team and seeking talent in this provocative and public way, Trump built attention for himself not only as a savvy football executive, but as a man.

Trump conveyed male dominance in other, more conventional ways as well. In December of 1983, Donald Trump organized a public tryout for the Generals' cheerleaders. The event was held at a Manhattan disco, where a panel of celebrity judges including Andy Warhol and LeRoy Neiman selected the roster for the Briga-Dears, as the cheerleaders would be called (not, as was briefly considered, the Trumpettes). As the Generals' director of cheerleading explained, the cheerleaders would be carefully monitored and reassessed for conformity to the organization's preferred sexualized ideal: "They must exercise," she assured the *New York Times*, "We will measure them constantly, and if they gain too much they'll be off the squad."[17] Trump would go on to exercise control over female bodies in his associations with beauty pageants. In both these cases, Trump positions himself as the exacting purveyor of hegemonic male fantasy. Revelations emerged during the campaign that Trump made unannounced visits to pageant dressing rooms, and had made denigrating, racist and misogynist comments about some contestants. These allegations undoubtedly damaged his credibility among many voters, but they further secured his hegemonic credentials for those most invested in a culture of white male entitlement.

After the demise of the USFL in 1985, Trump's self-promotion through what Michael Messner calls "combat sports"— a violent "cultural sphere defined largely by patriarchal priorities"—continued.[18] At his casinos, Trump took a visible role in promoting boxing matches. Later, in 2007, he would appear as part of World Wrestling Entertainment's WrestleMania 23 in the much-hyped "Battle of the Billionaires." He and fellow sexagenarian Vince McMahon "fought" through surrogate wrestlers—providing the footage that would be recycled in the tweet discussed at the beginning of this chapter. In 2008, Trump entered a partnership with Affliction Entertainment, a company competing with The Ultimate Fighting Championship (UFC) for the growing Mixed Martial Arts (MMA) audience.

Trump was taken with the sport's brutality, which he used to promote it (and himself) in media appearances. "Somebody dies!" he exaggerated excitedly in a radio interview with Howard Stern.[19] He endorsed the sport in part by noting its stark contrast with feminized sports such as gymnastics and figure skating. "I've never seen anything like it...It's not like, 'Oh, how are the judges voting?' OK? It's like, you know, somebody just—succumbs." The headliner for Affliction Entertainment was Russian Fedor Emelianenko, whose "thing," Trump insisted, "is inflicting death on people."[20]

These ventures in sport were not financial successes. Affliction Entertainment folded after only two events, and a planned reality show featuring Fedor never became a reality. The USFL lasted just two seasons after Trump began his involvement, its demise sealed by a disastrous antitrust lawsuit against the NFL led by Trump as a way to force a merger. Trump's Generals never even won a playoff game under his ownership. But they did allow him to very publicly associate himself with paragons of American masculinity and to publicly assert dominance over women. As the acquirer and deployer of athletic and cheerleading talent, Trump publicly asserts his dominance in the hegemonic male order. In *The Art of the Deal*, Trump writes that "having my own team seemed like the realization of a great fantasy."[21] Indeed, sport has long served as a space and practice constituted by, and constitutive of, raced and gendered fantasies for white men. More specifically, Ben Carrington details how sport provides "a homosocial space for the projection of white masculinist fantasies of domination, control and desire for the racial other," and "a stage for the white masculine imaginary to engage latent (and occasionally explicit) homosocial desires for and fears about the black male (sporting) body."[22] These aspects of sporting spectacle have become increasingly prominent in recent years. Through fantasy leagues, the popularity of the NFL and NBA drafts as media spectacles, and in video games such as *Madden NFL*, fans are encouraged to indulge fantasies that combine the satisfaction of managerial control with the taboo yet historically established license to openly look at, examine, admire, and assess commodified bodies.

Thus, Trump's entrepreneurial role in sport afforded the opportunity for him to publicly exercise control over the bodies of people of color, a hallmark of his later political appeal. Trump's promises to secure the borders, ignore reports of police brutality and racial bias, and inflict punishment on women procuring abortions all signaled this orientation on the campaign trail, but they were not new elements of his personality. From his earliest days in the public eye, as a defendant in a housing discrimination suit, or as a self-proclaimed playboy claiming access to women's bodies as a sign of his status, Trump has consistently lived his life as if society should put no limits on white men's prerogative to live life as they so choose. Significantly, these assertions have frequently been made through sport.

CANDIDATE TRUMP'S SPORTING ENDORSEMENTS

During the 2016 presidential campaign, Trump sought and received more endorse-ments from sportsmen than any other candidate in recent memory. While a few came from well-known African-American athletes, the bulk arose from white sportsmen. Trump deployed famously outspoken, old-school coaches like Mike Ditka and Bobby Knight as media surrogates.[23] While campaigning Trump fre-quently referenced local white male sporting idols to appeal to voters and position himself as a populist. In New England, he humble-bragged about his close friend-ship with New England Patriots' quarterback Tom Brady. In Pittsburgh, he name-dropped legendary Penn State University football coach Joe Paterno, and Steelers' quarterback Ben Roethlisberger, even though the latter later publicly denied any political allegiance to Trump. And although UFC President Dana White was the only sport figure who spoke at the 2016 Republican national convention, Trump reportedly had wanted to stage a "winner's evening" featuring American athletes because in his view "our country needs to see winners…We don't see winners any-more."[24]

Given Trump's tendency to construct his public persona through tales of sporting prowess, perhaps it should be no surprise he used white sportsmen to convey the notion that the restoration of a strong, tough, unapologetic, and guilt-free white manhood was an essential part of his project to "make America great again."[25] By employing white sportsmen as racial dog-whistles Trump commu-nicated a complex set of ideas that affectively resonated with the racial resent-ments of his white supporters without overtly mentioning race: (1) contempt for the putative erosion of institutional support and cultural respect for white men, (2) relief from status anxieties by revitalizing white male prerogative, (3) enthusi-asm for the return of unreconstructed white manliness, and (4) pride in re-center-ing white masculinity in American socio-cultural life. These ideas structured the tone, rhetoric, and performances of candidate Trump's white masculinity and were vital to his aim to ingratiate himself with aggrieved white men who were key to his electoral strategy.

For example, at a rally at the University of Iowa, Trump surrounded himself on stage with members of the football and wrestling teams.[26] Although plenty of athletes of color participate in Iowa athletics, all of the athletes invited on stage that day were white men. These white men were meant to visually signify Trump's ideal of strong, tough, American "winners." The display evoked nos-talgia of high school pep rallies where male athletes are given an exalted status the crowd is expected to affirm. Through these displays, Trump offered himself and his racially-exclusive sporting fraternity as saviors for white Americans who feel they've become "strangers in their own land" and deserve respect ahead of Muslims, immigrants of color, and LGBT individuals, among others.[27] Through lionizing white sportsmen and including himself within their company, Trump, like other strongmen politicians before him, demonstrates how easily American sport—institutionalized practices rooted in plantation relations and fantasies of American exceptionalism, national unity, and male dominance—can serve as a vehicle for white supremacist, fascist, and nationalist projects.[28]

Trump's most frequent athletic accomplice on the campaign trail was former college basketball coach, Bobby Knight. Knight explained Trump's appeal as his being a "tough son-of-a-bitch" that "no one is going to push around," while Trump gushed about Knight being an unbelievable leader.[29] Knight epitomized Trump's idea of a great white sportsman. Through his praise of Knight, Trump soft-ped-dled his predilection for authoritarian performances of white masculinity. Indeed, Trump featured Knight as a campaign surrogate because of, not despite, his refusal to adopt or be contained by the norms of political correctness, feminism, and multiculturalism. Lest we forget, Knight once brazenly staged a photo-op where he "jokingly" wielded a bullwhip on an African-American player.[30] On another occasion he answered a question about how he handles pressure as a big-time college coach by insensitively stating: "if rape is inevitable, relax and enjoy it."[31] And despite decades of reports of inappropriate and abusive behavior, Knight long evaded public condemnation because he embodied a performance of white male dominance that not only generated millions of dollars in revenue for Indiana University and the NCAA, but was instrumental to the social reproduction of white men's social and cultural authority.

Finally, in 2000, Knight was fired after another of his transgressions. His supporters were apoplectic. Implicit in their disbelief was the assumption that white sportsmen always deserve a blank check of institutional support and protection—especially if their teams win and they are imagined as uniting local communities and making men out of boys. So in Knight, Trump chose not just a coach who symbolized "winning sportsman" and "manly leader," but a white man whose long record of demeaning people of color and women registered his investment in wielding and upholding white male prerogative.

Yet, while stumping for Trump, Knight's controversial past was largely elided. Instead he was cast as a humble patriot whose love of his country admirably compelled him into service for Trump. That Knight's—and Trump's for that matter—previous racial and gender transgressions were not made to matter revealed how systemic white privilege was hardly eroding as those in the "white men are in crisis" chorus often bemoan.[32] Even further, it proved many whites' willingness to overlook a white man's racist and sexist wrongdoings so long as he promises to protect their privileges and wages of whiteness.

Finally, in addition to being recast as a "patriot," Knight consistently drew on a casual language of white cultural nationalism that emerged after 9/11 when speaking for Trump. This rhetoric can be heard in conservatives' racially-coded talk of "taking back *our* country." It relies on the logics of colorblindness to reauthorize white supremacist ideas in plain sight. Note Knight's comments on Colin Kaepernick's protest of police brutality and continued racial oppression during the 2016 NFL season:

> If I were the man in charge he'd be looking for another job. I wouldn't want that on my team… It has taken away from our objective and that's winning. To really discredit [the United States], as a citizen…is beyond anything what I could understand. I mean I don't know where in the world you could go whether you're black, white, green, Indian, whatever the heck you are and have a better opportunity to live than in the USA, that just boggles my mind.[33]

Through his comments on Kaepernick's activism, Knight dismisses the social meaningfulness of race to tacitly define US citizenship as white by default. Knight conveys a white supremacist's expectation that people of color subordinate their interests, voices, and will to freedom to an implicitly white team/nation that shows little respect for their rights and humanity. On another occasion, while addressing a virtually all-white crowd at a Trump rally, Knight explained his support for Trump this way:

> We need a Donald Trump. You need him. Your children need him. We need someone who is smart, tough, and loves the USA.… For the past eight years, we've had the worst prepared president for the job, its not his fault, but our fault for not finding someone who is better.[34]

While the racial meaning of the "we" and the positioning of Trump as a savior needed for "your children" is unspoken, it also is not ambiguous. Even further, close examination of the comments of this unapologetic white male authoritarian coach and his role in Trump's campaign evince how the semiotic potency of white sportsmen—to signify both fantasies of white male dominance and eroding institutional support for white men—was part of the Trump campaign's will to re-birth a (white) nation.

NO TIME FOR LOSERS: WINNERS AND LOSERS IN THE TRUMP ERA

In 2014, Donald Trump made a very public bid to buy Buffalo's NFL franchise. After being passed over in favor of another owner Trump saltily announced via Twitter "Even though I refused to pay a ridiculous price for the Buffalo Bills, I would have produced a winner. Now that won't happen."[35] Eight months later, he announced his candidacy for president. Since his election, pundits have struggled to understand the components of "Trumpism." As countless political commentators have noted, Donald Trump's governing style is erratic, inconsistent, and unmoored from conventional ideological commitments. He routinely makes forceful, provocative public statements, only to renege on them later. Often, he denies having made such statements at all, while adopting what is seemingly the opposite position.

So what, then, is Trumpism? Is there such a thing? And if so, does Trump's mobilization of sport help bring it more clearly into view? The range of positions Trump seems to take on many issues can obscure the fact that his policy positions communicate a consistent set of political commitments based on promoting tough, strong white guys portrayed as "coming straight from central casting" and/or being regarded as "the very best" our country has to offer, all the while making policies, programs, and pronouncements that both marginalize and seek to constrain the agency of people of color, women, and trans people in the body politic. Trump also consistently vaunts his background as a "dealmaker" whose triumphs in the unforgiving world of business demonstrate the perspective and mindset necessary for the contemporary moment. He has proven to be an advocate of privatization and corporatization, continuing a recent presidential tendency to position Wall Street financiers to shape the economy. While his worldview is not wed to any contemporary political program, Trump seems firmly rooted in ideas and logics that trace back to scientific racism, Victorian gender ideologies, and gilded age capitalism.

More than anything, the intensely racialized, gendered cultural project of "Trumpism," is a *style* of politics, one that unabashedly reasserts white, male, capitalist dominance. Trump's performance of white masculinity—one that imagines itself as dominating and extraordinary, even as innately superior and above the law—has already impacted American culture by reinvigorating many contemporary white men's resolve to push back on multicultural, feminist, and cosmopolitan logics, norms, and values. Surely, Trump did not invent this reactionary response. But his status as the leader of the free world has given it a new legitimacy, especially for whites angered and made anxious by economic changes and shifting racial and gender norms and values.

As Jackson Katz argues, presidential campaigns are always "a kind of referendum on the meaning of American manhood."[36] For Katz, presidential elections often turn on a candidate's ability to authentically embody the type of man voters value at that particular moment in history. Indeed, though he did not win a majority of votes, Trump's robust support (especially among white men) is based in a changing set of cultural values. Trump's connections to sport underscore the extent to which the personal and political values he articulates—a keen sense of the precarity of white masculine power, the pleasures of controlling non-white and female bodies, the glorification of "the art of the deal"—have saturated commercialized twenty-first century sport in quiet but widespread ways.

Contemporary sporting culture has long served as a kind of bastion against the encroachments of people of color, women, queers, and others who would challenge white male hegemony. In recent decades, as members of these groups have become increasingly visible in sport and their concerns and politics have grown more audible, entrenched forces have often responded by articulating a sense that white men are somehow the victims of structural disadvantages. For example, one of the major stories of 2006 involved three white male Duke lacrosse players accused of raping a black stripper their teammates had hired to perform at an off-campus house. After the allegation went public, the American news media and eighty-eight Duke faculty members famously rushed to judgment and transformed the players into symbols of the individual and institutional evils of white male privilege. All charges against the players were eventually dropped after the accuser's story changed multiple times and local district attorney Mike Nifong was found to have concealed DNA evidence that exonerated the players. The incident has become a potent rallying cry used by white nationalists and men's rights advocates, serving as "proof" that contemporary white men are being unfairly treated, demonized in a post-white and feminized America where they are supposedly no longer valued nor respected. The incident appears to have been formative for two figures who would later hold important roles in the ascension of President Trump—the white nationalist Richard Spencer and Stephen Miller, the advisor who reportedly authored and defended President Trump's travel ban for majority Muslim nations.[37] Spencer and Miller, who were both students at Duke during the scandal, learned that unapologetically and assertively defending white men against "elements of political correctness," "liberal establishment," and "social justice warriors" could be both a winning and career-enhancing strategy.

In addition to this incident, contemporary mediated sport provides other symbols in an ongoing struggle over identity and the nation's future. Twenty-first century sport scholarship has highlighted how the glorification of white American male athlete-celebrities like Tim Tebow, Lance Armstrong, Pat Tillman, Michael Phelps, and Tom Brady, sporting spectacles like Super Bowls and NASCAR races, and corporate sporting commerce have worked to re-center white masculinity in U.S. culture, often through narratives guided by paradoxical logics of victimization and valorization, overt populism and tacit supremacy.[38]

At the same time, contemporary sport provides ample opportunities for indulging fantasies of control over subjugated bodies and refining entrepreneurial skills. Whether admiring stripped muscular male athletes in photo spreads, preparing fantasy league strategies, reading about and watching athletic drafts, or consulting books on leadership by famous coaches and executives, consumers of mediated sport are routinely invited to indulge the pleasures of controlling mostly black male bodies—bodies that also circulate as paragons of male strength. Such pleasures echo Trump's attempt to define himself as a mogul positioned to stage and bask in hyper-masculine sporting spectacles. Such pleasures are available because, as Leola Johnson and David Roediger note, "sport has functioned as a spectacle in which the male body and the white mind are at once exulted and in which white men feel especially empowered to judge, bet on, and identify vicariously with African-Americans."[39]

Trumpism asserts the prerogatives of white, hyper-masculinity as a means to securing power—by insisting that only a dominant white man is suitable for the rigors of the presidency and leadership of the nation. While many policy objectives appear convoluted, contradictory, or deceptive, the promise to use state sovereignty to control the movement and freedom of women, trans people, and people of color are consistent, straightforward, and undisguised. Trump projects a vision of white male dominance, and sport is a vitally important backdrop against which he is attempting to manifest this vision.

This link helps illustrate the important (if sometimes subtle) political work that dominant meanings of mainstream sport can perform—and they highlight the urgent need to intervene in the telling of those narratives to offer new ones. While mainstream sport narratives seem to readily lend themselves to right-wing agendas—especially when driven by neoliberal logics seeking the generation of profits—we must not forget that resistive sporting cultures and personalities always exist, even if they are too often omitted from, or marginalized within, mainstream news coverage. Trumpism has, at least in part, spawned a renaissance of activism in sports as prominent figures like Colin Kaepernick, Megan Rapinoe, Serena Williams, Steve Kerr, Eric Reid, Gregg Popovich and others have rearticulated struggles for social justice in and through sports. And there are countless under-reported grassroots efforts all across the US where sport is mobilized to validate the lives and experiences of those that Trumpism seeks to cast as "other" to its vision of America: people of color, women, LGBT individuals, new immigrants, refugees, and those from lower income, under-resourced areas.

Contesting dominant cultures requires more than just identifying, as we have done here, what conjunctures have been exploited and how. It also requires crafting effective new narratives. Media workers and other critical observers who narrate contemporary sport have an important responsibility to examine how the gratifications they produce help construct the shared imaginary that Trump exploits. Challenging this does not require an abandonment of the pleasures of sport, but rather a reimagining of them. Notions of conquest, domination, and their link to masculinity are familiar modes of narrating sport, but they are not the only available enjoyments sport can offer. Indeed, the disruption and subversion of these dominant values provides not only opportunities for reflection and learning, but pleasure as well. The commitment to tell new kinds of stories about sport and to challenge the hegemonic conventions of mainstream narratives may seem daunting, but it is the ground on which a new, alternative culture of sport can be built. Feminist author Ursula Le Guin emphasized how dominant forces can be challenged through thoughtful, deliberate narratives that deliberately and carefully defy convention. In a 2014 address at the National Book Awards, Le Guin observed:

> I think hard times are coming, when we will be wanting the voices of writers who can see alternatives to how we live now, and can see through our fear-stricken society and its obsessive technologies to other ways of being, and even imagine some real grounds for hope. We need writers who can remember freedom. Poets, visionaries—the realists of a larger reality…Any human power can be resisted and changed by human beings. Resistance and change often begin in art, and very often in our art, the art of words.[40]

A better world is possible, both in sport and beyond. The example of Trumpism demonstrates the urgent need for all of us—athletes, critics, writers, and fans—to work collectively to bring it to life.

NOTES

1. Alison Hearn, "Trump's 'Reality' Hustle," *Feminist Media Studies* 17, no. 7 (2016): 657.
2. Naomi Klein, *No is Not Enough: Resisting Trump's Shock Politics and Winning the World We Need*, (Chicago: Haymarket Books, 2017), 33.
3. Stephen David Kantrowitz, *Ben Tillman and the Reconstruction of White Supremacy* (Chapel Hill, NC: The University of North Carolina Press, 2000).
4. Michael D'Antonio, *Never Enough: Donald Trump and the Pursuit of Success* (New York: Thomas Dunne Books, 2015), 40.
5. D'Antonio, *Never Enough*, 327.
6. Glenn Plaskin, "Playboy Interview with Donald Trump," *Playboy*, March 01, 1990, http://www.playboy.com/articles/playboy-interview-donald-trump-1990.
7. David Hochman, "Playboy Interview: Donald Trump," *Playboy*, October, 2004, https://www.playboy.com/read/donald-trump-interview.
8. D'Antonio, *Never Enough*, 46.
9. Donald J. Trump, Twitter post, March 19, 2013, 6:07 a.m., https://twitter.com/realdonaldtrump/status/313970051453710336.
10. Michael Scherer, "The Donald Has Landed: Why Trump's Latest Hit Show Is Driving the Political Elite Crazy," *Time*, August 20, 2015, http://time.com/trump/. A 2017 *Washington Post* article disputed Trump's claim. See Aaron Blake, "That Fake *Time* Cover Isn't the Only Thing Inflating Trump's Accomplishments at His Golf Clubs," *Washington Post*, June 28, 2017, https://www.washingtonpost.com/news/the-fix/wp/2016/10/28/donald-trump-claims-to-have-won-18-golf-club-championships-not-all-of-them-were-created-equal/?utm_term=.1d1b1a41a167.
11. Donald Trump, *Great Again: How to Fix Our Crippled America* (New York: Simon and Schuster, 2015), 9.
12. Jose A. DelReal, "Trump Says He and Clinton Should Take Drug Tests Before Next Debate," *Washington Post*, October 15, 2016, https://www.washingtonpost.com/news/post-politics/wp/2016/10/15/trump-says-he-and-clinton-should-take-drug-tests-before-next-debate.

13. Susan Jeffords, *Hard Bodies: Hollywood Masculinity in the Reagan Era* (Bloomington, IN: University of Indiana Press, 1995), 25.

14. Trump, *Great Again*, 1.

15. Ira Berkow, "Trump Building the Generals in His Own Style," *New York Times*, January 1, 1984, http://www.nytimes.com/1984/01/01/sports/trump-building-the-generals-in-his-own-style.html.

16. Dave Anderson, "By Sports of the Times; The $5 Million Contract," *New York Times*, February 27, 1983, http://www.nytimes.com/1983/02/27/sports/by-sports-of-the-times-the-5-million-contract.html.

17. William E. Geist, "Aspiring Cheerleaders Throw Body and Soul Into Their Tryout," *New York Times*, December 14, 1983, https://www.nytimes.com/1983/12/14/nyregion/aspiring-cheerleaders-throw-body-and-soul-into-their-tryout.html.

18. Michael A. Messner, "Sports and Male Domination: The Female Athlete as Contested Ideological Terrain," *Sociology of Sport Journal* 5 (1988): 208.

19. Michael Crowley, "Donald Trump's Other Blood Sport," *Politico*, August 30, 2016, http://www.politico.com/story/2016/08/donald-trump-mixed-martial-arts-227461.

20. Crowley, "Donald Trump's Other."

21. Donald Trump with Tony Schwartz, *The Art of the Deal* (New York: Random House, 1987), 274.

22. Ben Carrington, *Race, Sport and Politics: The Sporting Black Diaspora* (London: Sage, 2010), 4.

23. Charlotte Wilder, "30 famous sports figures who have endorsed Donald Trump," *USA Today*, May 30, 2016, http://ftw.usatoday.com/2016/05/30-sports-figures.

24. Nick Corasaniti, "Donald Trump Wants Sports Stars, Not Politicians, on Convention Stage," *The New York Times*, June 10, 2016, https://www.nytimes.com/2016/06/11/us/politics/donald-trump-republican-convention-sports-celebrities.html.

25. Kyle Kusz, "Trumpism, Tom Brady, and the Reassertion of White Supremacy in Militarized Post-9/11 America," in *Global Sport & Militarism: Contemporary Global Perspectives*, ed. Michael L. Butterworth (New York: Routledge, 2017).

26. *FULL Speech: Donald Trump AMAZING Rally- Iowa City, IA at the University of Iowa (1 26- 16)*, YouTube video, 36:14, posted by "Donald Trump News," December 3, 2016, https://www.youtube.com/watch?v=lkKqhViXrRo.
    An unscientific visual survey of the 2016 Iowa Football and 2016–2017 Wrestling teams' Media Guides suggests that approximately 59% of the Football team and 93% of the Wrestling team might identify as white.

27. Arlie Russell Hochschild, *Strangers in Their Own Land: Anger and Mourning on the American Right* (New York: The New Press, 2016).

28. Richard Dyer, *White: Essays on Race and Culture* (New York: Routledge, 1997).

29. *This AMAZING BOBBY KNIGHT SPEECH Will Get DONALD TRUMP ELECTED PRESIDENT Rally Michigan Grand Rapids*, dailymotion video, 13:38, posted by "FrancisWade61814791," August 13, 2017, https://www.dailymotion.com/video/x5wub9s.

30. Associated Press, "NAACP Decries Photo of Knight Putting Whip on Black Player," *Los Angeles Times*, March 28, 1992, http://articles.latimes.com/1992-03-28/sports/sp-4355_1_bob-knight.

31. Malcolm Moran, "Knight Is Criticized Over Rape Remark," *The New York Times*, April 27, 1988, http://www.nytimes.com/1988/04/27/sports/knight-is-criticized-over-rape-remark.html.

32. Matthew Hughey and Gregory Parks, *The Wrongs of the Right: Language, Race, and the Republican Party in the Age of Obama* (New York: New York University Press, 2014).

33. Fox Business, *Bobby Knight: If I were boss, Kaepernick would be out,* YouTube video, 5:31, September 23, 2016, https://www.youtube.com/watch?v=U-FDPqUrefA.

34. Dailymotion, *This AMAZING BOBBY.*

35. Donald J. Trump, Twitter post, October 13, 2014, 9:11 a.m., https://twitter.com/realdonaldtrump/status/521664598168977408.

36. Jackson Katz, *Leading Men: Presidential Campaigns and the Politics of Manhood* (Northampton, MA: Interlink Books, 2013), 8–9.

37. Reeves Wiedeman, "The Duke Lacrosse Scandal and the Birth of the Alt-Right," *New York Magazine,* April 14, 2017, http://nymag.com/daily/intelligencer/2017/04/the-duke-lacrosse-scandal-and-the-birth-of-the-alt-right.html.

38. See Michael L. Butterworth, "The Passion of the Tebow: Sports Media and Heroic Language in the Tragic Frame," *Critical Studies in Media Communication* 30, no. 1 (2013): 17–33; Michael L. Butterworth, "'Race in the Race': Mark McGwire, Sammy Sosa, and Heroic Constructions of Whiteness," *Critical Studies in Media Communication* 24, no. 3 (2007): 228–44; Grant Farred, "The Uncanny of Olympic Time: Michael Phelps and the End of Neoliberalism," in *Sport and Neoliberalism: Politics, Consumption, and Culture,* ed. David L. Andrews and Michael L. Silk (Philadelphia: Temple University Press, 2012); Daniel A. Grano, "Risky Dispositions: Thick Moral Description and Character-Talk in Sports Culture," *Southern Communication Journal* 75, no. 3 (2010): 255–76; Matthew Hawzen and Joshua L. Newman, "The Gospel According to Tim Tebow: Sporting Celebrity, Whiteness, and the Cultural Politics of Christian Fundamentalism in America," *Sociology of Sport Journal* 34, no. 1 (2017): 12–24; Samantha King, "Offensive Lines: Sport-State Synergy in an Era of Perpetual War," *Cultural Studies Critical Methodologies* 8, no. 4 (2008): 527–39; Kyle Kusz, *Revolt of the White Athlete: Race, Media and the Emergence of Extreme Athletes in America* (New York: Peter Lang, 2007); Joshua L. Newman and Michael D. Giardina, *Sport, Spectacle, and NASCAR Nation: Consumption and the Cultural Politics of Neoliberalism* (New York: Palgrave Macmillan, 2011); Thomas Oates and Zack Furness, *The NFL: Critical and Cultural Perspectives* (Philadelphia: Temple University Press, 2015); Michael Silk, *The Cultural Politics of Post-9/11 American Sport: Power, Pedagogy, and the Popular* (New York: Routledge, 2012); Michael Silk and Mark Falcous, "One Day in September/A Week in February: Mobilizing American (Sporting) Nationalisms," *Sociology of Sport Journal* 22, no. 4 (2005): 447–71; Gavin Weedon, "'I Will. Protect this House': Under Armour, Corporate Nationalism and Post-9/11 Cultural Politics," *Sociology of Sport Journal* 29, no. 3 (2012): 265–82.

39. Leola Johnson and David Roediger, "Hertz, Don't It? Becoming Colorless and Staying Black in the Crossover of O. J. Simpson," in *Birth of a Nation'hood: Gaze, Script, and Spectacle in the O. J. Simpson Case,* eds. Toni Morrison and Claudia Brodsky Lacour (New York: Pantheon, 1997).

40. Jeff Baker, "Ursula K. Le Guin's Fiery Speech, and the Overwhelming Reaction to It (Full Text and Video)," *The Oregonian,* November 20, 2014, http://www.oregonlive.com/movies/index.ssf/2014/11/ursula_k_le_guins_fiery_speech.html.

Index

POLITICAL COMMUNICATION

FRONTIERS IN

General Editors
Mitchell S. McKinney and Mary E. Stuckey

At the heart of how citizens, governments, and the media interact is the communication process, a process that is undergoing tremendous changes as we embrace a new millennium. Never has there been a time when confronting the complexity of these evolving relationships been so important to the maintenance of civil society. This series seeks books that advance the understanding of this process from multiple perspectives and as it occurs in both institutionalized and non-institutionalized political settings. While works that provide new perspectives on traditional political communication questions are welcome, the series also encourages the submission of manuscripts that take an innovative approach to political communication, which seek to broaden the frontiers of study to incorporate critical and cultural dimensions of study as well as scientific and theoretical frontiers.

For more information or to submit material for consideration, contact:

Mitchell S. McKinney: McKinneyM@missouri.edu
Mary E. Stuckey: mes519@psu.edu

To order other books in this series, please contact our Customer Service Department:
(800) 770-LANG (within the U.S.)
(212) 647-7706 (outside the U.S.)
(212) 647-7707 FAX

Or browse online by series:
WWW.PETERLANG.COM

Printed in the USA
CPSIA information can be obtained
at www.ICGtesting.com
LVHW010404101223
766053LV00004B/376